FIRST AID FOR FAMILIES

Most of us have been, to some degree, a hostage to past hurts, but if I can escape, then so can you. The stories, research, and professional advice offered in this book have enabled me to do what you will be able to do. I have given you the road map to take the same route I've taken. I believe the information contained in all the chapters of this book will lead you to reconciliation or to a healthy coping with a fractured relationship until it is mended. Now I have faith that I will travel from this position of healthy coping to the ultimate goal—a full reconnection with the person I love.

The emotionally draining ordeal of family estrangements will always be with us—it is so often woven into the fabric of human flaws and frailties. But hope and health are within our grasp. You're holding both in your hands right now.

—Barbara LeBey

"Fast-paced, to the point, and sensitive, *Family Estrangements* strikes quickly at the heart of the problem and may turn you in a new direction."
—Marlin Fitzwater
Press Secretary to Presidents Reagan and Bush

"Barbara LeBey makes a major contribution toward keeping families together."
—David Rosin, M.D.
Deputy Director, South Carolina Department of Mental Health

family
estrangements

how they begin
how to mend them
how to cope with them

Barbara LeBey

BANTAM BOOKS
NEW YORK   TORONTO   LONDON   SYDNEY   AUCKLAND

FAMILY ESTRANGEMENTS
A Bantam Book

PUBLISHING HISTORY
Longstreet Press, Inc. edition published 2001
Bantam trade paperback edition / January 2003

Library of Congress Catalog Card Number: 2001086511
ISBN: 0-553-38196-2
Published simultaneously in the United States and Canada

Bantam Books are published by Bantam Books, a division of Random House, Inc. Its trademark, consisting of the words "Bantam Books" and the portrayal of a rooster, is Registered
in U.S. Patent and Trademark Office and in other countries. Marca Registrada.
Bantam Books, New York, New York.

PRINTED IN THE UNITED STATES OF AMERICA

RRH 10 9 8 7 6 5 4 3 2 1

To my husband, David, and my children, Pamela and Daniel.

ACKNOWLEDGMENTS

This book would never have happened had it not been for my friend, Marge McDonald. Her faith in my ability to write this book and her encouragement to do so have made *Family Estrangements* a reality.

I am grateful to clinical psychologists Dr. Paul Hirschfield and Dr. Jim Fitzgerald for their continuous consultations. Because of their broad experience and immensely valuable insights, I have been able to offer the kind of professional advice people need most when they're going through painful estrangements. I am also grateful to Dr. Hirschfield for refining my skills in helping others.

I am grateful to Ann Kempner Fisher for reading and editing my chapters with me as they came rolling out of my printer. Her suggestions have been invaluable to me in birthing this book. And to my editor, John Yow, for always being positive, reassuring and instructive.

I am grateful to Gary Zweifel, an Atlanta estate lawyer, whose breadth of professional experience enabled me to offer sound and current legal advice in an area of law that is always changing.

I am grateful to my niece, Laura Sydell, whose journalistic background and broad experience as a radio personality have given me the comfort and assurance of knowing I can speak articulately on this subject of family estrangements even before a camera or a microphone.

I am grateful to my husband, David, for his love and patience during my years of consuming involvement in research and writing, and to my daughter, Pamela, who gives me the joy of a loving relationship. We sustain each other in the best ways possible, particularly during the estrangement we have had to endure from someone we all love very much.

I am grateful to my many family members and friends for just being who they are and offering to explore issues and give encouragement: Phil and Jan Sydell, Jerry and Roz Sydell, Carolyn Wills, Lyniece Talmadge, June Moseley and Nathalie Dupree.

Finally, I am grateful to a great many people who cannot be thanked by name—the men and women whose experiences appear in this book and whose privacy I have promised to protect. *Family Estrangements* would not exist without them.

CONTENTS

INTRODUCTION

Are you estranged from a loved one in your family? Someone who doesn't want to see or even speak to you? Or perhaps it's a group of relatives who want nothing more to do with you? There are myriad reasons for family estrangements—a messy divorce, an in-law problem, an interracial marriage, religious differences, a family business that fails, a conflict over an inheritance, an adult child's announcement that he or she is gay, the sole burden of taking care of aged parents falling on one sibling while another does nothing. Whatever the reason for the breakdown of a once-loving relationship, time is an essential component in the definition of *estrangement*. If you've been out of touch with a loved one for several months or years, and it has made you extremely unhappy but you don't know what to do about it, then you have an estrangement and this book was written for you. Even if the breakup is with a dear friend who was as close as family, the coping and mending strategies are the same as with a family member.

What has struck me as extraordinary is the fact that family

estrangement is a widespread problem that appears to be completely ignored. Is it one of those subjects that people don't talk about? Is a sense of shame involved, analogous to a teenage daughter who gets pregnant or a child who gets arrested for shoplifting? Families sweep those stories under the rug, but it's difficult to sweep an estrangement under the rug because it isn't a one-time event. It goes on and on. The pain of it goes on and on. How can you cope with it if you lock it in a closet and throw away the key? Or for some, is that the only way of coping?

And what does it mean to cope? According to the standard definition, "to cope" means "to contend with." To cope effectively, as the term is used in this book, means to minimize the impact of the difficult situation in which you find yourself. Such situations—cherished relationships broken through an estrangement—usually arise because of a problem with a particular family member. Trying to change the other person's personality or perception of the situation, though sometimes possible, is more likely to be the world's greatest hard-luck story. Coping, by contrast, has a much more limited and practical goal. It is a means of learning to function as productively as possible, learning to get on with your life, regardless of the difficult person or situation—regardless of the sense of loss from the estrangement.

Because I had a painful estrangement from my son, I searched for books or magazine articles to help me find guidance and comfort and to understand and resolve the heart-wrenching loss. But I could find no books on the subject—nothing in print, nothing out of print—not even a comprehensive magazine article. I decided to write this book in the hope that it would provide for others what I so badly needed and couldn't find. How to begin was the question—until I started talking to people about the subject. At first, whenever I mentioned my own estrangement from my son and the pain of missing him, almost everyone either had his or her own unhappy story or knew of someone who had one. In fact, many people told me they too had looked in vain for a book or article on the subject.

Until I embarked on the journey of discovery that led to the writing of *Family Estrangements*, I had no idea how pervasive the problem is. What has been even more disturbing is the number of families who are left with the inexplicable loss of loved ones who offer nothing more than the vaguest reasons for their decision to abandon their families. "Why are you doing this?" is a question they seem incapable of answering. This is especially true in the stories dealing with in-law rifts and sibling rivalries.

These stories will speak to you. Those who shared their pain, anger and frustration did so to help themselves move beyond a sense of defeat and feeling of despair. The real world is full of cautionary tales, champions and difficult hurdles to overcome. The best defense against stupidity, unkindness and despair is simply telling the truth with all its ambiguity and complexity. Each of us can make a difference by simply sharing our own stories with real people in real times and places.

We can all be grateful for all the people who did just that. After the first few interviews, I was surprised to learn how many people had never talked about their unhappy estrangement, and how cathartic it was for them to recall and relate the details even though it meant reliving a very painful episode. As the months of interviewing went on, I found so many men and women stuck in a place of confusion, helplessness and resignation—even despondency. It became clear to me that those who think they can't do anything to change their situation stop trying, and then they really can't change things. *If you think you are beaten, you are.* The feeling of futility is paralyzing. For those I spoke to, just *talking* about the estrangement had the effect of moving them from emotional inertia and discouragement to a place of hope and new options—even solutions. Whenever someone hesitated, tightened up or became embarrassed by what they considered their personal tragedy, I related some of the stories I'd already heard to show them that they were not alone. From those stories they were prompted to ask questions about the mending strategies that others had used. Eagerly, they seized on them, and the prospect of applying them to their own situations was now a viable option.

Families are woven together over decades of mutual experiences and history and blood—families are wonderful and aggravating and transitory and growing and diminishing all at the same time. In one form or another, they are here to stay, and they will always define the human condition. From that first sparkling minute of life, the family is the portal of entry, and if we're lucky, only with our last sigh do we depart its embrace. It is through family that we experience all those human feelings that prepare us for and insulate us from the outside world. Family is essential to our emotional health, so shouldn't we do everything possible to keep the family alive and strong?

We all realize the past is the past, indelibly fixed in the way it shapes the future. No amount of teeth gnashing or playing the blame game will alter what has already occurred. There is no perfect person; there is no perfect family. It is not my intention to dwell on who is at fault for family rifts, but to show how these estrangements developed and how the various individuals mended their relationships or learned to cope with their situations. Their stories vividly illustrate how many different ways there are for opening locked doors to reconnect with a family member that you love and miss. It's important to realize that a coping mechanism or a mending strategy can appear in a story in one of the chapters and be entirely appropriate for your situation even if your story is factually different from the one you're reading.

One of the mending strategies that appears often throughout the chapters and has proven most successful is one I call, "Never give up!" Also, the helpful guidelines that appear at the end of each chapter are applicable to most estrangements.

In writing this book, I have relied not only on the experiences of those who have to some degree triumphed over their emotional pain, but on the expert opinion and advice of clinical psychologists Dr. Paul Hirschfield and Dr. Jim Fitzgerald. Numerous other family counselors, therapists, clergy members and lawyers who wrestle almost daily with family problems have been kind enough to provide me with their knowledge and guidance. My twenty years of working as a lawyer and a judge have also proved to be of great benefit in understanding people mired in conflict. Finally, I have drawn on my own personal experience as a mother who has been estranged from her son.

Now, after several years, my son and I have finally resumed communicating with an occasional phone call or e-mail. Still I'm guarded, reticent and fearful of using the wrong tone or saying the wrong thing, but the door is now cracked open, and that's what gives me hope. Someday, I may even get to see the grandchild I've never seen. Through the anguish of it all, I came to realize that my own situation made me uniquely qualified to understand the struggle and the pain other families have had to face. My story is in the book, with my family accorded the same privacy I have accorded others. The identities of the people I interviewed, who gave so generously of their time and spoke so candidly of their emotions, have been protected. But nothing can protect them from the painful estrangement they are going through, in many cases far worse than my own. For me they have provided a source of strength and inspiration.

I hope they will do the same for you.

Chapter 1

———◦◦◦◦———

WHY ARE FAMILIES GROWING APART?

*Wisdom too often never comes, and so one ought
not reject it merely because it comes too late.*

~ JUSTICE FELIX FRANKFURTER

Are there more estrangements today than in the past? While there are no statistics on the subject, considering how easily I found people who have had an estrangement or are in the midst of one, it appears to be an escalating problem. We can only speculate on the reasons why.

There have always been rifts in families, but they seem to be more numerous, more intense and more hurtful than ever before. Sisters aren't speaking to each other since one sister took the silver when Mom died. Two brothers rarely visit because their wives refuse to talk to each other. A son alienates himself from his family when he marries the woman who hates everyone that was ever in his life before she was. A daughter never sees her mother because she can't stand another guilt trip. A family banishes a daughter for marrying outside her race or religion. A son repudiates a divorced father when he reveals his homosexuality. And so it goes—a variety of conflicts, misperceptions, petty grievances, prejudices and jealousies that can lead to one unhappy outcome: estrangements.

Today we are facing a rapidly changing family relationship landscape. Every assumption made about the family structure has been challenged, and once-narrow boundaries have been stretched to include single mothers raising out-of-wedlock children and gay couples having or adopting children. If the so-called conventional family is having trouble maintaining good relationships, imagine what problems can and do arise in less traditional situations. Looking back, we can see that fault lines in our family structure were widening throughout the last 40 years of the twentieth century. The cracks did not become evident until the early 1960s, when the divorce rate began to rise so sharply that it doubled by the mid-1970s. According to a 1999 Rutgers University study, divorce rates have risen 30 percent since 1970, the marriage rate has fallen faster, and only 38 percent of Americans consider themselves happy in their married state, a drop from 53 percent of happily married people 25 years ago.

Today, 51 percent of all marriages end in divorce.

How Americans managed to alter their concept of marriage and family so profoundly during those 40 years is the subject of a great deal of scholarly investigation and academic debate. In a *New York Times* magazine article (May 2000) titled "The Pursuit of Autonomy," the writer maintains that "the family is no longer a haven; all too often a center of dysfunction, it has become one with the heartless world that surrounds it." Unlike the past, the job that fits you in your twenties is not the job or career you'll have in your forties. Even the spouse you had in your 20s will probably not be the spouse you'll have after you've gone through your midlife crisis.

Starting with the 1960s, four sweeping societal changes have exerted an enormous influence on the traditional family structure. Many of these changes led to positive results, including but not limited to a strengthened social conscience, women's rights, constraints on going to war and a growing tolerance for diversity. But there has been a price to pay. Not only have these societal changes altered the structure of the family, but converging together, and as an unintended by-product, they fostered family alienation, exacerbated old family estrangements and created new ones. These major shifts in our American society were:

- ❧ the Me Generation of the 1960s,
- ❧ the women's liberation movement,
- ❧ the states' relaxation of divorce laws, and
- ❧ the ever-increasing mobility of American families.

ME, ME, ME!

The Me Generation of the 1960s perpetuated the notion that we are first and foremost *entitled* to happiness and fulfillment. In America, the business of happiness has always been a growth industry. It's positively un-American *not* to seek it! Which goes back to that early period of our history when Thomas Jefferson dropped the final term from John Locke's specification of human rights—"life, liberty, and … property"—and replaced it with what would become the slogan of the new nation: "the pursuit of happiness."

In 1961, an advertising executive working on the Clairol hair color account came up with the catchy line: "If I've only one life, let me live it as a blond." In a sense, this neon commercial distilled the basic nature of the 1960s. Tom Wolfe, in *Mauve Gloves & Madmen, Clutter & Vine,* had it right when he pointed out, "If I've only one life, let me live it as a _____! Throughout the next decade, everyone began to fill in the blank for themselves."

With the same vigor and determination demonstrated by Americans in their rush for gold, so too were these baby boomers in pursuit of their own individual destinies. This was a cultural revolution with a new perspective—whatever made *me* happy was acceptable. And the converse of that perspective was also true: if marriage made a spouse unhappy, the marriage was no longer acceptable. For that matter, any relationship that was failing to deliver happiness was being tossed out like an empty beer can. More recently, the pharmaceutical industry has learned how to cash in on the American obsession with feeling good by hyping mood drugs to rewire the brain circuitry for happiness through the elimination of sadness and depression.

Throughout the 1960s and 1970s, Americans were enjoying the most prolonged adolescence in their history. The predictable self-absorption of youth evolved into a philosophy of instant gratification that spread through our culture like a California brushfire. In fact, that's where it all started—at the Haight-Ashbury intersection in San Francisco where the "hippies" first congregated to be heard and celebrated. They gyrated to the music of the Beatles and the Grateful Dead, swayed to the songs of Joan Baez and Simon and Garfunkel. Yes, there were birth control pills and a sexual revolution, but also there was a growing social conscience. While longhaired women wearing headbands were reputed to be burning their bras, they were also marching beside their bearded men in opposition to the Vietnam War. Gail Sheehy in *New Passages* describes this generation of young people: "Pampered in the childcentric incubator of a prosperous period [the 1950s], with the invisible hand of Dr. Spock sparing the rod, members of the Vietnam Generation grew up believing they could do just about anything."

Young people fled from the confines of family to be a part of "the scene," and that scene included not only demonstrations and protest marches, but mind-altering drugs and sex for the taking. Families were frantic worrying about exactly where their adult children were and what they were doing. One thing was certain— they weren't abiding by the rules their parents and prior generations had lived by. In fact, the word was, "Don't trust anyone over 30." What better way to alienate than to believe that the parents couldn't be trusted? There were probably more estrangements between parents and their adult children during that period than ever before.

"I AM WOMAN, HEAR ME ROAR . . ."

In the wake of the civil rights movement and President Johnson's Great Society came the second of the four societal changes—the women's liberation movement, and what a fired-up role it played in changing perceptions about the family structure! Women who graduated from college in the late 1960s and early 1970s were living in a time when they could establish and assert their independent identities. In Atlanta in 1968, Emory Law School's graduating class had six women in it, the largest number of women the law school ever had in a graduating class, and all six were in the top 10 percent, including the number-one graduate. Thanks to their record of excellence, I was admitted to the 1970 law school class, and also graduated in the top 10 percent of my class. We were the trailblazers. We worked so hard, knowing how much influence our performance would have on future female enrollment. A point worth noting is that at least half of us were there not as unmarried college graduates, but as wives and mothers. In that same period, the all-male Ivy League colleges opened their doors to women for the first time. For example, Princeton's first coed class was admitted in 1969. No one could doubt the message Helen Reddy bellowed out—*"I am woman, hear me roar. . . ."* For all the self-indulgence of the "hippie" generation, there was a profound awakening in young people, a recognition that civil rights must mean equal rights for everyone in our society, and that had to include women.

Full equality was the battle cry of every minority, a status that women claimed despite their majority position. This individualism and demand for equal rights accounted for much of the drive behind the movement. As they had once marched for the right to vote, women again began marching, but this time it was for both sexual equality and for the same broad range of career and job opportunities available to men. As those options became accessible, women entered the workforce in droves. With this newly found financial independence, women were now freer to walk away from a marriage that was denying them their right to fulfillment and happiness. In the words of Sheehy, "[The Me Generation] expressed their collective personality as idealistic, narcissistic, anti-establishment, hairy, horny and preferably high." Without doubt, this was a dramatic departure from the puritanical sense of duty that had been woven into the American fabric since the birth of this nation. For all the good that came out of this movement, it also changed forever traditional notions of marriage, motherhood and family unity. Perhaps we threw the baby out with the bath water.

Even in the most conservative young families wives were letting their husbands know that it was now their turn. They were saying they'd like to go back to work or back to school. "Don't ask, don't tell" day care centers sprung up where overworked and undertrained staff and yuppie parents ignored the children's unhappy days—all in the name of equality so that women could reclaim their identities. They didn't want to do what they thought their mothers had done, become the appendages of their husbands. They wanted to be people in their own right, and now they had the opportunities to do just that. These were the parents who ran away from home.

DO-IT-YOURSELF DIVORCE

Before long, there were as many women in college as there were men. At this same time, the 1970s, divorce rates began to increase. Many states began to approve legislation that allowed no-fault divorce, eliminating the need to lay blame on spouses or stage adulterous scenes in sleazy motels. More than ever before, our legal system established procedures for easily dissolving marriages, dividing property and sharing responsibility for the children. Perhaps the most significant reason for the rise in divorce rates was predicated on increased numbers of married women working outside the home. This along with their newly found entitlements altered the role of women within marital relationships. Marriage had become a choice rather than a necessity, a one-dimensional status sustained almost exclusively by emotional satisfaction, and not worth maintaining in its absence. There were even do-it-yourself divorce manuals rolling off the presses. That's how easy it was to get a divorce, as long as there were no child custody issues and no substantial property to fight over. During these two decades, the 1960s and 1970s, attitudes about divorce were becoming more lenient, so much so that we finally elected our first divorced president in 1980—Ronald Reagan.

With few exceptions, most of the Western world is undergoing the same sort of family transformation that has occurred in the United States. Today Great Britain has a divorce rate that exceeds ours, and its single-parent families are at an all-time high. Similar increases are occurring throughout Western Europe, even in those countries where the populations are predominantly Catholic. In Belgium, Switzerland and France, divorce rates have doubled, while in Canada, England and the Netherlands they have risen threefold. With divorced fathers always running the risk of estrangement from their children, this growing divorce rate has had the predictable impact of increasing the number of those estrangements.

Though we have gotten away from communal living serving as a substitute for the traditional family, we are still feeling the impact of this chasm between the young and the old. Today, and probably for the foreseeable future, we will be searching for answers to the new set of problems we created by these societal changes. Can we be optimistic that we will eventually rectify these problems? Those who have studied and understood the American psyche have held firm to an optimistic perspective. About Americans Alexis de Tocqueville said, with only a tinge of French envy, "No natural boundary seems to be set to the effort of man; and in his eyes what is not yet done, is only what he has not yet attempted to do."

ON THE ROAD AGAIN

The fourth change, and certainly as important as any with regard to its impact upon the family, was the increased mobility of families over these four decades. Families were no longer living in close proximity to one another as they once did. The organization man now moved to wherever he could advance more quickly up the corporate ladder. College graduates took the best job offer even if it was three thousand miles away from where they grew up and where their family still lived. Likely, the person they chose to marry, instead of being the boy or girl next door, already lived where the young graduate had just moved to.

According to Lynn H. Dennis's *Corporate Relocation Takes Its Toll on Society* (*Workforce*, Feb. 1999), during the ten years from 1989 to 1999, more than five million families were relocated one or more times by their employers. In addition to employer-directed moves, one out of five Americans relocated at least once, not for exciting adventure but for economic advancement. From March 1996 to March 1997, 42 million Americans, or 16 percent of the population, packed up and moved from where they were living to another location. That is a striking statistic. Six million of these people moved from one region of the country to another, and young adults age 20 to 29 were the most mobile, making up 32 percent of the moves of that year.

What this produced was a disbursement of nuclear families throughout the country, radical disconnections and, ultimately, the death knell for the extended family—the clan and all its adhesive qualities.

With cell phones, computers, faxes and the Internet, the office can now be anywhere, including in the home, and therefore we can *live* anywhere we want to. If that's the case, why aren't more people choosing to live in the towns where they grew up? There's no definitive answer. But it does seem certain that, in spite of all the praise heaped on family values, staying close to family no longer has a substantial influence on our choice of where to live.

These relocations affect the emotional stability of household members, disrupt family unity and require individuals to invest an enormous amount of time to reestablish their lives without help from the family or even friends they grew up with. It is true that nothing compares to the experiences of immigrants who left their countries knowing they would never see their families again; nevertheless, the analogy suggests itself. The rootlessness caused by pervasive American relocation makes family relationships difficult to sustain.

Our culture tends to focus on the individual or at most on the nuclear family, downplaying the benefits of extended families, though their role is vital in shaping our lives. The notion of "moving on" whenever problems arise has been a time-honored American concept. Too many people would rather cast aside some family member than iron out the problem and keep the relationship alive. If we don't get along with our father or if our mother doesn't like our choice of mate or our way of life, we just move far away and see the family once or twice a year. Once we're married with children in school and with both parents working, visits become even more difficult. If the family visits are that infrequent, why even bother at all? Some children grow up barely knowing any of their relatives. How will they ever fully understand the benefits of an extended family? Contact ceases, the rancor doesn't resolve and the divisiveness germinates into a full-blown estrangement.

In an odd sort of way, the more wealth that's generated, the more families scatter and grow apart. It's not a cause, but it is a facilitator; tolerance levels decrease as financial means increase. Just think how much more we tolerate from our families when they are providing all our financial support.

One young woman related how her father expected her to come home from college every summer and work in his sporting goods store in exchange for her college expenses. As a journalism major, she would have much preferred to get a job with a newspaper, but Daddy was paying the bills so he was also calling the shots. When she was finally off Daddy's payroll, she moved away and curtailed her contact with him to a once-a-year visit. This went on for several years until she needed his money once again to pay for her wedding.

For many of us when we were growing up, Sundays were family days. We all piled in the car and drove off to visit the relatives—typically going to Grandma's house where everyone gathered for Sunday dinner. Recently, a well-known actress being interviewed in a popular magazine was asked if there was one thing she could change in her family, what would it be? Her answer was simple: "That we could all live in the same city." She understood the importance of being near loved ones and how, even in a harmonious family, geographical distance often leads to emotional disconnect. When relatives are regularly in each other's company, they will usually make a greater effort to get along. Even when there is dissension among family members, they are more likely to work it out, either on their own or because another relative has intervened to calm the troubled waters and thereby to prevent a family estrangement. But with families scattered all over the country as they are today, the matriarch or patriarch of the extended family is far less able to keep his or her kin united, caring and supportive of one another. In these disconnected nuclear families, routinely we observe certain trends—workaholism, alcoholism, depression, anxiety, isolation, escapism and a push toward continuous supervised activity for children. What happened to that family day of rest, relaxation and togetherness? We should mourn its absence.

Another unintended consequence of this mobility phenomenon is its negative impact on the elderly. Elderly people sometimes suffer at the hands of adult children who lead busy lives and rarely visit their parents because they don't live close by. Geriatric depression can be triggered or aggravated when aging parents need help and the children aren't there.

On the positive side, in the absence of children elderly people gain a sense of comfort and security when they know they have brothers and sisters to turn to. Studies show that at least 80 percent of siblings over age 60 enjoy closeness with one another. Rivalries forged in childhood become less and less important with time. Brothers and sisters know each other in a unique way during childhood and share a history that can bring understanding and perspective in adulthood. Loneliness is a major source of geriatric depression, and is it any wonder—with friends and neighbors moving away, coworkers forgotten, marriages broken up, parents deceased and children too busy with their own lives? Who's left? Brothers and sisters can rediscover the values and strengths of family, especially when a sense of mortality is upon us.

But again, we are more likely to have these close relationships— and more motivated to forgive hurts and grievances—when we see family members on a regular basis. Solid family relationships are much less likely when we live far apart and see each other only at weddings and funerals. By living apart we don't depend on one another, so there's less need to forgive and forget. When rifts occur, relatives often need a real jolt to perform an act of forgiveness.

On Yom Kippur, the Day of Atonement, the highest of holy days in the Jewish religion, Isaac, faced with a terminal illness, unable to attend synagogue services, delivered an unforgettable homily to his adult children. In a weakened, gravelly whisper, he said, "I want you to look into each other's eyes and ask for forgiveness for anything cruel and hurtful you ever said or did to each other, knowingly or unknowingly, and I want you to totally forgive one another." Twelve hours after muttering those words, Isaac died, but his wife, mother of the children, was there to remind them of their promise to their father.

Isaac delivered that request at a time when his children desperately needed to hear it, when their relationships were strained, with not much to say, too many unspoken resentments and too much hostility that seeped out in snide remarks on those holidays when they traveled from afar to be together. For over a year, two of the siblings had been estranged from each other. Their father's words helped them begin to reassess their relationships, and to handle the intricacies of their father's estate with relatively little conflict compared to what it might have been had he never uttered those words. Today, scattered families see each other so infrequently that the likelihood of keeping such a promise is virtually nil.

Often, absolving a family member can be the toughest act of forgiveness to pull off, probably because the emotional bonds are so much deeper and usually go all the way back to childhood. Could it be that blood is a thicker medium in which to hold a grudge?

For this widely dispersed Me Generation, with more financial means than any prior generation, commitment, intimacy and family togetherness have never been high on their list of priorities. How many times have you heard of family members trying to maintain a relationship via e-mail and the telephone answering machine? One young man now sends his Mother's Day greeting by leaving a message for his mom on *his* answering machine. When she calls to scold him for forgetting to contact her, she'll get a few sweet words wishing her a happy Mother's Day and his apology for being too busy to call or send a card! His sister can expect the same kind of greeting for her birthday—that is, if she bothers to call to find out why her brother hadn't contacted her.

There's No Family Like Our Family

A part in each of us needs to engage in a meaningful way with our family. To do that, we have to develop an empathy that recognizes how much we belong to each other—and how incomplete we are without the love of family. Even when families have grown so far apart, they have regenerative qualities and can grow back together again. But the first and most important step in reconnecting is to recognize our deep desire to do so.

Chapter 2

X-RAY THE FRACTURE

You can't shake hands with a clenched fist.
~ INDIRA GANDHI

Not all rifts can be mended, but *most* of them can be. The first step is to take an X-ray to know where the fracture occurred—the conflict that caused the break. Once you know what you did to drive the other person away, you can apologize and avoid making the same mistake again. That isn't to say apologies are always accepted, but it is usually the best way to begin the mending process. To say you are involved in an estrangement because you just don't get along with the other person is about as helpful as telling a doctor you don't feel well. It's too vague for him to diagnose the condition and recommend a treatment. Although we may believe nothing we did created the rift, if we think about it objectively and honestly explore the details of the situation, we can usually come up with some solid clues as to what caused the relationship to rupture. And just as importantly, how to prevent it from happening again.

Awareness of Hot Buttons

When you carefully reflect on the difficult or troubled relationships you may have had during the course of your lifetime, you will probably see a pattern emerge that sheds light on why you become entangled in conflict. Sometimes you may have to go all the way back to childhood. Maybe you had a friend who had promised to go to the park with you, but when invited to go to a party with someone else, he or she said nothing and abandoned you. Probably the playmate wanted to remain your friend but a better invitation came along. You probably wondered what kind of friend breaks a promise like that. Or maybe you found out your best friend talked about you behind your back and was telling others things you had said in confidence to that friend. Or maybe your friend threw a temper tantrum or teased and tormented you when he or she wanted you to do something you didn't want to do. You felt betrayed and eventually walked away from that relationship. Those rifts are minor estrangements, and likely the first ones you ever had.

From such episodes, you may be able to predict that disloyalty or betrayal or intimidation is, for you, enough of a hot button to trigger a breach in a relationship. For some, being compared to a sibling is a hot button—as in, "Why can't you be more like your sister?" Being unjustly accused of something—"Why are you always thinking of yourself?"—is a hot button for many people. Or maybe it sets you off when someone is transparently trying to give you a guilt trip: "You're going to upset your father if you don't do what he's asked of you. You're the only son—you have to take over the family business." And then of course threats and ultimatums are hot buttons for all of us. "If you marry that man, we will disinherit you." Any one of these comments may be enough of a hot button to spark your anger—and perhaps trigger a breach in a relationship.

Even in the best of parent/child relationships there is always a certain amount of disharmony, and sometimes it erupts into what could be called a mini-estrangement—one where communication stops, but the rift is short-lived. By retracing your steps back to those arguments, you might learn more about your tolerance level for a certain kind of conflict and what you do to bring it about. Try to discover your own hot buttons. Usually people manage these in-depth probes into their past with a therapist, but it's worth attempting on your own.

UNREALISTIC EXPECTATIONS

After we've begun to identify the patterns of our conflicts, disagreements and angry outbursts, and their origins and causes, we need to consider, as honestly as possible, what specific things we're doing to make matters worse. You will find the biggest part of the problem is centered on the unrealistic expectations most of us have. When we hold certain assumptions that seem reasonable to us but that others are not willing to fulfill, we are going to be perpetually disappointed, frustrated and even angry.

A typical complaint might be something like: "My brother's wife never helps to clear the table or do the dishes at Mom's house. All the rest of us pitch in. Why can't she do her part?"

Have you ever considered that she works full-time at a high-pressure job? Or maybe she doesn't understand why all the sisters help and the men do nothing. And is it important enough to create dissension?

Or: "Why can't your mother baby-sit for our kids? She never hesitates to take care of your sister's children?"

Try thinking of her situation and why she's not available for you. Is it possible that because she lives in another city and rarely sees these grandchildren, it's hard for her to manage them, as she's able to do with the grandchildren who live near her and are accustomed to being with her?

The problem with expectations such as these is that:

(1) People can't read our minds and know what we expect of them.

(2) Just because we abide by certain rules of conduct doesn't mean others have to do the same.

(3) These expectations lay the foundation for blame to be placed elsewhere when things don't work out as we wanted them to.

Some of the expectations that are most likely to create conflicts are those in which we make demands of other people based on standards we apply to ourselves. Maybe you visited your parents every week, and now you expect your son and his wife to do the same with you. When they fail to meet your expectations, you build resentments, and those resentments are usually directed toward the in-law rather than toward your own blood relative. This may cause you to behave too coldly toward your daughter-in-law until she no longer wants to be in your company at all. And don't for one minute think you can hide those growing animosities. Some in-laws are quicker to spot them than to spot a tornado at their door. Your attitude will also have the effect of alienating your son, who probably relies on his wife to arrange family get-togethers. If you attack your daughter-in-law for avoiding visits to your home, you can expect your son to defend his wife. After a time, you may find yourself in the midst of a full-blown estrangement from the son you love. Remember: This conflict started with a mother whose expectation was predicated on what she thought was reasonable based on her own history. Sadly, serious estrangements can grow out of our unrealistic expectations, and more often than not, for the flimsiest of reasons. Maybe some of your friends have had married children for a long time. You're likely to hear some stories that will give you the comfort of knowing your situation isn't as bad as it gets. You'll understand that in-laws don't always feel the same way about you as you do about them—or maybe they do!

One friend told another friend about the time she backed out of the driveway and hit her son-in-law's new Lexus. As soon as she told him what she had done, he reached for his mobile phone to call the police.

"What are you doing?" she asked. "I'm family."

"I don't believe in nepotism," he said, as he continued dialing.

Check with friends. Even if they can't give you answers to all your questions, you'll begin to put your own situation in perspective. Sometimes friends who have had years of experience dealing with married children can offer some valuable advice. They'll be able to relate the variety of ways they handled their situations. Rather than building up a storehouse of destructive resentment, consulting and commiserating with friends is the better alternative. They may tell you how they drop everything they're doing when their adult children telephone, because the one occasion of being too busy may mean a deep freeze for months on end. They may also remind you that your adult children may be in the busiest times of their lives while your life is growing more leisurely. We have to make the same allowances for them that we wanted our parents to make for us. It's worth it for the sake of family unity. In the words of Martha Stewart, "It's a good thing."

As parents, then, we need to be aware of easily unrealistic expectations that can poison relationships. If visits from the children are infrequent, try substituting e-mails, funny cards or telephone calls for face-to-face conversation. I've heard of grandparents and grandchildren who e-mail back and forth all the time and keep their relationships alive that way. It's better than no communication at all.

When it comes to death, wills and inheritance, unrealistic expectations often make for lifelong, bitter estrangements. The heir who expects more than he actually receives is usually being unrealistic and certain to be disappointed and angry.

One daughter whose father had just died suggested her mother contact her older brother, from whom she'd been estranged for more than 15 years. Her mother said she'd think about it.

The daughter didn't know the details, only that her mother and her mother's brother had clashed over the care of their own mother, the daughter's grandmother. After the grandmother's death, the mother's brother and his wife moved away. They never had any children, and when his mother's will was probated, he discovered that she had left all her money to the children of her two daughters in a generation-skipping trust. He and his wife were bitter about being entirely omitted because they were childless. They contested the will, but predictably, the courts would not overturn the wishes of the testator, in this case, the man's mother.

"Why is he mad at *you*?" the daughter asked her mother.

"To tell you the truth, I really don't remember," the mother replied. This family estrangement had taken on a life of its own. If family members reach the kind of impasse this brother and sister reached, every day of not seeing each other or talking widens the breach. Apologies are easier to make if you understand and accept your part in the controversy, but exactly what part this woman played in the controversy with her brother was vague. Of course, it's clear that the brother's expectation of inheritance was at the root of his anger, but focusing that anger on his sister was unreasonable. It wasn't her will that cut him out of a share of his mother's estate. Perhaps the brother unrealistically expected his sister to influence her children to renounce a portion of their inheritance. Whatever his reason for alienating himself from his sister, there's no question his anger was misplaced and his expectations were unreasonable. No one should consider himself entitled to anyone else's money, even a parent's. Sadly, we are so steeped in a mindset of entitlement that we tend to overreact when our expectations are not met.

One divorced father became estranged from his two teenage children by making repeated demands that they spend all their vacations visiting him in another city where he had moved after divorcing their mother. During their visits, the father continued going to work and left them alone in his sparsely furnished apartment with nothing to do but await his return at the end of the day. They wanted to be home and with friends during the holidays rather than sitting in an apartment in a strange city where they didn't know anyone. This routine continued until they finally refused to visit with their father, and their refusal, in turn, aggrieved the father, who stubbornly insisted that being with him for whatever time he could spare should have been enough for them. The children's relationship with their father disintegrated, and to this day, twenty years later, they have not seen or heard from him. Without an argument or even a discussion of the problem, he broke off communication with his offspring.

This father, an only child doted on by his parents, was used to having his own way and unrealistically expected that his children would be thrilled just to be in his presence. In short, he never considered *their* needs and desires. Unable to overcome the inflated view he had of himself, it cost him his children. The children, now adults, married with families of their own, are left with an inexplicable void in their lives. To this very day, they wonder if their father has ever figured out the part he played in this twenty-year, ongoing estrangement. He simply walked out of his children's lives when they refused to spend all their holidays with him on his terms.

A woman physician who was a lesbian and living with a partner whom she'd been with for 15 years refused to go to her brother's wedding when her invitation specifically excluded her partner.

Years have gone by and this brother and sister are still not speaking. Prior to the wedding, the brother had maintained a cordial relationship with his sister's partner, as did the whole family, but the family into which the brother married had strong objections to the lesbian relationship. Instead of insisting that his sister be invited with her partner, the brother gave in to the prejudices of his new in-law family. He expected his sister to understand the exclusion of her partner because he felt he was caught in the middle. Sure it was tough for him, but it was a defining moment when he should have demonstrated loyalty rather than weakness and hypocrisy. Given the long-term relationship of his sister and her partner and the brother's acceptance of them as a couple, his caving in to his prospective new family's insensitivity was hurtful to his sister. The brother was *disappointed* in his sister's reaction and her refusal to come to his wedding without her partner.

If many of your relationships fracture because people continuously disappoint you, then you have to examine the *reasonableness* of your own expectations. The key word is "disappointment." By probing your own history, you just might succeed in learning enough about yourself to avoid making unreasonable demands on loved ones.

Reversing any lifelong pattern, especially one that is an integral part of someone's personality, is a challenging journey, but one that is worth taking if that pattern has been an obstacle to harmonious relationships.

Dig Deep for Insights

As we expand our awareness of our typical reactions during conflicts, as well as what kind of disputes are likely to ignite strong emotional responses in us, we increase the likelihood that we can change that behavior—do something different from what we characteristically would do in those circumstances.

Try talking to yourself, but don't do it in front of other people or you may find yourself with a whole new set of problems you didn't anticipate. When you're alone, ask yourself: Why am I feeling so threatened, defensive or volatile? What do I think is at risk that makes me overreact to a seemingly inconsequential matter? What in my past is similar to this present conflict? Why does it seem to be hitting a nerve? How can I avoid doing these foolish things that engender anger and rejection? And if I've already done too many foolish things, to the point of total rejection, how can I repair the damage without a full understanding of what it is that I did in the first place?

THE NEED FOR CONTROL

In most situations, there are much larger issues at stake, concerns that reach into the depths of our being and, logically or illogically, threaten our sense of self-worth. *For most people the issues that lead us into knotted relationships boil down to two: the need for control and the need for approval.*

Looking at past conflicts to better understand ourselves will help us maintain a degree of vigilance over how control issues are fired up by the actions of others. Children have little control over the events around them. Growing up means struggling with parents, teachers and other adults for the right to make our own decisions and govern what happens in our lives. The desire for independence, freedom and autonomy is a major force within each of us. Anyone who's in a position to restrict our movements, any situation in which we feel less autonomy than we believe we have a right to have, is likely to elicit our fear of losing control. Once that control issue crops up, people tend to go into high gear, barreling directly into a conflicted relationship.

The son-in-law who takes his wife and children far away to another state or even another country is likely to trigger a certain amount of resentment in the wife's parents. Even if his career advancement requires this move, nevertheless he has taken away an important part of their family. Now in control over some of the most meaningful relationships of their lives, he's altering them to his will. Suddenly, the wife's parents have a change of attitude toward their son-in-law, a change that shows in what they say and how they say it. The son-in-law will sense it and react. He may act as one brash son-in-law did to his mother-in-law. "You're a pain in the ass," he said, never once empathizing with the sadness the mother was feeling over her only daughter and her grandchildren moving to a distant foreign country at a time when she was too frail to travel. He'll try to persuade his wife that her parents resent him and blame him for taking their daughter and grandchildren away from them. Now the daughter is defending her husband and turning against her parents. The wife's parents are no longer in control, and that is a circumstance they must learn to accept. It's the process of "letting go." Typically, both sides to a conflict have a point.

Extending ourselves to see the other person's point of view can work magic in avoiding estrangements.

Or maybe there's an ex-wife who's making it almost impossible for her former husband to have meaningful visitation with his children while at the same time he's paying generous alimony and child support. They're his children, but he's lost all control. He can't rant at his ex-wife without risking further alienation from his children.

Perhaps there's a mother-in-law who has an unusually close and compatible relationship with her son, and the son's wife feels threatened. When the mother and son are together, they have so much to talk about—so many interests in common. The wife feels left out because for whatever his reason, her husband doesn't communicate with her as he does with his mother.

Because the wife feels a loss of power over the situation, she begins to curtail the time she and her husband spend with his family. The mother becomes aware of her daughter-in-law's withdrawal and questions it. How can the son's wife explain a feeling of competition that she has with his mother without appearing foolish? Eventually the relationship deteriorates until the wife forces her husband to choose between his wife and his mother. The wife hopes that a ruptured relationship with her husband's family will solve all her problems. Though he chooses his wife, the husband is now put in an untenable situation that causes him to freeze his mother out of his life. By doing that, he can't spend time with his father, his brother and the rest of his family. Predictably, the husband harbors resentment toward his wife, even though he's choosing to side with her against his mother. Could the mother have seen this coming and done something to avoid it? Sometimes even when we're right, we have to alter our behavior for the more important objective. Loving relationships are too important to lose.

THE NEED FOR APPROVAL

Here is an example of a broken relationship between a mother and daughter that had its origin in the mother's own childhood and her need for approval. They might have avoided the break had the mother paid enough attention to what caused her problems in the first place.

The mother was especially hungry for love and attention. She felt that her own parents didn't love and admire her as much as they did her brother. Even if she misread the situation, her own perception of it had a lasting effect on her personality. She made sure her own daughter was always given the love and approval she had missed, but when the daughter became embarrassed by her mother's extroverted and attention-getting personality, the mother's childhood feelings of rejection were revived.

"And that wasn't all of it," the mother said. "When her father and I argued, she always took his side. I hated that she did that. It was as if she despised me for not being quiet and demure. My voice

31

is on the loud side, I'm too fat and I have a kind of guttural laugh. I know it makes people turn around. I try to modulate it, but sometimes I forget. I suppose it's been an embarrassment to her in front of her friends. She was rejecting my very presence, and this continued for many years. To make matters worse, this rejection was now coming from the one person I had least expected it to come from, the daughter I had doted on."

At first this mother was hurt, then she was furious, furious enough to trigger an argument about the daughter's scornful behavior. It led to her daughter's decision to break off their relationship. This first rift lasted for several months. They reconnected because the mother begged her daughter to speak to her and see her. The mother even apologized for whatever it was she had done, though she really couldn't be specific other than to say that she shouldn't have admonished her daughter for being so hurtful. And even though the daughter deserved to be told that her behavior was cruel and unwarranted, the mother was the one making the apology.

When pushed to examine how the ultimate estrangement could have been prevented, the mother was forced to explore these painful past memories. As a child, she had always felt unwanted and unloved. She wanted to do all the things for her daughter that weren't done for her. Her relentless insecurity even pushed her to indulge her daughter with material things.

"And I gave in to her, even when she made demands that I shouldn't have given in to—for example, letting her have some of my expensive jewelry that I still wanted for myself. Or the times when I would cancel my plans just to run an errand for her. She sensed this vulnerability in me, and exploited it to get what she wanted. I don't mean to say that this freeze between us is all her fault; on the contrary, I believe that by trying so hard to be the good mother, I didn't draw the line when I should have. But I know I don't deserve what she's doing to me."

Before this woman can expect to alter the pattern of conflicted relationships in her life, she needs to not only identify what upsets people who deal with her, but she has to figure out the origins of these troubled interactions. She needs to recognize how the difficulty with her daughter paralleled that of other disagreements she had experienced during her life—all in her pursuit of approval and validation that she could never get from her own parents. Wearing her neediness for the world to see had the effect of driving people away. Coaxed into that place of realization, the mother came to understand that in her desire to be liked and loved, she failed to stand up for herself when she should have.

"I knew my daughter had lost all respect for me. By giving her everything she wanted and apologizing for things I shouldn't have had to apologize for, I ended up appearing weak and spineless. I think the embarrassment she felt for me just grew until she couldn't stand the sight of me."

This kind of unresolved anger, combined with a longing for what might have been, is the kind of mix that keeps therapists in business. If the mother's own efforts to mend this estrangement fail, she should try to persuade her daughter to join her in seeking professional help, and if her daughter won't go with her, the mother should continue alone. The mother's first step in her own healing process should be forgiveness and acceptance of herself. As for the daughter, she must accept responsibility for her cruel behavior toward her mother, and she also had better face the prospect of living with long-term guilt if her mother should die before they're both able to mend their relationship.

Avoiding Guilt

Parents, especially cranky ones, have a scary habit of dying just before we make our peace with them. If you think it's difficult dealing with a cantankerous, demanding, aging parent, wait until you try dealing with his or her absence. Memory can play nasty tricks on us when we remember a deceased parent with whom we had an unresolved conflict. Even when we try to be objective in our thinking, we either remember only the good stuff—making us feel like monsters for what we've done—or only the bad stuff, leaving us with a guilt trip that is far worse than the one that the parent could have inflicted on us. It's the kind of guilt that can haunt you for the rest of your life, and another important reason for mending rifts with loved ones.

There we have some classic examples of unreasonable expectations, control issues, approval issues, overreactions and hot buttons that lead to estrangements. In order to find out what we're really fighting about with another person, we have to be sure of which of our own issues is at stake.

IRRECONCILABLE DIFFERENCES

Despite your best intentions and most dedicated efforts, not all controversies can be worked through. Even when you have counteracted all tendencies toward blame and resentment and transformed yourself into a benevolent and agreeable person, there is still that ever-present problem I refer to over and over again in the coming chapters—people who refuse to forgive and forget.

Often deeply ingrained patterns are irreversible. These are usually the unresolved issues from the past that can never really be laid to rest. You've known people who are unlikely to ever change their positions, whether it's on the issue of the unregulated right to bear arms or the right to life without exception. They're never going to change even if 100,000 children are killed by guns every year or if a woman's life is at stake by reason of her pregnancy. People of this ilk do not bend. When people feel so strongly about something that their whole value system is at stake, even incremental changes are unlikely to occur. And if there are two such inflexible people involved in an estrangement, they'll be unable to find common ground to negotiate a settlement.

Look at the situation involving Nancy and her mother-in-law Louise. Nancy believes that people are basically selfish and untrustworthy. Louise thinks that most people are basically good, and when given a choice will do the right thing. One day around the family dinner table, Nancy, a claims adjuster for an insurance company, related how she saved her company three weeks of interest on a car accident settlement that was to be paid to a young mother and her injured baby. A drunk driver insured by Nancy's company caused the wreck. Nancy boasted about how long she was able to stall the settlement and keep the money in the insurance company's interest-bearing account. Louise was appalled to learn that the young mother, without adequate health insurance, desperately needed that money to pay for her injured child's surgery. Delaying payment to the mother in order to benefit the insurance company's bottom line was an unforgivable cruelty, according to Louise. She reminded her daughter-in-law that in trying to do the right thing for her company, she put an innocent child's life at risk.

Over time, and on a host of other issues, each woman will probably become more entrenched in her position, more convinced that she is right and the other is wrong. When Louise tries to uncover the underlying reasons for their conflicts, she may run into a wall unless she fully understands the basic nature of her daughter-in-law. Louise must face the sources of their antagonism and the roots of Nancy's determination to take the positions she takes. Only then will Louise see that she and Nancy are so *fundamentally* different in their basic values and beliefs that disagreements between them are inevitable. The best they can hope for is to reduce the intensity of their struggles in order to prevent both of them from feeling wounded every time they deal with each other. Because their basic ideologies are irreconcilable, the warmth and intimacy of family may never grow between these two women, but they can at least avoid causing each other a great deal of pain.

Some conflicts are so complex or so ambiguous that it is virtually impossible to sort out all the variables involved, much less work out a blueprint for reaching a harmonious agreement.

Jackie and her sister Frances feel a certain grudging sisterly affection, but they have been feuding with each other for as long as both of them have been able to talk. Over the years, they have tried to smooth out their differences, but the differences persist and recently have escalated to a point of real hostility over who gets to keep their deceased mother's diamond ring. Jackie has two daughters. Frances has two sons. Jackie believes she should be entitled to her mother's most valuable piece of jewelry because she can pass it along to one of her daughters, failing to realize the same problem could arise again by choosing one daughter over another. Frances maintains that the ring should be sold and the proceeds evenly divided between the two sisters.

At least once a month they see each other at family gatherings, but each knows all too well that underneath the restrained civility there is a major eruption waiting to happen. Each time they've tried to figure out why they get on each other's nerves, they've only made things worse. It becomes a rehashing of all their differences and all the slights each has stored in her memory bank over the years. With this angry arsenal they fight their war. Unless there is an intervention by a family member they both respect or by an objective third-party professional who can reach the source of their antagonisms, they are unlikely to resolve their differences.

On the matter of the ring, there can be no real compromise; there is going to be one winner and one loser. In a situation where one person gets what she wants and the other person doesn't, conflict and resentment are part of the consequences for this irreconcilable difference.

Life is a puzzle, often with pieces missing or ones that don't fit together as they should. Unfortunately, interpersonal conflicts aren't always resolvable. Part of learning to think more constructively about controversies in your life is to recognize realistically what is in your power to change and what is not. A wiser mind than mine has said this so well: *God grant me the serenity to accept the things I cannot change, the courage to change the things I can, and the wisdom to know the difference.*

In your contemplation of the problem, it's prudent to accept that you may not have all the answers. It should be apparent by now that most of the issues we fight about are not what we're really concerned with; there are often other matters, some readily visible and some buried from view, that drive our behavior. If you can't figure out what is the source of your problem, seek advice and be receptive to it. There is the likelihood that someone else—another family member, a friend, a clergyman or a therapist—will have something in their reservoir to be of help where you have failed.

This book is filled with stories of almost every type of family estrangement, and each chapter offers many different means of coping and mending ruptured relationships. By exploring all of them, there is a good chance that you will find one that you never considered and yet has wonderful possibilities of working for you.

✕ HELPFUL GUIDELINES ✕

All guidelines that appear at the end of each of the chapters are applicable to estrangements that occur for any reason. Even if the subject of the chapter seems unlikely to fit your facts, remember that the coping mechanisms and the mending strategies revealed in the stories are useful for any type of rift.

Deal with strong emotions. Before you express your feelings, process them internally so that you have sorted out what part of your reaction is the result of your own unresolved issues. Only then can you begin to understand the emotional issues embedded in the struggle with the estranged family member.

Hot buttons need to be confronted and understood. Explore your own history until you fully recognize what your hot buttons are—the ones that when pushed will trigger heated emotions and overreaction. You can discover them by sorting through the years of your life and seeing how you reacted to other conflicts. Once you understand your own hot buttons, you can tone down your reactions to people who may be pushing them unintentionally.

Remain flexible. When you have worked through resentments that get in your way and taken responsibility for your own part in the conflict without blaming anyone, you are better positioned to address grievances in a conciliatory way.

Know the goals of the estranged family member. By careful introspection, figure out what the estranged person *wants*. What you want is easier to figure out—you want to reconnect. What the other person wants is to avoid you, but why? Once you figure out why you are being avoided, you will know what it is the other person wants. If you can provide that, then move to the next step and communicate your willingness to accommodate the other person's wishes.

Accentuate the positive. Communicate your desire to work things out by immediately conveying that you value that person and want to reconnect with him or her, that you hold no grudge. Be forewarned: resolving differences often means taking risks, baring your soul and again facing rejection. For most of us who want to reconnect with a loved one, it's worth the risk.

Keep your eye on the real issues. The object in deciphering the real issues that underlie your disagreements is so that you can deal with what is the heart of the problem rather than with superficial or irrelevant issues. Learn how your conflicts may be representing your attempts to relive dysfunctional patterns that were programmed in the past—i.e., keeping people at a distance to avoid being hurt.

Don't play the blame game. This should come as no surprise. If you are ever to bridge differences, you have to move beyond blame. On the other hand, if you are the one who wants to mend a relationship with a family member who instigated the estrangement, you may have to brace yourself for a diatribe of blame against you. Take it. Say you want to think about it, not necessarily that you accept the blame, but do not—I repeat, do not—retaliate with charges of your own. This will be hard to resist doing because you may feel that you are humiliating yourself, and in a sense you are, but this is one of those situations where the end does justify the means.

Note: This last guideline does not meet the usual standards for conflict resolution. Accepting all the blame is viewed as detrimental because it is considered to be encouragement for further hurling of blame in the future. Blame makes people feel defensive, which is usually a negative aspect of conciliation, but where family members are concerned the stakes are higher and the sacrifices will have to be greater, too.

Chapter 3

―――⋙◆⋘―――

FOR BETTER OR WORSE . . . AND WORSE . . . AND WORSE

DIVORCE-RELATED ESTRANGEMENTS

Because I needed to love my mother and father in all their flawed, outrageous humanity, I could not afford to address them directly about the felonies committed against all of us. I could not hold them accountable or indict them for crimes they could not help. They, too, had a history—one that I remembered with both tenderness and pain, one that made me forgive their transgressions against their own children. In families there are no crimes beyond forgiveness.

~ PAT CONROY, *The Prince of Tides*

Have you ever wondered how all those sacred marriage vows to love each other "until death do us part" become quaint but meaningless words for too many loving couples? It's like asking the question: when do fish sleep? There's probably an answer, but who knows for certain what it is. The breakdown of the nuclear family, which began with the increasing divorce rates of the early 1970s, has accelerated to become a virtual chain reaction. While people still cling to the ideal that marriage should be a lifelong commitment, couples, even as they stand hand in hand at the altar, are becoming aware of the dismal statistic that more than half of all American marriages end in divorce. A sad truth, especially when there are children.

When divorce occurs, not only do the spouses part, but also many other family and friend relationships are broken. In this chapter, several different family estrangements are presented to show how these individuals coped with their painful predicaments. Some of these were resolved, others were not, but they are all useful in showing how estrangements occur and how people learn to cope with them, particularly those that seem irreconcilable.

In her book *The Dance of Intimacy*, Harriet Goldhor Lerner writes: "Distance or cutoff from family members is always a trade-off. The plus is that we avoid uncomfortable feelings that contact with certain family members inevitably invokes. The costs are less tangible but no less dear."

What are the costs? If one of the parties to the divorce doesn't want the marriage to break up, that person may be on a mission to punish the spouse who has decided to leave. Revenge is like a tornado that may destroy or damage everything in its path. Just remember that an eye for an eye will eventually leave everyone blind.

These specific situations may not totally mirror your own, but they will give you a framework to help you consider changing your perspective. Not only will you see how others have coped with the anguish of losing contact with loved ones, but you may see and be able to avoid certain pitfalls on the path to reconciliation.

POISONED MINDS

A vengeful parent or even a grandparent can poison the minds of children so that they no longer want to be with one of the parents. The first two stories show the damage that occurs when young minds are poisoned. Each father dealt with the loss in his own way, and both managed to reestablish contact with one or more of their children.

At the time of this interview, Doug, a 72-year-old reserved and dignified banker and father of three adult daughters, said, "The pain of not seeing one of my daughters for 25 years has been tempered by the passage of time, but it was very painful at first."

When asked to discuss how the estrangement came about, Doug could only provide a skeletal version of the rifts with his daughters.

"We just don't see each other," he said, then paused and took a deep breath. "It's been hard. And there wasn't only the estrangement with two of my three daughters, but also with my mother and me. That lasted until she died."

His eyes turned away. "I was her closest relative, and when she was dying I had to be the one to give permission to take her off life support. It was really hard, but it was what she wanted according to her living will. Strange—by law I was the closest to her, but we barely spoke for more than 20 years. It wasn't what I wanted. It was her choice."

Doug has three daughters from a first marriage. Because of his divorce from their mother, initially he became estranged from the two younger daughters who remained in their mother's custody. The oldest daughter avoided the conflict because she was away at college. The relationship with the youngest daughter resolved itself several years ago, but the estrangement from his middle daughter has never mended. She is now 38 years old, married with two children of her own, and Doug has had no contact with her or her family for all these years.

When Doug first told Vickie, the mother of his three daughters, that he "wanted out," she threatened to destroy him financially. Although she had a history of infidelity throughout the marriage and had abused Doug, she was unwilling to give up the financially secure life he had provided. Over the course of a 23-year marriage, as both Doug and Vickie gradually increased their drinking to a point of excess, they found contrasting ways to torture each other. She became verbally and physically abusive while he grew more and more passive and unresponsive. Doug admits that in the later years of his marriage he could barely tolerate his wife, but continued to remain in the marriage for the sake of the children. He didn't want to break up the family for fear it would be more devastating to their daughters than the dysfunctional situation they experienced at home. In retrospect, he admits he should have left years before he did.

Vickie's abuse finally became intolerable. Doug had even spent hours in a hospital emergency room because of a knife wound she inflicted. Doug moved out of the house while the two younger daughters, 9 and 13, remained with their mother.

"I didn't really relate to my daughters," Doug said, "not as I probably should have." He hadn't been very involved in the activities of their day-to-day lives, and when out of the house, his involvement became even more limited.

When Doug told Vickie he wanted a divorce, her reaction was "predictably hostile and aggressive." She took scissors to the clothes Doug had not yet packed and a hammer to the sports car he left in the garage. Uncomfortable and unskilled at being an active parent, marginalized by infrequent contact, Doug began to focus on building a new life.

The Victorian Code

In all the years of his wife's abuse, mental and physical, Doug never told anyone about her behavior, including his mother. "I was ashamed of it all," he said, "ashamed of her and ashamed of myself for putting up with it."

When he visited his mother to tell her that he was going to divorce Vickie, his mother strongly objected, but not half as much as she objected to Doug's announcement that he had met another woman, Beth, and was planning to marry her. "My mother never approved of Vickie, in fact never liked her, but for some reason, she now sided with Vickie."

It was at this point that the seeds of his estrangement from his two younger daughters were sown. Doug's mother told him to "cut off all contact with this other woman," a professional woman with a young son and daughter. His mother required that he not be seen with "the other woman" for at least a year. "And if you continue to see her," she said, "I will have nothing further to do with you." Then she declared her intention to do whatever she could to prevent her son from seeing his own children if he disobeyed her. Doug knew she would do exactly what she did do—threaten to disinherit him, but he didn't care. What he didn't expect was her cruelty in collaborating with his estranged wife to alienate his children from him. At the time of the divorce, Doug was 47 and a well-respected member of the business community in his town. It was an affront to him that his mother was trying to dictate how he should live and with whom.

He paused. "In looking back, I see now my escape from that marriage may have saved my life."

When he made it clear that he had no intention of following his mother's ultimatum, she carried out her threats, trying to turn the children against him and cutting him out of her will. They were unsuccessful with the older daughter, who continued to have a relationship with her father, and it has strengthened over the years.

Throughout the interview, Doug repeatedly blamed his mother for the estrangement from his daughters. He felt his ex-wife would never have succeeded in driving his daughters away without the support and collaboration of his mother. He called her "a Victorian lady," someone who was "living in another time, more concerned with appearances and the family name than with anything else." His mother knew of her daughter-in-law's heavy drinking and incidents of embarrassing behavior, including her daughter-in-law's suspension from their country club because of several humiliating drunken incidents. Doug felt that his mother's threat to prevent his contact with his children was motivated far more by her desire to break up his relationship with the woman he planned to marry than by a desire to do what was best for the children.

Doug divorced his wife and married Beth. The divorce decree granted him visitation with his two younger daughters every other weekend. Beth did all she could to welcome his children into their family. She went to great lengths to plan activities that would appeal to all four of the children, her son and daughter and Doug's two daughters. This "new family" went to amusement parks, the zoo, movies, hikes in the mountains and trips to the seashore. The children got along very well together.

But in less than a year, Doug's middle daughter, the 14-year-old, announced that she no longer wanted to visit him. Doug realized that his daughter had been "brainwashed" against him. The 10-year-old daughter told him of the hateful things said about him and Beth by her mother and grandmother. She revealed that her sister had been telling the grandmother outrageous lies about their visitation weekends and even made up accusations of inappropriate sex by her father and Beth in the presence of the children. When the youngest daughter said her sister was lying and that nothing had ever happened, the grandmother scolded the youngest child for calling her sister a liar. Doug's mother chose to believe her granddaughter's shocking stories despite the fact that she knew her son was not capable of such bizarre behavior. If anything, she knew he was rather shy and reserved, and she had often chided him for his reticence.

Forced to Let Go

After a time, Doug's youngest daughter began to feel comfortable with Beth and her two children. She told her father she wanted to live with him, but he realized it would be virtually impossible to change the custody agreement. He'd never win that battle without revealing the sordid details of his marriage to Vickie and disgracing her publicly.

There would also be the ugly scene of his 14-year-old daughter being called as a witness to refute the horrific lies she had been telling. When he told the youngest daughter that as much as he wanted her to live with him, the courts would never allow it, she was deeply hurt. His explanation for why she could not move in with him did not satisfy her, but she became resigned to the fact that she would have to continue living with her mother. It was then that she announced she no longer wanted to continue seeing her father. She explained how difficult it was for her when she returned home from those weekend visits. She felt rejection by her mother, her grandmother and her sister. It was as if they were punishing her for wanting to see her father and betraying them in their mission to isolate Doug from his entire former family. Doug said that Vickie and his mother put the child through "a torturous third degree every time she came back from one of her weekend visits." Finally Doug stopped insisting on those visits. "I felt she would be better off not having to go through all that." At this point, the real estrangement began.

Constructing a Wall

Doug missed his daughters. He tried to resume some contact with them by going to their school to see them when classes were out. It was then that Vickie began a campaign of late-night drunken phone calls to his home, with threats of physical harm to Beth's children, and made repeated slanderous remarks to business associates of her husband and people that both families knew. She even called the school where Beth's children went and related horror stories to the principal. Then she went to the extreme of placing an anonymous phone call to the County Department of Family and Children's services accusing Beth of abusing her children. The situation became so intolerable that Doug ceased all contact with both daughters.

During this time Doug began drinking again to mask his own pain. It was the same escape route he had taken during his first marriage. "I had all sorts of physical problems, my work began to suffer and so did my relationship with Beth. She hated the drinking and urged me to get help, but I didn't. I didn't see any point to it. I'd been to counseling with my first wife. It didn't do a bit of good. She was just as violent as she had been before she started therapy. If anything, she got worse." But when Beth threatened to divorce him if he didn't stop drinking, he stopped.

Over time Doug developed a close and loving relationship with his two stepchildren, and ultimately he adopted them legally. He realized that his relationship with Beth and her children was his life raft in a stormy sea. "They made me feel good about myself again."

Though he was not seeing his daughters, and the pain of that estrangement never really went away, Doug continued paying alimony, child support and tuition for private schools and their college. Nine years after the divorce, when the youngest daughter was away at school and out from under her mother's wrathful control, she made regular visits to Doug's office to collect her living-expense money. Though she resumed a relationship with her father, it has never reached the level of closeness he hoped it would, but he's grateful for whatever communication there is. Doug says the strain of the rift continues to affect the relationship. The oldest daughter, who was in college at the time of the divorce, maintains a warm and constant relationship with him. Doug feels closest to her and makes a conscious effort to keep in touch with this daughter and her family. When asked how he felt about losing his middle daughter, he said, "At first it was painful, but in time I adjusted to it. The struggle with divided loyalties, guilt and disappointment were at times so difficult that I finally welcomed the loss of contact as a way of having some peace."

When asked if he thought there was any way of reconnecting with the middle daughter, he said he didn't think so. "We would all have a very difficult time being with her. It would be hard to forget the terrible lies she told. She hurt a lot of people. She doesn't even get along with her own sisters. I don't want to risk more trouble. I suppose it's been so many years now that I don't really think about her anymore. I don't have the will to deal with all her resentments and hatefulness. I guess I've constructed a wall." (You will see how two other men who were interviewed for this chapter temporarily erected the same kind of wall.)

Recently, Doug learned for the first time about the threats and verbal abuse his oldest daughter had to endure from her mother, one sister and her grandmother (her father's mother) every time she defied them to see her father. The grandmother would threaten her with disinheritance to discourage the visits with her father. This daughter told Doug that his mother was obsessed with the middle daughter and would have done anything to keep that daughter with her as much as possible. This middle daughter had few friends her own age because she tattled and gossiped and said mean things about people behind their backs. Now that all these daughters are grown with families of their own, it's no surprise to learn that this middle daughter is so difficult to deal with that her sisters want nothing to do with her.

Throughout Doug's account, I was struck by his apparent lack of anger at what had been done to him by both his first wife and his mother. When asked if he had difficulty expressing anger, he replied, "I suppose so. My mother didn't like scenes. As a child, if I got angry or displayed any kind of temper, she'd criticize me."

Remember, this was the mother who was more concerned with appearances than in what was in the best interest of her only son and his children.

What became apparent from Doug's story and his behavior was his use of silence and restraint as a way of coping with painful emotions such as anger and frustration. Many men, especially of his generation, often find it very difficult—they don't even know *how*—to become intimate in close relationships. Many men of Doug's age were raised by fathers who were conspicuous not by their presence, but by their absence, both emotionally and physically. As a result men often distance themselves from their children as a way of controlling or avoiding very intense feelings. According to Harriet Goldhor Lerner, a breakdown of communication between members of a family may be a way of managing anxiety. It should not be construed as a lack of love or feeling.

Fade-Out Fathers

Many fathers, perhaps a majority, fade out of their children's lives during the first few years after a divorce. This is true even when fathers have visitation rights and are paying child support and alimony. Rarely do they participate in raising their children. It is usually the mother who makes most of the decisions about the children's lives. Fathers, including those still married, often relate to their children primarily through their wives. If the marriage breaks up, the ties between father and children are at risk. And when the divorce is messy and acrimonious, those ties seem all the more fragile. Less and less of the father's time is spent with the children when it means the father has to regularly encounter the angry ex-wife—particularly if he has moved on to another family. By the time these extended separations take place, it may be too late for the contentious parents to tone down the ugly rhetoric.

MORE POISONED MINDS

Joe, a 60-year-old successful business executive, has had to deal not only with estrangement from his two sons, but also from his mother. I chose to tell both Doug's and Joe's stories because they reflect a common and growing problem men face in maintaining relationships with their children during and after a particularly bitter divorce. Like Doug, Joe also had to endure the rejection of his own mother during some of the most stressful times in his life. And again like Doug, Joe managed his pain by erecting a wall.

Joe married Sandy when they were both in college. When Sandy told Joe she was pregnant, he agreed to marry her. Joe had a difficult time preparing what he would tell his parents, but when he told them Sandy was pregnant and they were going to get married, his parents said, "good," and nothing more. Joe was shocked at their abbreviated reaction. "I went up to my room, fell on the bed and cried. I wondered if my parents understood what I just told them."

From the very beginning of the marriage, Sandy stayed at home and Joe worked, not only holding down two jobs, but also going to graduate school. Their first son was born a few months after the marriage, but their relationship steadily deteriorated.

Thanks in part to Joe's travel schedule, they fell into a pattern of little or no contact during the week, then on weekends too much partying and too much drinking. On countless occasions, Sandy would accuse his friends of making passes at her.

"She knew how to hurt me," he said. "We weren't compatible. Soon we weren't even speaking, but I stayed with Sandy until my older son was a freshman in college and the younger son was 12."

Finally Joe announced to his wife that he was leaving and filed for divorce. The actual divorce didn't occur for several more years because of legal wrangling over the division of property, but shortly after the separation Joe met Sara, the woman who was later to become his second wife.

Joe felt he mishandled the situation with his sons. "Sandy and I should have sat down with the two boys and told them their father and mother were getting a divorce." It soon became clear that Sandy regarded his involvement with Sara as the reason for the marital breakup. The result: His sons didn't want to have anything to do with her and, ultimately, with him.

Joe tried to see his sons, but they kept rejecting him. "This hurt unbearably. I really missed them," he recalled. After about a year of dating Sara, they moved in together. His ex-wife also met someone and began living with him. Joe described him as "a good guy, no hidden agenda, and my sons liked him, had a good relationship with him."

Sandy put their oldest boy in an expensive private school. Despite the fact that Joe was paying for it, plus generous alimony and child support, his ex-wife went to see his mother and asked for money, claiming Joe had left them inadequately provided for and she needed the money for *food*. "This was a calculated effort," he said, "to turn my mother against me, and it worked. My mother stopped talking to me. That hurt."

The breach with his mother lasted for nearly two years. Eventually one of his brothers intervened to explain to their mother that Sandy's story of Joe abandoning his family was untrue, and that Joe was paying handsomely to support his former family. His mother relented and began once again to communicate with Joe, but not on any intimate basis. In fact, they never actually discussed why she had chosen to alienate her son. To this day, Joe is unable to fully forgive his now-deceased mother for what she did and for failing to give him her compassion and support when he most needed it.

"I was damn angry," he said, "that my own mother would have believed Sandy and would just stop talking to me without ever giving me a chance to tell my side of the story."

Exiled from the Family

As was true with Doug, Joe's mother sided with his former wife. Joe was one of three brothers. Joe recalled an incident with his mother and one of his brothers, who was quieter and more reserved than the others. At one point, when this brother was going through a difficult time and seeing a therapist for depression, he went to his mother and asked her if she would tell him about himself when he was a child. His mother said, "I don't remember you at all."

"That kind of brutal cut was typical of my mother," Joe said. "So I guess I shouldn't have been surprised when she rebuked me."

And then Joe said something curious that was once again similar to Doug's childhood situation: Doug was not allowed to display any anger or disagree with his mother about anything. Joe said his family would gather at the dinner table where there would be lively discussion about politics and the events of the day, but the children were not allowed to disagree with the parents or they would be sent to their rooms. Neither Doug nor Joe was allowed to have a mind or opinion of his own. In both of these stories, the men had to endure estrangements not only from their children but also from their own mothers. In both cases the men were exiled from their families and in both cases they were prohibited from speaking out as children if they didn't agree with their parents.

Losing My Sons

Joe attempted to maintain contact with his two sons, but his oldest son wanted nothing to do with him. The youngest boy began to have gastrointestinal problems, stomach pains and vomiting. He told Joe, "You cheat people every day. That's what Mom says. That's what everyone says."

Joe responded, "I have people who like me and people who don't like me, but no one I know would ever say I cheated them out of anything."

Nothing helped. The boys were not interested in maintaining contact with their father. Joe began to grieve. "I cried a lot," he said. "And then about two or three years after the separation, and after a lengthy period of not seeing my sons, I began to have suicidal dreams, driving off a cliff or into a highway median. I decided to see a psychologist. She helped me understand what was happening."

The psychologist saw his preoccupation with suicide as a way of venting the anger he felt toward his ex-wife, children and mother. He wanted them to feel responsible and guilty about what they were doing to him. And just as Doug had walked away and turned to alcohol as a way of dealing with his frustration and anger, so did Joe. Also similar to Doug, he turned to the embrace of another woman, and in that new relationship both men found the solace and support they could find nowhere else. Joe's loss of contact with his two boys went on for many years. In that time, Joe could never completely immunize himself to the sadness of losing his sons, but his life with Sara gave him the joy and happiness to withstand the loss.

When the 12-year-old was 21, he contacted his father and expressed an interest in seeing him. This was the moment Joe had been waiting for. At Joe's suggestion, they both saw a therapist and were able to work through their problems to a healthy reestablishment of their former relationship.

The 16-Year Rift

The oldest son continued to refuse to see his father for another six years, thus extending the void created by his absence. Joe continued to try to repair this relationship, but all his efforts were rebuffed. Joe invited his oldest son to meet him for lunch, dinner, a drink or a walk in the park. Nothing worked. On countless occasions, his wife Sara would urge him to try a different approach, less confrontational, but Joe resisted her suggestions, believing he knew best. Finally he followed Sara's advice and asked his son to join him for a game of golf. Surprisingly, his son agreed. They went out to play a couple of times, but avoided any discussion of their long estrangement. They just played golf. And they enjoyed each other's company. Then Joe's son asked his father to play with him in a golf tournament. They came in second. After the match, Joe said, "We were in the parking lot, and he came over and suddenly put his arms around me. You'd have to see it. He's six-foot-four and over 200 pounds, and I'm six-foot-two and 220 pounds. So there we were, these two big men standing in the parking lot, hugging. And he said to me, "Dad, I love you." As Joe spoke, his voice was filled with love, pride and gratitude that the relationship with his oldest son was, at long last, after 16 years, finally on the mend.

There is a striking pattern here of locking up the anger and frustration, and then not dealing with it. This was the behavior of Joe's mother, then of Joe himself, and finally the behavior of his oldest son.

When asked what advice Joe would give to others in a similar situation, he said, "Never let them go. I probably gave up from time to time. I remember telling my brother I've cried all the tears I'm going to cry—the hell with them! I regret that, and I don't advise others do that. I'd say if you have to put a noose around their necks to hold them close, then do it. You just can't ever let them go."

He stopped and reflected. "In the early years when they were young, I think the kids thought I left them. I should have constantly reassured them that I wasn't leaving them, that I wanted them. And it was a difficult message to get across because of what they were hearing from their mother. She kept saying I'd left them."

It's difficult to persuade children that the father hasn't left them because the message is there anyway. The father's long absences and, ultimately, his leaving are inevitably going to be considered a rejection of them and a reinforcement of their mother's claim that their father has abandoned them.

The big question is: how does a father counter the message that he's leaving the children when he and their mother divorce and he moves out of the house?

It makes sense to follow Joe's advice: *Be persistent in telling the children you're not leaving them.* Repeated efforts to mend the relationship offer the best chance for a happy resolution. Would this reconciliation between Joe and his sons have taken place if Joe had responded to their cutoff with more anger and cutoff? Probably not.

Recall that Doug's handling of the estrangement with his daughters was not ultimately as successful as Joe's. Doug's coping mechanism was, in effect, to protect himself with a passivity that led to a permanent estrangement with one of his daughters, a superficial relationship with another daughter and a close relationship with the one daughter who took the initiative to maintain contact with him. Doug's personality prompted him to the path of least resistance whereas Joe's personality prompted him to constantly seek contact with his sons. Joe's means of coping proved more effective—and produced a full reconciliation. These two stories contrast so well because they show how a divorced father's persistence paid off.

The reason you can't hug a porcupine is because when he feels threatened or angry, he puts out his quills and retreats to protect his soft underbelly. People, especially men, have been taught to do the same thing. When they feel threatened, they armor themselves with quills and retreat. The solution is to understand that angry feelings always have other feelings attached, such as hurt, helplessness or fear. If you can learn to recognize and express those other feelings to an estranged loved one, you have a far greater chance of being "hugged" than if your quills are out.

THE CONFIDENT FATHER

Michael and Claudia had been married for 22 years, but in the last two years, the marriage was a sham. They had three teenage children. Michael said that Claudia had begun to "hang out in bars and wouldn't come home until after midnight, sometimes not until the wee hours of the morning." Michael asked her to stop. She suggested he might want to accompany her because it was "fun meeting new people." Michael tried it once or twice, but soon discovered it was not for him. Claudia continued her nightly sojourns. "The kids became totally undisciplined—they went wild," Michael says with anger. To make matters worse, Michael's home-building business went into a decline along with the entire real estate market in the 1970s. While money was tight, Claudia used credit cards to give the children anything they wanted, regardless of the cost.

"She was buying their love with my money," Michael said. "She even bought a whole set of golf clubs for one of my sons and another set for his friend."

Michael asked Claudia for a divorce. "I'm keeping the house," he said. "You're getting out, and I'm keeping the children."

The children stayed for a brief time, but they rebelled at his demands that they be home for dinner, do their homework and be in bed at a reasonable hour during school nights. Claudia moved into an apartment, walking distance from their house. One by one the children left and went to live with their mother. Michael laments, "When they were with her they were free to do whatever they wanted to do. So they became uncontrollable and destroyed their options for the future—I mean their chances to be successful professionals."

For a year or two, Michael was completely estranged from his children. Claudia moved to California. The children went with her. They would call occasionally when they needed something.

Michael began to see another woman, Helen, and he married her when he heard Claudia was coming back to try to reclaim the house where she intended to live with the children. Michael said he loved his children and was disappointed at the loss of them, but he described himself as a person who was "pretty good at adjusting to whatever happened and not letting it crush me." He wished he "could have done more—done something to turn things around. Maybe I should have left Claudia 10 years earlier before she had a chance to ruin the kids. Maybe I should have worked less and spent more time with them or maybe tried to turn Claudia around. Finally, I decided I had to learn to live with it. I would stay the course, do what was right and they'd come back. And they did."

When asked how that happened, Michael said it occurred when he and his second wife were divorced. Helen left because she wanted to live a different lifestyle. When his youngest daughter, who was then 25, found out her father was living alone, she called him and asked if he'd like to have a roommate. He was delighted. She lived with her father for almost four years before finally getting her own apartment.

"It was great having her there," he said. "We're very close now. We always will be."

During that same period of time, his first wife Claudia remarried and moved back from California. The other two children voluntarily resumed their relationship with Michael. Now they are both in business with their father. They're all happily married and have children of their own. Michael sees them or speaks to them every day. When asked why he thought they returned to him, he said he didn't know the answer, but he always believed they would one day realize that he was only trying to do the right thing for them, and when they did, they would reconnect with him. Also, he said he had to accept them as they were, not as he had hoped they would be. He was prepared to educate them so that they would one day have professional careers, but their years of skipping school and running wild had dimmed their prospects for higher education.

"They don't have lofty positions," he said, "but they do well, and they are making good lives for themselves and their families. What more can I ask for?"

What was striking about this father's situation and the way his relationship with his children mended had much to do with the absence of anyone poisoning their minds against him as Doug's and Joe's ex-wives had done. Also, unlike the other two, Michael's parents stood by him, as did a large circle of friends and business colleagues. He coped in the best possible way. "Sure I was frustrated," he said. "I thought they were throwing their lives away, and I missed them, but what could I do?"

He kept busy, had an active social life and kept a positive attitude, always certain that he was doing the right thing. He never sought professional help during their estrangement but instead relied on the closeness of family and friends.

"Children have an instinct to survive and survive well. They knew their father was in the best position to help them reach their goals, and that I had always tried to do what was best for them." That, together with the absence of the destructive influences in Joe's and Doug's lives, allowed Michael to have a relatively short period of being cut off from his children and the most favorable resolution of their problems.

In our imperfect world, family structures inevitably lead us to deal with the frailties and disappointments of human life. Sometimes it's necessary to let go of certain unrealistic expectations in order to achieve more important goals. Michael did just that.

Defusing Anger

On the matter of fathers and children of divorce, it is important to do everything possible to defuse the anger of the custodial parent who is fighting for more of the marital property. All three fathers had to deal with resentment over money. In two of the three situations, the ex-wives' anger translated into a poisoned atmosphere where they denounced the fathers and turned the children against him.

Settlement is generally preferable to a lengthy and destructive litigation process, even if it costs a little more. The children are worth it. It's unfortunate that the court system and divorce attorneys makes divorce such an adversarial and bitter process, but progress is being made as more and more states are handling divorce in family courts where the adversarial system is minimized in the interest of the children.

THE ADDICTED MOTHER

It's interesting how people react when you tell them you don't talk to your mother. One woman told a story of having dinner with an old friend from college and mentioning that she and her mother weren't on speaking terms.

"What do you mean you don't speak to her?"

"We don't speak. I don't see her."

"How long has this been going on?"

"A few years."

The friend was shocked at first and didn't know what to say. After a long silence, she said, "She can't be all that bad, and what good does it do to blame your mother?"

Our society frowns on sullying the image of the "good mother." A bad relationship with a mother is almost a taboo. But often an adult daughter's bond with her mother may be one of profound ambivalence. To most of us the word "mother" conjures up the loving caretaker, the woman who bakes cookies and stays up all night with a feverish child. That's what motherhood is perceived to be—either in how we know her in our memories, or how we wish her to be. And fortunately, many mothers are that way, but some children have more somber visions.

Chloe is the only daughter in her family. She has a younger brother. When her parents were divorced after more than 30 years of marriage, Chloe was enlisted by her mother to be a foot soldier in her mother's war against Chloe's father. Chloe had always been her mother's "friend and confidante," and she had never been close to her father, so the estrangement that ensued between Chloe and her mother made them "both miserable," as she put it. Oddly, that's a good sign, because it means they each have enough invested in the relationship to want to repair it.

She described her mother as "once beautiful, vivacious and the life of the party. But now her looks are ruined by her drinking and smoking. My mother was always in charge of the household and the children. She wanted all our love and adoration. It was us against my dad all my life."

Chloe described her mother as someone who coped with life

through her addictions, and she attributed to the addictions the problems with her parents' marriage.

"My father said he wouldn't leave if my mother would stop drinking and cut down on her smoking, but my mother made bad choices and wouldn't change."

When Chloe was in her 20s, she too started drinking. But then she stopped. "I grew up," she said. "I decided to take responsibility for my life. I'm in charge . . . so if something is wrong, it's probably my fault. I need to go back and correct what I've done wrong, but my mother won't do that. And that's the root cause of my separation from her. She takes no responsibility for what goes wrong in her life. She's a victim, and life is railroading her."

She described her father as "quiet, introspective, a man who never talked about his feelings as many men don't. He would just come home and talk to my mother—never came to the children to ask what we did that day. He never had a relationship with us," Chloe said, "and I think I know why. My mother never asked him to spend time with us—never said 'be with the children.'"

Though she admitted her father had committed adultery several times, Chloe persisted in seeing her mother in the more negative light. She related how her parents went to a marriage counselor, but it did no good. "My mother refused to listen to anyone. She wouldn't do any of the things she was asked to do."

In that year of her parents' divorce and Chloe's forthcoming marriage, she and her father had reason to spend more time together planning her wedding since he was paying for it. She and her mother argued repeatedly whenever Chloe asked her father for advice about the wedding. Her mother was angry and maintained the money was hers, too, because it was accumulated by both parents during the marriage.

"No," Chloe said, "'Dad's holding the purse strings, not you.' My mother was furious. She felt she should be the one telling me what to do. I was supposed to obey her. She didn't respect me as an adult."

When asked if that was the basis for the estrangement, Chloe said, "That's just part of it. My father was seeing someone and eventually he married this woman. The estrangement came when my mother gave me an ultimatum, that I was not to see my father's new wife. She regarded her as the cause of the divorce."

Chloe refused to say she would not see her father's second wife, a woman Chloe likes very much. And she attributed her father's happiness to his second marriage. "He's a different person from the one I knew growing up. He smiles now—he's happy."

Her mother reacted to Chloe's refusal by saying, "If you see 'that woman,' I'll have to cut you off."

For over a year Chloe and her mother didn't see each other. Chloe felt she had to stand her ground, but she was terribly stressed and unhappy during that year. She cried often and experienced "long bouts of moodiness." It began to affect her own marriage. Eventually, she sought help from a counselor at her church.

"It helped," she said. "I learned to release my own feelings and not be paralyzed by them. He gave me the comfort of knowing that my first obligation was to do whatever was necessary to preserve peace with my husband, but to also see some of the good in my mother."

Chloe's brother, who was still in his mother's favor, begged Chloe to call her. He said he couldn't take it anymore, meaning the late-night phone calls he had to endure from his inebriated mother. Chloe refused.

Finally, Chloe received a phone call from her mother; she was withdrawing her ultimatum. But Chloe said it took several more months before she could trust her mother because "she withheld her love from me, just took it away."

Although Chloe viewed her mother's demands of obedience as a lack of respect, it was really a part of her effort to regain the control she was losing, not only over her children but also over her own life. When a person is weak and addictive, it is sometimes best to try to see them as someone who is handicapped. We try not to be angry with a handicapped person. We try to be more tolerant, less argumentative and more realistic about our own expectations of this person.

Chloe said she was also able to acknowledge how much she and her mother loved each other and to remember all the good things her mother had done for her in the past, and the happy times they shared. This allowed Chloe to accept her mother's gesture of reconciliation and to begin a new relationship with her mother, one in which they would treat each other as adults, rather than as mother and young child.

All of us feel powerless at times. Triumphant survivors, however, trade in the victim's role for a decision to take charge and search for options. Chloe did just that, but her mother was unable to draw on the kind of inner strength that Chloe could draw on in herself. It's likely that Chloe will always have to be the more tolerant one in the relationship.

The question that arises from Chloe's story is whether or not the father's adultery had anything to do with her mother's escape into alcohol. Chloe never addressed that issue—it's there like a door that's still locked, but if opened, might hold the answer. Chloe could have been more tolerant of her mother's behavior had she fully understood the pain her mother must have felt over the father's pattern of adultery. Perhaps Chloe's myopic view of the situation resulted because her mother's drinking was more immediate than was her father's adultery.

It's easy to blame events or other people for our suffering or missed opportunities. We can attribute our misfortunes to the actions of one or both of our parents, our spouse or ex-spouse, or our in-laws, or we can refuse to relinquish the core of power and control that we need to make choices. This leads me to the case of Jan, a daughter who had a 25-year estrangement from her father.

THE TRIUMPHANT DAUGHTER

When Jan was 10 years old, her mother threw her alcoholic father out of the house. Jan had a younger sister, but she described herself as "Daddy's girl, the one he favored." Jan's mother never told her children that she had kicked their father out of the marriage.

For years Jan experienced enormous insecurity. As is typically the case, Jan believed "had I been a better girl, he never would have left me." And she was so afraid her mother might also leave that she would not spend the night with girlfriends for fear she'd come home to find her mother missing. She explained her father's absence to friends by saying he was away on business.

Her father had remarried and lived in a neighboring town, but Jan didn't see him for 13 years until her grandmother's funeral, which he attended. When Jan was in college, one of her professors urged her to contact her father; she warned that Jan might be adversely affected in later relationships if she didn't work out the problem with her father. Her father was a successful executive in a large public corporation. "Even when he drank, he never missed a beat with his job."

She contacted him and made plans to meet him, but he cancelled the meeting, offering illness as an excuse for not being there. She learned that her father had concealed his first family from his colleagues at work. He believed the situation with them might hinder his climb up the corporate ladder. Jan was distraught that he had never showed up for their meeting. At her own wedding she broke down in tears: "My dad wasn't there to dance that one dance fathers dance with their daughters."

Years later, Jan, who was then divorced from her first husband and remarried, had another chance to meet her father. He was now a widower, retired and living in another state. Her second husband went to see her father and urged him to see Jan. He agreed and they finally met. Jan said, "I like him but there's an emotional void. He can't talk about the feeling side of his life. It's hard to touch his soul. All he would say by way of explanation for the lost years was 'but for the drinking, I never would have left my family.'"

Now Jan talks to him on the telephone a few times a week. To protect her mother, she doesn't bring up the restored relationship with her father. Though her mother never said anything bad about him, she was upset to learn that Jan, and more recently her younger sister, had reconnected with him. Her father made a lot of money. Her mother resents what he did for his second wife and her children while allowing his first family to struggle financially.

When asked what words she could offer to others who were trying to mend a relationship with a father who had virtually abandoned them, Jan said, "While it's easier to tread water than it is to swim against the current, I would take the challenge every time. It's worth it even though it's especially hard to reconnect with a person who's not in touch with his feelings."

Pursuing her father and confronting him was a courageous expression of Jan's adult self. She said, "You can't change the past; you can only go forward."

Jan felt compelled to say she had no anger toward her father. Whether or not anger is there and being suppressed isn't important. What's important is that she is a happier person because she was able to reclaim a relationship with her long-absent father.

Do You Know and Understand Your Father?

In all of these stories, the children did not know much about their own fathers. It's easier to disconnect from a relationship that lacks intimacy. Do you really know and understand that person you no longer see? Do you know his heroes, what makes him laugh, what he likes least about himself or most about himself, what he tried to do but failed, what his relationship was with his own father? Fathers need to open up and share the details of their hopes, dreams, interests and disappointments with their children if they want to keep a close and enduring relationship with them. Since the risk of losing relationships is exacerbated in the context of divorce, it's important to establish real intimacy to reduce that risk. Sharing the details of one's life is a way of promoting intimacy.

In the larger realm of our lives, it's emotionally healthy to have warm and close relationships with family members and to know who they really are. It's easier to mend a relationship with a loved one when that person can be seen in his or her totality. It may not always be possible, but it's worth a try.

Unfortunately, not everyone is able to mend an estrangement, which brings us to the final story in this chapter.

THE LOST GRANDMOTHER

Glenda is a grandmother in her early 50s who holds a responsible managerial position with a large department store. About 10 years ago, her 19-year-old son, Jeff, became involved with a woman, Fiona, who was 17 years older than he was. She had been married and divorced twice before and had two teenage boys from her previous marriages. When she told Jeff she was pregnant with his child, he married her. Although Glenda gave them her blessing, she was not optimistic about the marriage, not only because of the age difference, but also because of a religious and nationality difference. Fiona was a British subject and had no intention of becoming an American citizen, anymore than she was willing to convert to Jeff's religion.

Despite these potential obstacles—mainly the age difference— Glenda and her family welcomed Fiona into their lives. When the child, Elizabeth, was born, she was Glenda's first granddaughter and the "joy of my life." Glenda doted on the child, and Fiona gave Glenda all the time she wanted with Elizabeth. Seven years later, the marriage soured and Jeff wanted a divorce. Fiona, knowing how much Glenda loved her granddaughter, began a campaign of legal extortion. The child became the pawn in the conflict over the terms of the divorce. If Glenda wanted to see the child, she would have to "up the ante," and contribute the better part of Jeff's alimony and child support that he was not financially able to pay. Jeff had to turn over virtually all his earnings to Fiona and move back home with his parents.

Shortly after the divorce was final, Fiona began to refuse to allow Elizabeth, now eight years old, to be with her paternal grandmother. Glenda begged for contact with her granddaughter, and was finally permitted to see the child after having had little or no connection for almost a year. She took the child to a family gathering at another relative's house. Other young cousins were there along with the grandparents. The children were playing together in the basement, when suddenly Elizabeth, visibly upset, came running upstairs to Glenda. She explained that one of her cousins, a 10-year-old boy, had made her pull her underpants down so that he could "play doctor." From what Glenda was told, she concluded that there was some touching but nothing more than that. All four children offered the same story. The children were disciplined and remained in the presence of the adults for the rest of the day.

The next day, Elizabeth apparently told her mother what had happened, and this began the three-year estrangement of granddaughter from grandmother. As if this wasn't bad enough, Fiona filed a criminal rape charge against the 10-year-old male cousin. She also accused Glenda of attempting to conceal the "rape," and as a consequence considered Glenda to be an "unfit" grandmother who should not be allowed to see Elizabeth.

Glenda can barely talk about the situation without crying bitterly. "That child had become my life. I missed her terribly. And all during the time this was going on, I lost my husband and my father. They died within months of each other. I know the heart attack that killed my husband was in some measure brought on by what we'd been going through to see Elizabeth and to keep my son from deep depression. These days, Fiona is threatening to go back to England and to take Elizabeth with her. If the courts let her do that, Jeff and I will never see Elizabeth."

Glenda tried everything possible to repair her relationship with Fiona, even agreeing to only see Elizabeth in Fiona's presence, but that, too, has failed. "I've tried and tried," Glenda said, "but I can't make Fiona do anything reasonable. I can't control her irrationality. I can only control myself. I've seen a therapist and been told I have to let go."

Resolution of deep anguish from missing a loved one is one of the most difficult adjustments to achieve. "I can no longer allow it to consume my life," Glenda said. "I've even stopped keeping the journal I had been writing in for the last several years. In it, I documented everything Fiona was doing. I keep expecting the court to prevent her from taking Elizabeth out of the country, but I don't know how long I can finance these legal costs. I've already mortgaged my home to the hilt."

When asked what she's doing to overcome her emotional pain, Glenda said she's trying to rid herself of the hatred she feels for Fiona, she's praying and meditating, and most important of all, she's spending more time with her other grandchildren and the rest of her extended family.

Glenda is so kind and gentle, it's hard to imagine why anyone would deliberately set out to hurt her and to deprive a child of her goodness and grandmotherly love. But as the other stories show, divorce can be as ugly and destructive to the human spirit as war. As long as divorce remains a battleground, casualties will be a risk.

⚹ HELPFUL GUIDELINES ⚹

Be conciliatory for the sake of the children. Don't allow the adversarial legal system to drive a wedge between your soon-to-be former spouse and yourself. Be fair in property division and generous with visitation. And don't ever use the children as pawns. It does more long-range harm to the children than to the target of your rage.

If you're suffering from an estrangement, get help. Help can come from other family members, friends, clergy and professional therapists. Don't alienate yourself from the people around you who love you and want to support you. And build another family if that's possible. The embrace of another family can be a wonderful antidote to loss.

Don't hate. Hate is a destructive force that has a habit of boomeranging against the hater. Try to see the other person's side, and try to create out of your unhappy history a whole and optimistic future. And remember if you are a victim of someone else's hatred, they are the ones to be pitied because they may very well self-destruct.

Stay healthy. If you're depressed and crying all the time, you're likely to begin to have physical symptoms. If they appear, seek help and most of all explain to your doctor what it is you're going through so that he or she can make better decisions about your health care. "Eat well, exercise and get sleep" may sound trite, but it's often the best advice anyone can receive. Take vitamins to keep up your strength. Get involved in social or educational activities, join walking or hiking groups, join a book club, take a class in writing memoirs (very therapeutic) or cooking or learning how to paint.

A short period of separation may prevent a long estrangement. Sometimes a short period of separation can help lower the anger and anxiety level, and help you sort out the highly charged reactions. But if you choose to do this, tell the other person about it. Sometimes it may possibly jolt him or her into examining their role in the conflict. When someone knows exactly what the consequences are of his or her destructive behavior, there is a greater chance it will be corrected. And at least there is an end date to the period of separation, so that it doesn't take on a life of its own.

Check out support groups. While you're going through the pain of estrangement, talking about your situation and getting feedback are valuable. Open the floodgates and reduce the weight of despair. Others are having problems, perhaps of a different sort, but if the support group is for people going through a divorce, you'll find an opportunity to vent and get some good advice even if the purpose of the group is not specifically directed toward estrangements.

Plan the first meeting to repair the relationship. In setting up a meeting to reestablish contact with an estranged loved one, plan the meeting around an activity, as Joe did with his son. Suggest something you know both of you like to do and may have done together in the past. In this way, the discomfort of a face-to-face encounter with nothing to do but talk is avoided. The fear of confrontation is minimized, and the other person has more incentive to restart the relationship in a relaxed setting.

Don't allow distance to mean family disconnection. When families are living far apart from each other, it's more important than ever to remember to stay connected. Honor birthdays, holidays and other celebrations. It takes so little effort and money to place a long-distance call on Sunday or to send a card for that special occasion.

Hang on to hope. Even when the situation appears hopeless, remember that old cliché: where there's life there's hope. As long as you and the loved one you're estranged from are alive, there is the likelihood of a reconciliation, especially if you want one badly enough. On the other hand, one person I spoke with said he wasn't sure there was any chance for reconciliation with his aged mother because she was so forgetful that she had to run through the names of all three of her children and her four brothers before she got to his. Remember: If the relative who has cast you aside knows your name, there's hope!

Chapter 4

---✦---

WHOSE THEORY OF RELATIVITY?

In-Law Relationships

When I was young, I set out to change the world. When I grew a little older, I perceived that this was too ambitious, so I set out to change my state. This, too, I realized as I grew older, was too ambitious, so I set out to change my town. When I realized I could not even do this, I tried to change my family. Now as an old man, I know that I should have started by changing myself. If I had started with myself, maybe then I would have succeeded in changing my family, the town, or even the state—and who knows, maybe even the world!

~ A STORY TOLD BY AN OLD HASIDIC RABBI

Real life has a way of intruding on the marital bliss two people believe they will automatically experience once the marriage vows are exchanged. In-law relationships, however, *begin* at the wedding and—for better or worse—go on for more than a generation.

Do you have a mother-in-law who gave you a steady diet of advice you didn't ask for until you finally said to your husband, "I can't stand your mother, and I don't want to have anything to do with her"?

Is your wife's brother borrowing money and not paying it back? Has it reached the point where you're not talking to him anymore because he won't honor his obligations?

Did your daughter-in-law decide she didn't want to spend

holidays with you and your family? Has it happened year after year so that you've lost touch with your son?

These are just three of the various dramas that play out in in-law estrangements. Most of the complex situations faced by the people whose stories are told in this chapter illustrate that there are no simple solutions. From these stories, you will see that your situation is not unique—you are not alone. And some of their solutions may be your solutions.

One young woman, who had not seen her in-laws for two years since the birth of her second child, told how her rich father-in-law offered the same toast at all family gatherings. "Here's to all my money and to those of you who stand to inherit that money if you're smart enough to act nice to me for the rest of my life."

"Don't believe for one moment that he intended to be funny," she said. "My father-in-law was dead serious." Despite the obvious incentive to maintain a good relationship with her in-laws, this daughter-in-law could not bear to be in their company. When asked what they had done or said to make her feel so hostile, she could not relate anything specific. "I just can't stand them," she replied. "My mother-in-law's emotions run from polite to polite. In politically correct terms, she's reality-impaired, if you know what I mean. And when she tries to hide her disapproval, I can always see through the tact to the fact. As for my father-in-law, well—you can certainly see what he's all about."

On the flip side, Susan, a 50-year-old mother-in-law, related her story. Someone had given her a business card that read, "You Don't Want Your Parents to End Up in a Nursing Home, Do You?" On the inside of the card was an advertisement for long-term care. She handed the card to her son's new wife, who glanced at the front cover and responded too quickly, "So what are you going to do when you get old?"

At first Susan was "dumbstruck." She composed herself, smiled and retorted, "I'll hire a nurse, and we'll just have to move into the Ritz Carlton Hotel where, no doubt, I'll be using up your inheritance."

There we have the radioactive tone of too many in-law relationships. How often have you heard people say, "You can choose your friends, but you can't choose your relatives?" Never was that more true than in the choice of in-laws. This extends from parents-in-law to sisters/brothers-in-law, and even to grandparents-in-law. Sadly, warm family relationships with new in-laws get little chance to develop; they're smothered with mother-in-law jokes before they can draw a natural breath. All too soon, those who laughed may find themselves a target of the same jokes they once laughed at. *If only we could remember that in-laws are the very same people who raised, nurtured and influenced our chosen spouse, the ones with whom he or she had the closest and most meaningful ties before marriage.* Like it or not, their genes flow in your spouse, and in light of modern medical research, we all know the power of genes.

And remember, too, that our own family is also filled with imperfections. Uncle Lou is an obnoxious braggart, Aunt Mary drinks too much, Mom is a travel agent for guilt trips, Dad relates to the kids as an oracle instead of a father and Cousin Joan's rebellious teenage daughter is oversexed, over-tattooed and undereducated. Recognize any of these relatives?

Each of us wants the unconditional love of family—a nurturing, approving, giving and happy family—though most of us will settle for less. If we can keep a sense of humor and be ready to laugh at the ubiquitous foibles of relatives, particularly the in-laws, we can minimize the resentments and grudges that lead to alienation. If your son describes his wife as having a personality that bubbles like champagne, smile and nod. Don't say, "You mean like Drano," even if you think it.

Much of the time, in-law relationships go reasonably well or they bump along but continue to move forward. Unfortunately, there are still too many instances where these relationships can cause untold heartbreak and bitterness. Years, even decades, of alienation triggered by a new in-law constitute the ring-any-doorbell secret scenario of many a family's life, the hidden drawer in the old desk we prefer not to open up.

PAY UP AND PAY NOW

Sharon and Tim, brother and sister, are both in their late 40s. She is a professor at a small college and lives in a large northeastern city. Tim has a furniture repair business in a coastal town about two hours north of where Sharon lives. Tim has been married for 20 years and is a devoted husband and father of two teenage boys. Sharon is married to her second husband, a neurosurgeon, who is also heir to a family fortune.

Sharon and Tim are having their monthly visit at a neighborhood coffee shop near the university. They reunited two years ago after a 10-year rift. Their estrangement began shortly after Sharon married her second husband. Tim was having financial problems getting his business off the ground and asked Sharon for a short-term loan at a current interest rate. Since Sharon's new husband-to-be disapproved of ever lending money to relatives or friends, Sharon dipped into her own funds and gave the money to her brother. She told him it was a loan *without* interest, and he should pay it back whenever he was able to.

About a year later, with Sharon now married to the doctor, Tim offered his sister half of what he had borrowed. Sharon's husband jumped into the discussion, demanding that if Tim wanted his respect, he should pay back the entire amount of the loan *with* interest. Discussion escalated into confrontation. A shouting match erupted between Tim and his new brother-in-law. When Sharon failed to stand up for Tim, he stormed out of their house. Not long after, Sharon's husband telephoned Tim and again demanded payment of the loan and called Tim "a loser and the family embarrassment."

Another year went by, and Sharon telephoned Tim in hopes of patching up their differences. He refused to discuss the rift. He was much happier with the family he had married into than with his biological family. He saw his own family as so troubling he wanted to forget them. His parents, who were then deceased, had been disappointed in Tim's career choice and in his failure to finish college. Even his older brother had little contact with Tim over the years though they had not completely severed their ties. Tim began to see his family as a threat to his happiness and to the security of his marriage. He saw them as high achievers who had far less respect for him and for his wife than they did for each other. When two people Sharon loved had come to an impasse that placed her in a position of conflicted loyalties, she chose not to stand up for her brother because she feared her new husband's disapproval. Sharon admits to having been weak. "I should have told my husband it was none of his business; that it was a private matter between my brother and me."

After Sharon's phone call to Tim, she remembers how the days of not seeing him became weeks, then months, and then years. She tried to talk herself into forgetting her brother, but memories of their childhood closeness gnawed at her. She missed him. Each summer when she and her husband drove to their beach house, she knew they were minutes away from where Tim lived. Almost 10 years had gone by since she and Tim had talked to each other, and no one else in the family had heard a word from him for the past three years. One week, when her husband left early for a medical meeting, Sharon drove to Tim's furniture repair shop. She persuaded him to have lunch with her. They spoke for more than two hours and then agreed to meet again the following week.

"It was like having a person you love come back from the dead," she said. "You don't know what you've missed until you get it back."

Sharon and Tim regained their relationship, and with it, a

renewed friendship and the sibling closeness that had been lost for so long. Tim forgave Sharon and acknowledged he had been too extreme in cutting his family out of his life, particularly his sister, whom he loved and missed all through the years of their estrangement.

Their reconciliation brought the whole family closer together. Sharon's husband had grown and matured over the decade and was now able to apologize to Tim for his unwarranted interference in a situation that should have been exclusively Sharon's concern.

Sharon and Tim's story had the kind of ending we all wish for, but it took Sharon's persistence and her own admission of wrongdoing to bring her brother back into her life.

Like Them or Not, In-laws Are Family

For many of us, in-laws are strangers who have been thrust upon us. These in-law problems cannot all be painted with the same palette; the solutions to them are unique and filled with as much variety as the people involved. When a couple marries, in-laws become part of the package. You can choose to work for a certain company, maybe even for a particular boss, but you can't choose the other people around you. A work situation is a good illustration for how you will have to deal with your in-laws. The problems may be more about *you* than about failings on the part of your in-laws.

It's wise to remember that in these in-law relationships, the history of familial bonds is absent, so that when the lines of communication cease, it's not as easy to reopen them as it is with blood relatives. Allowing a rift with an in-law to cause a total breakdown of communication for any extended period of time may just lead to a lifetime estrangement. In such cases, everyone is the loser, particularly the children who miss the whole sense of continuity. Nothing is more destructive to a marriage than the alienation of a spouse from his or her family. Uproot a living thing, and it may soon wither and die. Divorce is often a result of a marriage that goes awry because of a continuous state of turmoil over in-laws. Invariably the strife begins during the wedding and escalates over the issue of holidays or where to live or how to rear children or any one of a variety of issues that arise in families. More often than not, it is the family of the groom who loses a loved one—a son or a brother.

HOME FOR THE HOLIDAYS

Where the newly married couple will spend Thanksgiving and Christmas can be a source of enormous disappointment to the respective families of the couple. Consider this joke:

A mother who lived in Florida wanted her married son to be with her on holidays and at times went to great lengths to ensure that would happen. She called her son in New York and said, "I hate to tell you this, but your father and I can't stand each other anymore. We're getting a divorce. I'm telling you now so you won't go into shock later when I throw him out of the house."

Her son hung up the phone and immediately called his sister to tell her the bad news. His sister said, "I'll handle this." She called her mother. "Mom, don't do anything till we get there. We'll be there tomorrow night."

The mother hung up the phone and hollered to her husband, "Okay, they're coming for Thanksgiving. Now what are we going to tell them for Christmas?"

Here's Allen's story, a newlywed who unwittingly orchestrated an estrangement by failing to meet the reasonable expectations of his family.

Maybe you're as close to one of your siblings as Allen was to his brother Paul—close in age, close in interests. You grew up together, shared the same friends and spent every holiday together. One day your brother marries, and gradually, contact with him diminishes. You haven't seen him in months, but Thanksgiving is just around the bend, and you'll all be together, the whole family gathered for a big turkey dinner. Then your parents break the news that your brother is going to be with his wife's family for Thanksgiving. That first little tinge of resentment sets in. You try to rationalize. After all, his wife has a family, and they had the same expectations that your family had. Oh well, you'll see him for Christmas. But Christmas comes and goes, and your brother is with his wife's family again. How can that be? Why should he be with his wife's family when they live in the same town and see them all the time? It isn't fair. Your parents are upset. *Reasonable expectations go unmet, violating a crucial standard for family cohesiveness: meeting the reasonable expectations of other family members.* You try to console your parents and yourself at the same time with, "Next year will be our turn."

Next year comes and goes, and your brother is still spending all holidays with his wife's family. It's time to confront him. His response makes you furious.

"I'm sorry," he says, "but Kate's not comfortable being around our family during the holidays."

"Can't you see how upsetting this is for Mom and Dad?" Paul says. "It's not fair. Why don't you alternate? Everybody else does that."

"I'm between a rock and a hard place." Allen says, unable to even make eye contact with his brother. "Don't make it more difficult than it is. Kate says she hasn't been made to feel welcome."

"What did anyone do to Kate?"

"Nothing specific. It's just the feeling she has." Allen shrugs helplessly. "She wants to be with her own family on holidays."

"And what about you? Don't you count?"

Allen doesn't answer. Paul also keeps silent, but he loses a certain respect for the brother he had always looked up to. He thinks to himself, *What a wimp*. The message is clear. Allen doesn't value his own family enough to stand up to a wife who has shown a total disregard for his feelings and those of his family—the very same people who raised and loved him.

At that moment Paul begins to side with his sister, who felt from the beginning that Allen's wife wanted to alienate him from the family. And now Paul dislikes his new sister-in-law intensely. The whole family, once so eager to welcome her, dislikes her. And so it goes. The resentments became the seeds of an estrangement that continues to this day.

FOOD FOR THOUGHT

Maybe it should be the way it used to be at great Aunt Minnie's house. After a few canapés and cocktails, Aunt Minnie would pat her daughter-in-law on the hand and say, "It's so lovely to get together for the holidays, even though we can't stand each other the rest of the year."

You would have to do a double-take to realize the truth of her words. A long time ago, Aunt Minnie learned when you obsess about your enemies, you're letting them live in your head without paying rent. This approach works for Aunt Minnie, but what happens when there is a new in-law who wreaks havoc on the family and no amount of cajoling works? Whose theory of relativity is it anyway? Not yours! How do you keep a relationship with your brother when you can't stand his wife? Or maybe it's your son-in-law, or daughter-in-law or brother-in-law? Whoever it is, it's the source of so much conflict that the family is faced with a profoundly disturbing dilemma. Do you tolerate the slights and continue to maintain some kind of relationship at great discomfort to yourself and the rest of the family, or do you allow the ties to break and deal with the painful consequences? Whatever the circumstance, and wherever culpability lies, it's important to remember that once a relationship with a loved one is severed, it's sad, painful and always difficult to cope with. Each time you hear that relative's voice on the telephone, you'll stiffen with apprehension, alert to possible attack. It will invite a knot in your stomach that's hard to ignore.

Regrettably, estrangements arise for reasons just as trivial as the ones described above. When they can't be mended, how do we contend with the loss of contact with the family member we love and miss because he or she married someone who wants nothing to do with the spouse's family?

The following three stories convey the complexities of in-law tension that ultimately causes families to come apart.

A GIFT-WRAPPED INSULT

Patricia and her brother John had always been close, and Patricia believed they would always remain that way. She was wrong. When John told her he intended to propose to Olivia, Patricia felt a pang of sadness, because she had never experienced any bond of friendship with Olivia and wondered what that would mean to the relationship she had with her brother. Patricia got to know Olivia during the months her brother and Olivia were dating.

Olivia was a driven overachiever who worked on her body almost as much as she worked at her career as an accountant. Patricia belonged to the same health club as Olivia, but never had she seen anyone work out as much as Olivia. Olivia was more than dedicated—she was obsessed. Six days a week, she spent two or three hours doing step classes, aerobics and weight training. If Patricia ran into Olivia, their conversation always centered on Olivia, who expressed no interest whatever in how Patricia might be doing. Patricia found Olivia to be the height of selfishness and superficiality but never said anything to John for fear of jeopardizing her relationship with him.

Unlike most couples who plan to marry, John and Olivia seemed particularly undemonstrative toward each other. No intimate glances passed between them, not even an occasional gesture of warmth. What was even more curious was John's decision to marry a woman for whom he had no sexual attraction, a complaint he had repeated to Patricia on more than one occasion. When John first met Olivia, he was living with a couple of other young bachelor lawyers from his firm. Olivia began a serious pursuit of John by showing up at his apartment with baked goods, casseroles and clean laundry until she had completely won over the support of his roommates with her indulgences. Slovenly and disorganized about their personal habits, John and his roommates were happy to be taken under this mother hen's wing.

Olivia was indefatigable in her pursuit of John. One friend said it was like the proverbial "casserole brigade" that often accosts recent widowers. Invariably, the man will marry the one of his deceased wife's friends who captures his heart with the best casserole! Similarly, Olivia was patient and persistent, and the "catch" she went after was finally hooked.

Soon after John and Olivia announced their engagement, Patricia and her boyfriend Richard announced theirs—they would be married a few months after John and Olivia's wedding. From that moment on, until John and Olivia's actual wedding, whenever Patricia saw Olivia at the gym, she had to listen to every excruciating detail of Olivia's wedding preparations. Olivia never asked Patricia for her opinion or input. Patricia didn't even get a chance to mention her own upcoming wedding. Her brother definitely was marrying the shallowest woman Patricia had ever known.

John wanted a formal, seated rehearsal dinner for the huge bridal party, close family and out-of-town guests. Though his parents knew the cost would be great, especially with Patricia's wedding a few months later, they agreed to host the rehearsal dinner. When Olivia announced she was sending out invitations to nearly 500 people, of which 300 were out-of-town guests, John's parents were speechless. They informed John that they had no intention of hosting more than 50 people at the rehearsal dinner—it was just too expensive. A week or so before John's wedding, his parents received several calls from family and friends asking what event they were supposed to attend, the rehearsal dinner or the party given by the bridesmaids that was being held at another location and at the same time as the rehearsal dinner.

Patricia and John's parents were understandably upset that their future daughter-in-law had orchestrated a competing party hosted by the same bridesmaids who were to be guests of the groom's parents at the rehearsal dinner. Because John's family was eager to avoid having problems with their future daughter-in-law, they buried their feelings of resentment. They hoped the bridesmaids would not leave in the middle of the dinner, and that the guests would find their way to the right event.

Their new daughter-in-law never acknowledged the insensitivity of her actions anymore than she acknowledged the obvious dilemma she had created for hundreds of out-of-town guests by scheduling her wedding on Thanksgiving weekend. More than two hundred people who sent gifts declined the wedding invitation so that they could be with their families over the holiday. Could that have been her intention all along? It would be consistent with her other strategies, Patricia thought.

And as if that wasn't enough, the weekend of the wedding, John informed his mother that Olivia's parents were unable to have anyone but their own family for Thanksgiving dinner. This left John's family to fend for themselves in an unfamiliar city or remain at home and celebrate their own Thanksgiving. They chose to stay home. Olivia's family had excluded John's family even after his parents had hosted a dinner at their home for Olivia's relatives when the couple was first engaged. More importantly, it was a lost opportunity to reciprocate the hospitality of John's parents and to begin to blend the families together. Instead Olivia's family erected a wall that John's family had no intention of climbing.

The tendency for relationships within a family to become

polarized during the preparation and excitement of a wedding can happen all too easily. The new spouse may be subtly rejected for having the wrong religious or cultural background or opposing political preferences or for not being suitable in some other way. Discord at the time of a wedding can be a valuable indicator of fundamental family values, fears, prejudices and allegiances. Previously, at the engagement dinner, John's mother was quick to notice that Olivia's family barely engaged in conversation with each other and then only on the most superficial level. John described Olivia's mother as a "kind of country bumpkin" who had married "above" herself, but then worked hard to acquire the veneer and snobbishness of the class she had aspired to. And it was this attitude that set the stage for so many of the problems that could have been avoided.

Olivia's parents never once approached John's family to introduce themselves to the handful of his well-educated and accomplished relatives who had traveled a great distance to attend the wedding. This was not just a cold shoulder—it was one of sculptured ice, and continues to this day . . . but that gets ahead of Patricia's story.

For John's sake, Patricia continued to be polite to Olivia—until Olivia showed her true feelings for Patricia. Several friends had arranged a bridal shower for Patricia and of course, Olivia, now her new sister-in-law, was invited. As is the custom at bridal showers, the gifts were opened in front of the guests. One present stood out among the rest. It was splendidly wrapped with a puffy white silk ribbon around a powder blue Tiffany box. Patricia read the card. It was from her new sister-in-law. Carefully, Patricia began to undo the wrappings, and as the guests watched with anticipation, Patricia opened the box and removed a glass dish from the mounds of crisp white tissue paper. It was the size of a small candy dish, but without a top.

It was the very same glass dish Olivia had received as a wedding gift months earlier! It was easily recognizable because it had an odd opening that ran down the side of it almost as if the glass didn't quite meld together along one side. When Olivia first received it, she had commented to a friend in Patricia's presence, "How absurd to have this opening. It won't hold anything—it would come out the side." She went on to say that it was useless except as an ornament "and not a very attractive one at that. It looks like a manufacturer's mistake."

She said she would return it if she could, or she'd trash it. Obviously, when Olivia couldn't return the dish, she decided to trash it by *giving* it to Patricia. Olivia had obviously forgotten that Patricia was there when she talked about its uselessness. It was symptomatic of the whole problem; namely, Olivia placed little or no value on her husband's family. How could anyone feel good about receiving a gift intended for the garbage?

Communication between the two sisters-in-law diminished from infrequent to none at all. The by-product of the frosty relationship meant virtually no real contact between Patricia and her brother John. No words passed between them, harsh or otherwise, until Christmas.

Christmas dinner was held at John's parents' home. And wouldn't you know it, both Olivia and Patricia decided to bring English trifle for dessert. Patricia spent hours preparing the elegant gourmet affair with layers of homemade sponge cake soaked in Chambord and sherry, homemade custard, assorted berries and freshly whipped cream. It was all presented in a tall crystal compote dish. When Olivia offered her trifle—a concoction of vanilla pudding, bananas and Kool Whip—Patricia declined to eat it. "I'll just have some of my own," she said to her mother, who had tactfully offered to give everyone a little of each dessert.

John, who continued to remain aloof, grew stone-faced and said, "I'll just have Olivia's dessert." The battle lines were drawn ostensibly over a trifling trifle, but that was simply the culmination of a long period of slights by Olivia toward Patricia and, in fact, by Olivia toward the whole of John's family. Patricia's refusal to eat Olivia's trifle was her one and only retaliation for the shower gift and all the other insults, manipulations and deceptions that had been going on for too long.

Within weeks Olivia and John ceased all contact with John's family, though his parents had *done* nothing to provoke this cruel cutting off. It went on for several years. Patricia told her parents that she felt she had lost the brother she always loved. "And we've lost our son," the mother said. On the surface, this was an estrangement over a shower gift and a trifle, but those were just two of the early symptoms of a deteriorating in-law relationship that had started, as they often do, at the time of the wedding. How sad and ironic that just when two families are supposed to be celebrating a happy union, and creating an extended family, it is instead the beginning of disunion and family rift.

Patricia admitted that given a second chance to deal with her sister-in-law, she would have tried to overlook Olivia's spiteful-ness, shallowness and self-absorption. And now that she knows how manipulative Olivia can be, Patricia says she "would have choked down the damn trifle with mushy bananas," rather than lose her brother.

But it's too late now. Olivia seized the opportunity to instigate an estrangement of Patricia's brother from his entire family. It has gone on for five years. Other family members have tried to mend the rift, but Olivia ignores all conciliatory gestures. Several times Patricia has made overtures with gifts and phone calls to her brother, but nothing seems to be enough to repair the relationship. Olivia remains intransigent—convinced that her husband's family is not worth her time or interest, an attitude she and her family displayed almost from the very beginning. John claims he is caught in the middle and rather passively goes along with his wife's decisions and choices in order to keep peace in his own family—they now have two children who have not been seen by his family except for their birth announcements with pictures. Patricia feels badly that she played a pivotal role in Olivia's early attempts to begin the estrangement.

Unless John takes measures to convince Olivia that he will no longer tolerate her rejection of his family, the chance of mending this estrangement is not good, because (a) she has no desire to reconnect with them and (b) she has nothing to lose by continuing her rejection. Olivia's behavior shows a mean-spirited and highly narcissistic personality. Though she is perfectly capable of seeing her own and other people's needs with 20/20 vision, she has deliberately chosen not to see the needs of her husband and his family—a case of malicious emotional blindness. Her need to control her husband and be the center of his universe has taken precedence over everyone else's needs.

THE MOTHER-IN-LAW I LOVE TO HATE

Although connections with all in-laws are important and serve a vital function in a marriage, most of the problems that arise revolve around the mother-in-law/daughter-in-law relationship. This is the relationship that is crucial to maintaining harmony for all members of the new extended family. When there is a breakdown of communication between these two women, there is little chance for a good relationship for any of the other members of the merged families. Why is that? Primarily because most husbands leave the social obligations to the wives. How many men arrange get-togethers with friends and family? How many men buy gifts for Christmas and birthdays without the reminder and suggestions of their spouses? Thus, a social void is often created when the mother-in-law and daughter-in-law are not in touch with each other.

Most mothers of sons want their sons to marry, "to settle

down"—to start raising a family of their own. But what no mother wants is a daughter-in-law who completely rejects the husband's family and bans them from her life. *Rarely do men take this course with their wives' families.*

When a wife is determined to drive her husband's family away, and the husband allows the breach to occur, there is usually no easy way to mend the split without professional intervention. And that course is difficult to follow because it would expose the daughter-in-law's motives and pose the added risk that she might have to resume the very relationships she worked so hard to terminate.

If the husband is unwilling, too busy or too weak to demand they seek professional help, the estrangement will likely continue for a long time, even for the rest of their lives. It is interesting to see the dynamic of this type of estrangement in light of the psychological profile of the truly malignant daughter-in-law who cannot tolerate any competition for her husband's attention, particularly from the people who have been closest to him all of his life, his own biological family. We've all heard comments about how men who admire their mothers marry women similar to their mothers. Conversely, the ones who have less than comfortable views of their mother tend to marry women who are very different from their mothers.

During courtship, when a woman pursues a man by acting the role of a super-giving, nurturing mother, that man may not feel a sexual attraction to her. Clinical psychologist Dr. Hirschfield offers interesting insight into this dynamic. Since most adult males are not sexually attracted to their mothers, it is clear that the basis of such a relationship might be more mother-son than husband-wife. If that kind of courtship results in marriage, the husband may be shifting his focus to his wife, *not as a wife but as a substitute mother.* Invariably, it is this mother-figure wife who triggers estrangements with her husband's family. There is a certain constellation of factors usually present in estrangements precipitated by this type of daughter-in-law. She tends to be strong-willed, a "take charge" person, older or at least close in age to her husband rather than much younger, and she assumes most of the authority and the decision-making in the marital relationship. Growing up, this woman is usually her father's favorite, a spoiled little "Daddy's" girl who learns very young how to be demanding and get her way. These women want no competition in this role even when they've grown and gotten married, which leads them to manipulate their husbands and remove their husband's family, particularly his mother, from any position of influence over him. Even if the mother-in-law were completely benign, it wouldn't change the dynamic. The estrangement serves as the complete elimination of the competition.

The behavior of a husband who acquiesces to this type of wife tends to be a reflection of how his own parents behaved toward one another: in this case, a father who was unassertive, even passive, and who demonstrated how to get along with his wife by deferring to her dominance. There are also instances where the role model is an argumentative father or mother who causes upheaval in the family. This causes the son to learn early in childhood to avoid conflict at all costs.

Though the mother-son relationship is not fragile, and it would take an extreme situation to inflict lasting harm, a skilled, manipulating wife can still rip it apart by playing on the small resentments everyone feels at one time or another against their parents.

It bears mentioning that the daughter-in-law's perspective is not included here since, in almost every instance, it is the family of the estranged son who suffer the alienation of their loved one. The daughter-in-law does not require skills in coping because she usually has the option of mending the relationship at any time. Her husband's family would welcome any overture toward repairing the rift.

The following two stories involve *alienating wives and enabling husbands*. I selected these two—from dozens of similar ones—because they raise issues that arise so often and cause so much frustration and unhappiness.

THE IRON CURTAIN

Paula is a devoted mother of three grown married children, and the head of a successful catering business. When she spoke in-depth about her relationship with Jake, her youngest child, her sadness was evident and poignant.

"I once heard that in every family there is a lost child," she said. "There's always one child in a family who leaves the fold. Sometimes they just move away, and you lose touch with them. Often these lost children view their upbringing so differently from their brothers and sisters. Maybe it's true that you can't enter the same stream twice. But Jake lives right here in town—where we all live, his brother and his family, his sister and her family, aunts and uncles, even my mother.

"Just to show you how extreme this is, my mother-in-law, Jake's grandmother, is ninety-one. It's hard to believe, in his withdrawal from the family, that he could have cut this sweet old lady out of his life. All of this happened since his marriage to Kathy. It's as if she pulled an iron curtain down on our family. My mother-in-law is well off. She's always given my children everything: cars, trips to Europe, money for education. The only thing she wanted for her 90th birthday was for the whole family to be with her. We were all there except Jake, his wife Kathy and their son. It's been three years now since any of us have seen him, with one exception.

"One day my husband Larry was out in the front yard. At the time, I wasn't at home. A doctor friend was driving by. He saw Larry outside and pulled into the driveway. He told my husband that he'd seen our son Jake in the hospital and wondered how he was doing. We had no idea our son was in the hospital! We didn't even know he was ill. Larry jumped in his car and drove to the hospital. Jake had pneumonia and a collapsed lung. When Larry walked into the room, Jake ordered his father out, told him to just leave! Larry said he was so mad, he wanted to punch Jake in the mouth. Of course he didn't *do* anything—he just said, 'Jake, since you have no contact with anyone in our family, we won't know if you're alive or dead until you die.' Then my husband left. Now Jake won't even speak to the doctor who also happens to be a family friend." Paula kept shaking her head and interjecting, "None of us can understand it."

She explained that Jake's withdrawal from the family began when he was first married. She described her daughter-in-law Kathy as "a sweet-looking girl, like a little brown wren." She grew silent, then said, "Before she ever knew Jake, she'd been in therapy. We do know that, but we don't know why. Something tells me she has a lot of problems. Larry says she's lethal."

When Paula first met Kathy's family, she learned that Kathy and her three sisters were not close. Even on a superficial level, Paula could see a certain jealousy and competition among the sisters that she had never seen among her own three children. Shortly after the marriage, Jake stopped telephoning his brother and sister though the three had always been in close contact. Then he stopped calling his mother and father.

Paula asked him, "Why are you doing this?"

All he would say was that his parents had "not been there" for him when he needed them, that they were always too busy. When pressed for an example, he said they didn't come to his track meets or pick him up from after-school activities when he was a boy.

Paula was shocked by the triviality of his reason for such radical behavior; after all, he had completely cut himself from his family. Paula recalled the horrible raw hurt that she felt when Jake revealed his resentments.

"I never realized he felt that way," she said. "I treated all my children the same way, equally; the others have no complaints. Larry and I did everything we could for the three of them. We loved our children. There was no abuse in our family—we never even spanked our children or deprived them of anything. We worked hard to provide for them. My mother-in-law helped pay for their college education, because they were all in school at the same time and tuition was unbelievably expensive.

"We were a close and loving family. None of us could understand this sudden change in Jake's behavior. And all we have to explain it is his vague complaint that we had somehow short-changed him when he was young. The only new element in the equation was his marriage to Kathy and the birth of their child within that same year. That's when he first shut us out—that's when estrangement began. It's odd because we treated Kathy so lovingly until she grew distant and cold toward us."

When Paula was asked if she ever tried to talk to Kathy, her response was, "Yes, but Kathy simply reiterated something we had already heard from Jake. She believed we showed favoritism toward our other four grandchildren: that his child was not being treated the same as the others. This was completely untrue, but I guess it was Kathy's perception of us and Jake bought into it. Also Kathy told us she was uncomfortable around my daughter and my daughter-in-law. I couldn't figure this out either because they were always so nice to Kathy. My daughter is very down to earth—there's nothing threatening about her. My other son's wife is so friendly and lots of fun to be with. We're crazy about her. And I'm sure I would have felt the same way about Kathy if only she had let me."

Paula has a difficult time accepting the estrangement from her son. She has turned to the embrace of the rest of the family as they have turned to each other in their search for answers, or if not answers, then resignation to the loss of Jake in their lives. Paula also saw a therapist for a while. It proved helpful, mostly in learning how to go on with her own life and not blame herself for what Jake had done.

During these years of separation, Paula also had to survive a battle with breast cancer and the nightmare of a double mastectomy. Her son's continuous alienation added unnecessary stress, and the family worried about the effect Jake's behavior would have on his mother's full recovery. Jake's sister pleaded with her brother to reconnect with his family if only for the sake of his mother's health and well-being. No amount of persuasion could change his mind. His attitude was relentlessly cruel and punishing.

But Paula remains amazingly philosophical about it. "My family may not be perfect," she said, "but parts of it are wonderful. I try to focus on those parts." She pauses. "In science you learn that acid is more damaging to the container than to itself. With the help of a therapist, my family and friends, I was able to expel the acid. Yes, I have had to learn to live with this sadness. It's never been easy, but I won't give up hope. I know Jake will come back to us someday. I just want us all to be there when he does, not only for our sakes but also for his. *No matter how much he has pushed us out of his life, I can't help but believe he would suffer enormous guilt if something were to happen to any of us during this period of separation.* You see his grandmother is quite elderly. I don't want him to struggle with that kind of guilt." She paused to gather her thoughts, then said, "He's my son. No matter what, I'll always love him and wish him the best."

Even if more attempts to reach out to Jake end in rejection, Paula and her family know that they left the door open, and Jake might one day walk through it. The hurt won't disappear, but not to attempt reconciliation would be worse. How Paula reconciles her son's failure to visit her when she was undergoing treatment for breast cancer with her concern about his possible guilt over the death of a family member, particularly the grandmother, remains an unanswered question. Maybe she *doesn't* reconcile those two matters, but what she has learned to do is hope for the best while denying the obvious cruelty of her son. It is a mother's best defense. And many of us use it.

Mothers and Sons

Too many stories have sons banishing themselves from their families, thus raising more questions than just the issue of a daughter-in-law influencing her husband's radical break from his family. Literature and life are filled with stories of sons and mothers losing touch with each other. In his practice, Dr. Hirschfield has seen these alienations arise all too frequently. The walls are erected brick by brick by some sons who know they're hurting these women who gave them life and reared them to manhood. Why do they construct these walls and exclude their mothers from their adult lives? It's as if the mother is demoted to the basement storage room to be deleted from memory. Her advice and presence are no longer welcome. Could it be that boys are trained from early childhood by these mothers to become independent, tough-minded, to hide their emotions, to not cry and to go forth into the world fueled by testosterone? Maybe the message is so strong that it gets misunderstood, misinterpreted to the point of altering behavior. They leave with a vengeance, and they don't look back. Maybe mothers have to find a way of tempering how they cast their sons from the nest.

THE NARCISSIST AND THE CHAMELEON

Beth had a close relationship with her son Andrew and never anticipated that she would ever be estranged from him.

"I couldn't digest what was happening," Beth said. "It didn't make sense. Sometimes I can't believe how hard I tried and how miserably I failed for such a long time. I was operating from a position of faith that, if you are willing to assume some of the responsibility for the rift, to forgive the slights and rejections, to persist in communicating your wish to heal the wounds, even the most stubborn person will come around. That was my honest belief, but now I know there are some people who cannot and will not forgive and forget and move on. I had to learn to cope with the loss of a son who hadn't died, but lived a thousand miles away from us."

Her own words brought tears to her eyes. When asked if she thought the rift was permanent, she said she hoped not. "He says he loves us and doesn't want to lose his family. I want to believe that, but his actions say the opposite."

Beth explained how the problems surfaced at Andrew's wedding to Ilene. At the wedding, Ilene and her family never even came over to meet members of Andrew's family. Repeatedly, Beth approached them and invited them to meet her brothers and sisters, but during the four-hour reception, they never managed to find a few minutes to meet the groom's family.

Beth tried to give the relationship time, but the situation continued to deteriorate. Beth honestly could not understand what caused either her daughter-in-law or her son to want to pull away from his family.

"Ignoring the problem seemed to make it worse," she said. "Even with my daughter-in-law's obvious attempts to alienate my son from his family, in my heart I knew it would never have happened unless he allowed it to—an *enabler* in the classic sense. His passivity was a complete mystery to all of us, because he'd never been that way before."

Because Beth didn't want to lose her son, she was willing to try anything. She requested that they see a therapist together, hoping the intervention of an objective third party would be a means of bringing mother and son back into a loving relationship.

They started therapy, but unfortunately, it lasted only a few sessions because Andrew suddenly announced that he and Ilene were moving out of state. Beth wasn't just shocked at his news; she was disappointed and saddened because the badly needed therapy came to an abrupt end. And she knew how helpful it had been. She recalled that in the first session where they were together, the therapist asked Andrew to describe his wife in one word.

"She's a narcissist," he said, and then reflected. "Self-absorbed. Once she's made up her mind, there's nothing anyone can do to change it." When asked what word would best describe him, Andrew said, "A chameleon. I give the outward appearance of fitting in. I guess I need to be accepted and liked."

The therapist urged that Ilene participate in the sessions because she was a major cause of the problem and should be part of the mending process, but Andrew said he knew she wouldn't participate. When the therapist asked why, Andrew said, "Ilene doesn't think she needs therapy."

Once Andrew and Ilene moved away, nothing Beth said was able to penetrate the wall of silence Ilene had erected to ensure that the estrangement would be irreversible. Andrew told his mother that Ilene wanted no further contact with his family and there was nothing he could do about it.

Beth was heartbroken. How could the relationship with her son that had been strong and loving unravel to the extent that she would hardly ever see or hear from him? She persisted in wanting to know why this was happening. All Andrew would say was that his wife had long "lists of grievances," one against Beth, another against Andrew's sister. Beth had no idea of what was on the list of grievances, and all Andrew would tell her was that they were petty things.

"My daughter-in-law won't communicate at all. I can't speak to her because she won't speak to me. Her side of the story is missing. It's never really been aired, even to this day. I can't imagine what she would say to justify her behavior. She and I never even had a real argument."

Beth explained that the other members of the family were as

perplexed as she was. Beth began questioning herself. The only dis-agreement with her daughter-in-law that Beth could recall occurred when Beth telephoned to speak to her son but Ilene said he was out of town. Beth asked for a number where he could be reached. Ilene wanted to know why Beth needed to talk to Andrew and what was it that she had to say to him that she couldn't say to Ilene. When Beth refused to say what it was, Ilene wouldn't give Beth the number where he could be reached. Sometime later, Andrew telephoned Beth. Apparently Ilene called Andrew, and told him that his mother wanted to speak to him. About a month earlier, Beth had agreed to take care of her granddaughter for the weekend while her son and his wife went to a wedding. Prior to the time of the event, Beth had a broken ankle. When she first agreed to baby-sit, Beth thought the cast would be removed and the ankle healed, but her leg was weak and she couldn't climb steps. Still, she wanted to be able to baby-sit because she rarely saw her granddaughter. For that reason Beth delayed saying anything to her son and daughter-in-law about her problem. Her reluctance to speak to Ilene about the problem was based on Ilene's total lack of concern for Beth while she was incapacitated. Finally, when Beth did speak to her son, she explained that her delay in telling him was because she so much wanted to be with her granddaughter and kept hoping her leg would be strong enough for her to walk on it without crutches. His focus was on the need to have a babysitter. He was furious and refused to accept her explanation. That was the only incident Beth could think of that might have angered her son and daughter-in-law, but she still can't imagine that could be a reason to spark an estrangement from his whole family. To this day it puzzles Beth.

The longer the estrangement went on, the more Beth questioned her own behavior. "Did I reach out enough to my daughter-in-law? Did I do enough to emphasize the good things about her that make her special? I thought I had, but it's possible I hadn't done enough to praise her for her accomplishments. She has complained that I'm too 'dramatic.' I have a lot of interests and I'm enthusiastic about them, maybe too much so. I tried to tone myself down in her presence. Did I do enough of that? By her own description she is 'ultra right wing' politically, but because she and my son have such different political views, she kept her opinions to herself. Our family, on the other hand, is quite vocal on political issues—we love to debate them. But maybe we never should have done so in her presence. Maybe it made her feel like too much of an outsider around us. Or was she just looking for a reason to remove all of us from their lives? I kept asking myself, was I the mother-in-law from hell or was she the daughter-in-law from hell?"

When asked whether there was anything in her daughter-in-law's background that might shed some light on Ilene's overreaction, Beth said there were two things. "Ilene's parents have a strange relationship. They live together but separately at two different ends of their house. They may be married, but they're not together. My son says they even send Christmas cards individually."

Beth had also learned that her daughter-in-law had once stopped communicating with her own mother for almost two years. She and her mother had quarreled about Ilene's leaving the country to pursue a young man who traveled all over the world. When Ilene's mother objected to this costly pursuit, Ilene cut off all contact with her mother. When they finally reconciled, there was no discussion of their estrangement—they reconnected by merely being once again in each other's company.

Was this typical of her daughter-in-law to cut off a relationship with someone just because they were not in complete agreement with her? Was this her means of retaliation? Still, the question persisted—why take such an extreme and punitive course of action?

"Our estrangement wasn't just mother-in-law/daughter-in-law friction," Beth said. "Ilene was intolerant of our *whole* family—all she could say was that she didn't like us. Her attitude, her prejudices, her intransigence and her unwillingness to see a therapist, all of it made me realize how hopeless the situation had become. Whatever her exact reasons for this alienation from our family, it is now my strong belief that my son has been playing more than a passive role."

When asked to expand on that, Beth said her son's relationship with her and with his sister was complex, but that there had always been an overriding feeling of love for his family prior to his marriage. She explained that he hadn't been any different than most teenage boys—"car accidents, too much partying, not always telling the truth"—but there was never a failure of communication or the cold indifference that has characterized his relationship with the family since marrying Ilene.

Beth said that when her son and daughter-in-law moved out of state, based on Ilene's demand to be closer to her family and to live in a place where, as Ilene said, she could "be someone," holidays became more important than ever. Beth was crushed to learn her daughter-in-law had adamantly decided to spend all holidays with her family, and Beth and Andrew's father were not invited. In fact, their son conveyed the message that they were unwelcome at *any time.* This was more than unfair. It was cruel—the ultimate rejection. Beth hoped her son would object to his wife's mandate, but, as with all of her mandates, he gave in.

After the move, Beth sent gifts that often were not acknowledged unless she called to see if they had arrived. On one occasion she was told the gifts didn't arrive at all. Her son informed Beth that his wife considered invitations to spend some holidays with Andrew's family to be "pushy and manipulative." She even considered the gifts Beth sent to be "pushy." Every gesture was deemed to be threatening. Beth was in a no-win situation.

Beth noticed that Andrew had grown "increasingly restrained, artificial and ceremonious." She hated the "new phoniness" he had inflicted on their relationship. She hated walking on eggshells, but felt powerless to do anything about it. Soon, there was a total breakdown of communication—no visits, no phone calls, no e-mails and last year, for the first time, her son made no contact with her on Mother's Day. She said she probably would have been better off to feel anger, but instead when she was alone, she cried. She had little incentive to do much of anything. Depression was setting in. "I tried to cover up my hurt, but I was constantly shaking. I didn't want to see or be with anybody. All I wanted to do was stash myself away and wallow in self-pity."

When asked how she finally overcame the depression, Beth said, "I realized my only recourse was to bring about a change in myself, a change in the way I perceived the estrangement and a change in the way I lived with the situation. That was the beginning of my realization that I was not powerless because I could *alter my view* of the problem and not feed on this misery. And that was when I crossed over from an attitude of failure to one of empowerment. I started going out more, being with friends, getting lots of healthy exercise. I did some volunteer work. Seeing some of the problems of others made mine seem less significant. I began to spend more time with other family members and with women friends. I learned how to open up and confide in them. This helped enormously."

Her women friends shared their own stories of family problems, and they were genuinely supportive of each other. (Most men tend to shortchange themselves by neither expecting nor offering this kind of male friendship.)

Beth said she wasn't happy about the relationship with her son, but she was no longer suffering from it. "It was tolerable," she said. "Maybe for that time it was the best I could hope for. I no longer allowed the estrangement to disable me. I felt I owed that to myself and to the rest of my family. But I also coped by knowing that I would never give up trying to mend the breach."

In looking back, Beth said the ability to finally talk about it was the real beginning of the healing process. Until then, she had been enveloped in sadness, resentment and depression. Her daughter and her brothers and sisters-in-law were there for her. Family members offered a willing ear and some wise, albeit unsuccessful, suggestions to patch up the estrangement.

"I learned that most people have enormous compassion and want to do whatever they can to put families right. It was at this point that I called Andrew, and once again invited him to visit because my daughter, her husband and their child were coming to stay with us for part of the summer. It had been nearly two years since my son had seen his sister. My daughter also called and reinforced the invitation. He agreed to bring his daughter and spend a weekend with us. Without his saying so, I knew Ilene would not be coming with them."

During this visit, and for the first time, Andrew told his family how unhappy he was about the situation and how powerless he was in dealing with his wife. He was not coping well at all, even though the estrangement existed in large measure because of his inability to stand his ground and persuade his wife to keep the promises she had made to him. For example, once again on the issue of holidays, Beth said Ilene had agreed she would spend holidays every other year with Andrew's family if he would relocate to her hometown, but as soon as they moved, Ilene announced that they would spend all holidays with her family.

Beth came to understand that she had choices, and saw that Andrew, too, had choices, but he wasn't making very good ones. It seemed everything was happening by default. Beth suggested that Andrew and his wife go for counseling to try to work on their marriage. He told Beth he doubted Ilene would go, and it would be pointless for him to go alone.

Some weeks later, Beth returned to the therapist she and Andrew had been to. Beth was advised to call her daughter-in-law and be as conciliatory as she could—to tell her she'd missed seeing her and wanted to let her know how much she enjoyed seeing the baby. If her response wasn't antagonistic, then Beth was urged to try reopening communication by asking her daughter-in-law to tell her what was bothering her about Andrew's family. Beth was not to refute anything Ilene said, but to let her talk. "When Ilene is finished," the therapist said to Beth, "tell her you want to think about what she said, and that you'd like to call again in a week or two."

The situation had reached such an impasse that Beth had nothing to lose by calling her daughter-in-law. But Beth wanted first to run it past her son because she didn't want him to feel that she was doing anything behind his back. The therapist suggested that if she did that her son should be cautioned not to prepare his wife for the phone call—she might think some sort of conspiracy to manipulate her was going on. It was the therapist's view that people who harbor grievances need to air them first in order to allow the relationship to breathe again. When Beth phoned her son and told him what the therapist advised her to do, Andrew's immediate response was, "No, don't do that, don't call Ilene. It'll just make the situation worse."

For the first time, Beth wondered if her son wanted the estrangement to mend. She remembered something the therapist had said to her. "What better way to be controlled than to give up your identity?" Was Andrew becoming estranged from *himself*, from who he was and where he came from so that he could be totally controlled by his wife? Not only had her son withdrawn from his own family, but also from many of his friends.

Beth then had a new concern: questions about her son's motives and his participation in the rift. But the therapist pointed out the relationship with Andrew was the one that was important. "If I can't heal the breach with my daughter-in-law, I know I have to keep trying to heal the breach with my son. I must keep communication and the healing process going on at the same time. For now, even though I have little access, I'm just grateful to continue contact with him on whatever terms are offered. In the words of Anton Chehkov, 'Any idiot can face a crisis: It is this day-to-day living that wears you out.'"

Beth's friends told her that when children marry, there are inevitable ups and downs with new in-laws, but in time everyone usually settles into some sort of relationship, maybe not what you hoped it would be, but even a lesser relationship is better than none at all. All Beth wants for now is to speak to her son on the telephone and at least be with him and his child once in a while. Despite her daughter-in-law's accusation that Beth's gifts are pushy, Beth continues to send them.

Self-Exiled

Every child wants his parents to be perfect, and to no one's surprise, there are no perfect parents any more than there are perfect children. But adult children and their parents often try to change each other, particularly when new in-laws are introduced into the family.

In each of us the desire to have "good" parents is what also causes many to believe that those parents have failed them in some profound way and then to alienate them. Recall, Jake felt his parents, Paula and Larry, had "shortchanged" him in some way, and he exiled himself from them. Whether the causes are real or imagined, children's resentment, hurt and lack of fulfillment can be so deep-seated and primal that the alienation becomes a protective shield from pain. They can cut themselves off by maintaining an intense anger toward their parents, and/or by having nothing more to do with them, and telling themselves they have no need of their parents. What they fail to see is the damage they are causing themselves by taking this path. *A complete estrangement is as destructive to the person who initiates and maintains it as to those who are cast aside.* Those who forsake family relinquish a part of themselves and bury feelings that will inevitably resurface at some point in their lives.

In extreme cases, where the relationship is truly toxic, a lessening of contact can actually be a healthier course, *but long-term estrangements are not in anyone's best interest*.

Mother-in-law bashing is widespread and always has been. But we can't ignore the problem of a mother who, overly protective, doubts that anyone is good enough for her son or daughter—the one who, with the best intentions, becomes meddlesome and domineering. This type of in-law is often perceived as a threat to the marriage and must be driven away to reduce stress on that marriage. The situation devolves into a power play. We have another variation on the theme in the following story of Claire, but here we have a mother's alienation from her daughter and grandchildren, and once again we see the same dynamic of the new in-law's insecurity and need to control.

THE POWER PLAY

Because of a son-in-law's insecurities, Claire, a woman in her 50s, with three children from her first marriage, endured a five-year estrangement from her daughter, Dorothy, and two grandchildren. They had been a close family, not only when Claire was married to the father of her children, but also during her second marriage to their stepfather, Harlan. Fortunately, the divorce from their biological father and Claire's remarriage had presented no apparent problems.

When her daughter Dorothy married Tom and had two children, Robert and Lisa, Claire became a devoted grandmother who spent a great deal of time with her grandchildren when they were growing up.

Though Claire had never been close to her son-in-law Tom, she managed to get along with him enough to maintain a "pleasant and civilized relationship." But when Robert and Lisa were eight and five years old, suddenly Dorothy told her mother not to spend so much time with the children. Claire was dumbfounded and deeply hurt.

When Claire asked why and wanted to know what the problem was, her daughter told her that Tom did not want Claire to have so much "influence" over the children. He wanted them to go to public school, and believed Claire was putting ideas in their heads about private school.

"But Dorothy," Claire protested, "that's what *you* wanted. That's why I offered to pay for a private school. Have *you* changed your mind?"

All her daughter would say was that she agreed with her husband.

Claire was completely defeated at this point. "All right then," she said. "I'll never bring the subject up again."

For another six months, Claire continued seeing her daughter and the children, but her relationship with her son-in-law was strained. Despite Claire's promise to never again mention private schooling for the children, Tom continued to freeze Claire out, barely acknowledging her existence until, one day, Dorothy informed her mother that she was no longer welcome in their home. And she was not to see the grandchildren anymore! Claire was heartsick at this unexpected news. She could not understand why her daughter had taken this drastic and extraordinarily hurtful step. What on earth had she done to cause this? Repeatedly, she tried to discuss the matter with her daughter, but Dorothy refused to talk about it or give any explanation for the decision to abruptly cast Claire from their lives.

Claire continued to have a loving relationship with her two grown sons. She enlisted their help and asked them to talk to their sister, to try to find out why Dorothy had chosen to isolate her mother. But Dorothy would not tell her brothers any more than she told her mother. It wasn't long before Claire's communication with her daughter stopped altogether. When Claire's husband, Harlan, attempted to reconcile the families, Tom told him to "mind his own business."

Was Tom's insecurity at the heart of this? For a long time he felt that he was not the husband Claire wanted for her daughter. Claire had substantial assets and the benefit of a good education, as did her three children. Tom came from "a poor family," but had been able to educate himself by working and going to night school. Did Claire not appreciate this? She said she actually admired Tom's ability to achieve on his own, but admitted she had never expressed that admiration directly to him. In fact, she confessed that she had had very little interaction with her son-in-law over the years. Claire described him as sullen, given to pouting, a harsh critic of most people and an autocrat with Dorothy and their children. Clearly, she was not fond of her son-in-law and he knew it.

"People really don't like him," she said. "He has few friends and doesn't get along with people at work. He doesn't earn much money, and he has this constant chip on his shoulder."

When asked if she thought her daughter was happy with Tom, Claire shook her head. "No, Dorothy's not happy. Over the years she's often talked about divorce, but she didn't want to put the children through that ordeal. I think he knows how she feels, but he also believes she won't do anything about it. Dorothy is capable of going out and getting a good job if she really wants to, but Tom forbids her from working even though they have a tough time making ends meet. I often gave Dorothy money for the children's clothes and other things. I know she didn't tell Tom, because he would have been furious."

Claire began to cry. "For almost five years I couldn't see the children. Tom stopped Robert's piano lessons. He stopped Lisa's ballet classes."

When asked what finally ended the five-year estrangement, she said, "My grandson, Robert, called me one day and cried bitterly. He begged me to meet him after school. I did, not once but several times, until little Lisa inadvertently mentioned our meetings to my son-in-law. Then Tom tried to get a restraining order against me to keep me from seeing my grandchildren! My daughter wouldn't see or speak to Harlan or me. It was a horrible situation, and I couldn't bear it. But I had to learn to go on with my life, hoping each day that they would relent. In fighting the restraining order I managed to obtain grandparent visitation rights. Imagine! This wasn't even a *divorced* couple and they were *legally* forbidding the grandparents to see their grandchildren! All through the conflict, I was so depressed. Robert began to act out. His schoolwork began to suffer. He often refused to speak to his father. He told the judge that he wanted to see me—that he missed me and hated his father for what he was doing. Of course, from what Robert had said, I knew it was mainly Tom who initiated the complete break. The court granted me one visit every month. I had hoped for more, but I was grateful for that."

Claire thought the reason Dorothy went along with Tom had as much to do with her own jealousy over the closeness Claire had with Robert as it did with obeying Tom. And Claire took some of the blame for excessively interfering in her daughter's life.

"I was too close to Dorothy for her to know where I left off and she began, and I also had too much control. So, she turned her back on me and cut me off from her and her children in one surgical slash. I remember some dim-witted excuse was used, something about my giving the children chocolate cake, too many sweets. A ludicrous ploy; that's all it was. They shut me out and over the years took away from the children every memento given by me, every evidence of my existence. I was eradicated."

Claire became physically ill as a result and required a period of hospitalization. But then as she puts it, "A miracle occurred. Last year when Robert was twelve, he left home after an argument with his father. He came to me. He said he took his mother's side when his father was shouting in his mother's face. His father whacked him on the head. Then the court put pressure on the parents to sort it out. My daughter was shattered by Robert's departure. He refused to return home, and Dorothy allowed him to stay with me rather than have the court put him in foster care. To comfort her, I said I thought Robert would return home very soon. With my encouragement, he did. I tried to persuade my grandson to mend the rift with his parents, and my daughter appreciated my attempts to reconcile Robert with her and his father. Dorothy and I found our way back to each other, prodigal-son style. Now we have a deeply spiritual relationship that is exclusively ours. No one can damage it, not now, not anymore. I know my boundaries, and she knows hers. Even Tom knows that what was done was harmful to everyone. Our journey was a productive, if bitter one."

Claire described her "five years of exile" as a time of "immense sadness, loneliness that nothing and no one could ease." She and Harlan moved to another country during two of those years and tried to build a new life, but that proved to be an "unsatisfactory escape," so they returned home. And that was when her grandson was in turmoil and the conflict with his parents led to his moving in with Claire and Harlan.

During the years of estrangement, Claire wrote in a journal and became aware of her role in the situation, particularly her excessive influence on Dorothy and her unwitting intimidation of her son-in-law that led to the perception of her as a meddlesome authority figure. Because her son-in-law was fearful of his own inadequacies, he was threatened by Claire and the hold she had on Dorothy and the children.

Claire sought therapy to help herself better understand and come to terms with what was happening. Slowly, she began to cultivate a friendlier relationship with Tom. Her tone became less strident, and she initiated new avenues of communication. At first, Tom resisted, but over time he became receptive. Now, they have what Claire describes as "a healthier interaction, adult to adult."

And now, too, her daughter was able to achieve her own maturity. Dorothy was no longer simply Claire's child, but an adult daughter who was on equal footing with her mother. Dorothy was allowed to see Claire's frailties, her profound sense of loss and her need to be useful in order to feel worthy. Through Dorothy, Tom also "discovered" his mother-in-law and was less threatened by her. Now they lean on each other in times of need as a family should. This extended family—this *mended* family—is a stronger family, not by mere numbers but through a carefully constructed mutual support system.

Can We Talk?

In Claire's story, everyone failed in their ability to communicate and to be honest with each other and themselves. Claire, who found herself cast from the lives of her daughter and grandchildren, should have immediately gone to Dorothy and Tom and admitted some of her own failings in dealing with them. Knowing of Tom's insecurities, Claire should have gone overboard to make her son-in-law feel better about himself, particularly in his role as Dorothy's husband. Tom, like most men, probably thought he should be the family provider and was threatened by his in-laws' financial help. He needed assurance that he was worthy of Dorothy, and Claire should have given him that assurance. Men like Tom, perhaps lacking self-esteem, are likely to be intimidated by highly competent people like Claire.

Dorothy and Tom needed to be equally honest with Claire. They should have told her right up front that they didn't want their children's heads filled with thoughts of private school. Claire needed to know what she was risking by having so much influence over her grandchildren. Had there been more talks, especially between mother and daughter, maybe the situation would not have deteriorated to the point of an estrangement.

There is also the possibility of some hidden agenda at work here between Dorothy and Claire. Perhaps Dorothy needed to cut the umbilical cord with her mother, but foolishly chose the wrong way to do it. Candor and compassion might have prevented a five-year estrangement.

❧ HELPFUL GUIDELINES ❧

Be open and forthright, but do it with sensitivity. Distancing prevents new in-laws from knowing you and your family. If distance is maintained, misunderstanding and friction will result. If family members are too repressive about family issues, new members will be dissuaded from saying much about themselves. If you never get to know each other, you'll never be able to work out problems when they arise. And what is the likely scenario in such an event? Too frequently, it's the beginning of alienation and long years of estrangement.

Don't make the wedding an end unto itself. Too many brides consider the wedding a show in which they are the stars instead of viewing it as a time to celebrate, to take vows and to *blend* families. If one family refuses to consider the feelings of the other family, the wedding can become the opening salvo for two warring factions instead of the joyous event it should have been. Yes, the wedding is within the province of the bride and her family, but the groom's family deserves to be included as a most important part of the celebration. Maybe the mother of the groom has no daughter and may never have the opportunity to plan a wedding. Therefore, wouldn't it make sense to include her in some way? The inclusion could help pave the way for a closer relationship in the future.

Even if the groom's kid brother throws rice pudding instead of rice, the bride must smile and forgive the little brat. He will grow up and be her brother-in-law for a long time. He might even turn out to be her best ally. Brothers-in-law often are.

Alternate holidays. Every family wants some time with the child they raised. Don't hog all the holidays by insisting on being with your own family—especially if you and your family live in the same city. If that's the situation, the out-of-town family deserves to see you for Thanksgiving and/or Christmas and, at the very least, every other year. Whenever possible, have the out-of-town family stay with you so that everyone can be together for the holidays. It's usually only once or twice a year and worth the effort. If there are small children, think how happy they will be with both sets of families present. Make the holidays a time for family rejoicing and togetherness. And remember what it could be like if you were the one who had to spend all the holidays without your children. Recall the old maxim, "What goes around comes around."

Be receptive. Give your in-laws the gift of understanding by listening to what they have to say with a minimum of impatience, defensiveness or criticism. In-laws who learn to listen to each other with tolerance and kindness may find that they do not need to change each other. If we want an honest relationship with our in-laws, we have to make it safe for them to speak truthfully—not hurtfully, but truthfully. If you act upset or shocked when they tell you how they feel about a situation, you will close the door to more open dialogue in the future. For most of us, our history teaches that it is best to keep our thoughts to ourselves until we know how the other person would react to our words. However, in the case of a new in-law, it is important to take risks and trust that this newcomer will be able to deal with family issues and problems, recognizing that some are universal to all families. Reserve taking those risks for occasions when the issue is important.

Communicate. Communication is more than just talk. Often what is left *unsaid* conveys more than the spoken word. *Body language speaks volumes.* Arms folded over the chest and legs crossed often mean someone is tense and trying to protect him- or herself. Clenched fists, tears, lip biting—all send their own messages. Since we are communicating so much of the time, it seems prudent (even practical) to improve communication with those around us, especially our in-laws who really don't know us all that well. A failure to speak or a failure to look at a person is also sending a message. A mixed signal is a basis for misunderstanding. Make sure your physical behavior is congruent with your words.

Be observant. If your in-laws do not express their opinions to their own family, there is no reason to expect they will open up to you. If they are argumentative with the people closest to them, chances are they will argue with you, in which case it is best not to take it too personally. Learn to overlook some of the traits you don't like that you know are not directed at you.

Be respectful. Remember the connection that made you in-laws. You both love the same person, and that person will be happiest if you all respect each other and get along.

Don't hold grudges. Everyone makes mistakes, especially during times of crisis and change. Don't maintain a list of grievances. Don't hold grudges. Give up thoughts of slights and rejections that you probably exaggerated in your own mind. *Take a look at your own attitude and feelings.* Consider making a U-turn and see what kind of response you get. It's never too late to forgive or to ask for forgiveness. And don't go through the litany of grievances when someone apologizes. Allow that apology to wipe the slate clean.

Don't end the relationship. Look at the continuum of relationships. Realize that over time you will change and/or the in-laws with whom you are having conflicts will change. Just because a farmer has a bad crop doesn't mean he should sell the farm. Next year might be the bumper crop. If you cut off the in-laws, you won't be able to see the changed attitude that could make all the difference in the relationship. We can all put up with a lot more when our goal is to keep the family from falling apart.

Healing the rift. This is a complex and unpredictable process. If you feel the desire to take the first step toward healing a family estrangement, it's best to start slowly. You might try writing a brief, newsy letter in which you try to establish some common ground. Then you will have to wait to see if there's any response. A phone call with words of contrition might be the better course of action, because then you'll have an immediate response, one way or another. If a phone call is likely to cause nothing more than a rehashing of the original conflict, it might not be the best icebreaker.

If you've tried everything, including an apology, and still the problem persists, try a departure from your usual solutions. Most of us have mended fences with family members and friends, but our range of problem-solving strategies is usually not expansive. We tend to use the same techniques over and over again—writing a polite note of apology, a phone call or sending a gift.

When the feelings are running high, sometimes nothing seems to work, even logic and common sense. If a recalcitrant in-law has caused what appears to be a permanent breach with your blood relative, one that is causing you great heartache, you may have to try an entirely new approach. Writing a letter is a way to crack open the door, but not one of those etiquette-book boilerplate notes that sound insincere. Instead, say something neutralizing like, "I'd really like us to make a fresh start," or "You're my family, and I miss being with you." Try writing one that bares your soul, that lays out how deeply you want to resume a relationship and make it clear that you care about and understand the other person's feelings. You might say, "I suppose we've both been carried away." This canopy interpretation of past events tactfully skirts the issue of blame by distributing it evenly on both sides. A letter allows the other person to think about what's been said without having to react right away.

What if you really don't care about or appreciate the in-law's feelings? At that point, you must decide what is most important: reconnecting with your loved one or perpetuating the rift? Once you answer that question, everything else flows from it.

Even if that in-law expects the opportunity to berate you and blame you for the rift, it might just be worth it, especially if it allows your relationship with a loved one to continue. What's in your heart is more important than *how* you go about mending an estrangement.

Avoid the notion of quid pro quo. It's not giving in or diminishing yourself, but sensing that you're part of something larger, that you are not alone in the world.

Keeping the important relationship alive is the real triumph. When you're traveling down a road and you see that you're not getting closer to your destination, you may have to pull to the side and check a map to see if you're going in the right direction. If not, turn around. Do a mental list of all the objections your problem in-law has expressed. Is there a common theme? It will be linked to either what you are doing or what you are *not* doing. Maybe you're not hearing a cry for approval and acceptance. Try to think of words and actions that will convey the right message, the one being sought by the new in-law who wants your support. Nothing you've done has worked so far, so take a chance on doing something different. And remember what Einstein had to say on the subject: "Insanity is when you do the same thing over and over again and expect a different result."

Chapter 5

~≫≡≪~

"OUT" ISN'T ALWAYS "IN"
ESTRANGEMENTS CAUSED BY SEXUAL ORIENTATION

Home is not where you live but where they understand you.

~ CHRISTIAN MORGENSTERN

To dream of the person you would like to be is to waste the person you are.

~ ANON.

One of the worst fears human beings have is that if people find out who is really lurking under our surface, we will no longer be loved. According to Dr. Jim Fitzgerald and other mental health professionals, people in fear of being unmasked rarely share their sexual fantasies with anyone other than their therapists. A homosexual—a gay man or a lesbian—is likely to hide his or her sexual orientation even from those whose support they should most be able to count on, their parents. Whether gay or straight, the possibility of losing the family's love poses the biggest threat of all.

Though gays and lesbians enjoy more rights and protections than ever before—last year Vermont approved same-sex partnerships akin to marriage—homosexuality is still not fully accepted by the church, the synagogue or the mosque.

As recently as June 2000, the United States Supreme Court ruled that forcing the Boy Scouts of America to accept homosexual troop leaders interfered with its constitutional freedom of association and its "expressive message." As a corollary to the decision, a rationale was put forth that no homosexual group would be constitutionally bound to hire a heterosexual because they, too, have a particular agenda and an identity that may be maintained. The homosexual community views this latest decision as an infringement of their right to equal employment, but the Court made it very clear that this Boy Scouts of America decision in no way affected the right to equal employment except in this narrow area that they were careful to define.

Yes, society is becoming more understanding, but homosexuality is still stigmatized. One gay lawyer maintains that there is another aspect to the Boy Scouts of America decision. Parents fear that homosexuals who are in positions of trust and authority may try to influence these impressionable young people toward homosexuality.

"Because there's been so much information revealed about Catholic priests seducing boys and girls in their churches, I sympathize with their concerns," he said. "But it's also been shown that 88 percent of child molesters are heterosexual."

The question of "whether children are at greater risk for sexual abuse by homosexuals" was addressed by a group of researchers and reported by C. J. Jenny in a 1994 issue of *Pediatrics*. Of 269 children involved in the study, 82 percent were female and 18 percent were male. Of the 82 percent of girls involved in the study, 77 percent of them involved molestation by a heterosexual man also involved with their mother or other female relative. Of the 18 percent of boys involved in the study, 74 percent of them were allegedly molested by a man who was or had been in a heterosexual relationship with the child's mother or other female relative.

The gay lawyer went on to say, "Being gay isn't a matter of

being in an exclusive club. It's a beleaguered status. You have to learn to negotiate it as best as you can. As I contemplated confessing to my family, 'I'm homosexual,' I realized those words could banish me forever—could sentence me to a life of isolation. If I crossed the line, could I ever go back?"

The subject of sex is an uncomfortable one for parents and children. Add "homo" to that mix, and you have one of our culture's great taboos. Every gay man and lesbian knows their family will be disappointed at best, shocked, disgusted and angry at worst, when they learn their son or daughter, sister or brother, husband or wife is homosexual. It's a real stretch to imagine a family that is overjoyed with the news, particularly one where an orthodox or fundamentalist religion plays a dominant role in their lives. The stories in this chapter run the gamut from adult children revealing their homosexuality ("coming out") to their families, to men and women "coming out" to their spouses and their children. An estrangement occurs in every story, but with recourse to a variety of strategies, and usually with help from others, most of the relationships eventually mended.

RELIGION, MY COVER AND MY NEMESIS

Donald is now a successful lawyer living with his partner Jason, a computer programmer, but Donald's road to this point in his life has been filled with a painful family estrangement, denial, misguided aspirations and a gigantic overdose of guilt. The guilt was not only rooted in society's intolerance of the homosexual lifestyle, but in his deep religious conviction that grew out of his family background. Before choosing law as his career, Donald was on the verge of fulfilling his dream of becoming a Baptist preacher. It wasn't only Donald's dream, but also that of his mother, the person closest to him all the years of his growing up.

One day, he studied the image he had of himself that he foresaw in the future: "a preacher, a church, a wife, a couple of kids and a house with a white picket fence." But something was very wrong with this picture and Donald knew it. There wasn't going to be a wife and kids because Donald never had even the slightest interest in women as sexual partners. He had never had any sexual contact with females, not even a passionate kiss. In an honest moment of self-awareness, he acknowledged the truth. His agony spilled into the open. Depressed and desperate, he had begun for the first time to conclude that the church was wrong.

"And another realization occurred. The time had come when I knew being a Baptist was no longer going to give me cover. Being a Baptist made it easy for me to conceal my homosexuality. The religion strictly forbids any intimate physical contact between men and women before marriage. It allowed me to *look* perfect when I was the antithesis of *being* perfect according to the literal translation of the Bible. Finally, I had to come to terms with my dilemma—I was a homosexual, and that meant I was an abomination according to my religion. There was no other way but to give up my plans of becoming a Baptist preacher."

Donald still had to reconcile his religious convictions with his emotions. On an intellectual basis he could reject Baptist teachings on homosexuality, but on an emotional level he had to struggle for a longer period of time.

Donald told his parents of his decision to switch career plans. His father was actually happy about his change, but his mother was disappointed—still, she accepted his choice to go to law school. While in law school, Donald resolved the conflict between his religion and his emotions so that he could accept himself and reveal his homosexuality to his friends, both gay and straight. Now, he had to decide whether he would also let his family know the truth. He went to see a university therapist who specialized in gay and lesbian problems.

"The therapist was helpful," Donald said, "but my friends were the most help. Both gay and straight, they accepted me."

Donald was the youngest of three sons and knew his oldest brother, a medical researcher, was also gay but their parents knew nothing about his homosexuality. The middle brother was heterosexual but he also knew about the older brother's sexual orientation. Donald told both of his brothers of his intention to let their parents know the truth about himself—that he was gay. Despite his assurance that he would confine his disclosure to his own situation, the oldest brother objected and tried to persuade Donald that there was no reason to ever reveal the truth to the family. Over the objections of his oldest brother, Donald decided he would have a long talk with his parents. He was planning a trip home for Christmas and e-mailed his mother to let her know he wanted some private time with her to talk. She asked him to let her know what was bothering him. At first he explained that he had changed his religious views, but there was more he wanted to talk about.

"She was very insistent that I tell her whatever it was I had to say. Looking back, I can't believe I let her push me into saying what I had to say through e-mail, but I did. I told her I was gay. I regret I did it that way, but it happened. That was the day when I became the family pariah, no longer welcome in my mother's home. Not only did she request that I not come home, but that I not tell my father. I refused her request to conceal it from my father. In fact, I wrote a long letter to him revealing the truth. I didn't go home that Christmas. I had solved the religious dilemma, but not the homosexual one. I thought I had made it worse. I became horribly depressed. I was so confused and scared of the prospect of being alone and miserable."

Donald turned to his friends at law school and they were there for him, but that was not enough to make up for the loss of a family he had always been close to. His father responded to his letter affirming his mother's decision not to see Donald.

Donald phoned his father and cried uncontrollably, "You can't know how painful it is to be told not to come home anymore, not even for Christmas."

Surprisingly, his father relented and told him to come home, but not to talk about it to anyone. Donald refused those terms and spent the holiday with some friends from school, a young married couple who invited him to stay with them for the Christmas weekend.

After a period of several months, Donald's middle brother intervened. He convinced their mother to go with him to see their minister. The mother was persuaded by what the minister advised: Don't approve of his homosexuality, but welcome him home.

For the time being, those terms form the basis of Donald's relationship with his parents. He was not with his partner Jason when this estrangement occurred, but now that he is living with a partner, he and his partner can no longer stay in his parents' home. His parents refuse to allow Donald to share his bed with Jason under their roof. Fortunately, he and Jason have been invited to stay with his grandmother, his mother's mother, who lives near his parents. Teary-eyed, Donald related what his grandmother had to say, "Honey, it wouldn't matter to me if you were a pink, polka-dotted aborigine. You and your friend are always welcome in my home."

Donald is a classic example of a person who, while suffering a deep internal struggle about his sexuality, also had to struggle to keep his family's love and acceptance, particularly that of his deeply religious mother who could never reconcile her religious beliefs with her son's being gay. Even without the religious factor, families often become fearful and guilty, expecting their community may place blame on them for having fostered the development of a homosexual offspring. In a more rational moment, a family is apt to fear that their loved one will be scorned in an unsympathetic world, so they urge outward conformity even if inward conformity is not possible. Donald had two nonnegotiable terms: (1) that he would not be "closeted," and (2) that he would not allow anyone to affect his relationship with his partner.

Jason, Donald's partner, was present during the interview and had a different view of working through their problems with family.

Jason said it had taken him 28 years to come to terms with his sexuality, and he believed both his own family and Donald's were entitled to take more time, if they needed it, to come to terms with their son's homosexuality.

As of the time of the interview, both Donald and Jason are working toward a complete reconciliation with their respective families, but still there are boundaries that may never be crossed.

When Did You Choose to Be Heterosexual?

When someone reveals intolerance to homosexuality, you might pose this question: "When in your life did you decide to be a heterosexual?" At first, the person will be puzzled as they ponder the question. And if that person is honest, he or she won't be able to answer the question, because as most of us know, that moment doesn't exist. No one actually makes that decision—it just happens, as it does with homosexuals. It just happens without a deliberate choice. If anyone were able to make that choice, it's highly unlikely that he or she would choose to be a homosexual. Life is never easy for those who don't live within accepted standards of behavior. What we do know is that millions of experiences inherent in living in an unpredictable world build our character and temperament and create our unique personalities. No one knows for certain why that unique personality sometimes is attracted to members of his or her own sex.

Most gay men and lesbians don't fit neatly into the stereotype of being homosexual. Every day many of them pass as heterosexuals—indistinguishable from their neighbors, coworkers and other family members. Despite the "don't ask, don't tell" policy of the military, there is an entirely different call to action in gay communities across the country. Gay men and lesbians are being urged to "come out of the closet." They are being asked to tell the truth and be willing to stand up for that truth rather than perpetuate lies, myths and stereotypes. Telling the truth, first to oneself and then to others, is regarded as a necessary step for homosexuals who want to liberate themselves as whole and complete adults. According to Dr. Fitzgerald, most therapists who deal with the issue of homosexuality believe withholding the truth generally leads to depression and feelings of hopelessness. Whenever people conceal aspects of themselves, it means they are unable to cope with the consequences of the truth. Several homosexuals interviewed for this chapter expressed their fear of the reactions of others, and of their own ability to function effectively in the face of those reactions, especially from the people they have always been closest to—their families.

Dr. Fitzgerald regularly deals with "coming out issues" in his practice. His views, based on long years of experience, are summarized in this chapter. Coming out is not only premised on good mental health for the homosexual population, but on the notion that the more members of the general population disclose their homosexuality, the more society will come to accept same-sex relationships as just another aspect of a diverse population. As a corollary to that, the more out-of-the-closet homosexuals there are, the more families there will be with a loved one who *happens* to be homosexual. With increased numbers who come out, there is less likelihood of those foreboding consequences—rejection and alienation—and in time, perhaps the stigma will go away. This may be the answer over the long term, but as is true with any new movement—where acceptance is sought for an idea or a status that has always been considered unacceptable—there is the inevitable period of difficult transition. Where that manifests itself most is with the families who are unable to absorb the news of their relative's homosexuality without feelings of guilt, resentment and even rage.

But parents and siblings are not the only ones who must deal with the disclosures. Often it's a husband or a wife who reveals his or her homosexuality to the family for the first time, and generally the disclosure occurs when that person is seeking a divorce in order to pursue what for that individual is a natural way of life. So not only do parents and spouses have to absorb the news of something they may find repugnant, but sometimes the children of a homosexual parent will have to deal with the worst kind of trauma— divorce and a parent's homosexuality, both occurring at the same time. It's a perilous road, filled with sinkholes.

There are right ways and wrong ways of coming out to families, and both are illustrated by the stories in this chapter. The downside of a wrong way is rejection and damage to loved ones. That isn't to say the right way will always produce the desired result, but if there's any chance at all of minimizing painful reactions, the disclosure had better be done the right way. All of these scenarios are fraught with risk. And the biggest risks are harm to a child and estrangement from family—whether short-term, long-term or, tragically, permanent. But perhaps, as someone once said, "The greatest risk is not taking one at all."

Most lesbians and gay men have dealt with their sexuality for many years before disclosing it to others. They have usually gone through sadness, disappointment, regret, resentment, anger and confusion before being ready to responsibly come to grips with their orientation. The impact on families is predictably painful and shocking, but often it is temporary.

TO THE LETTER

At age 38, Phyllis mustered up the courage to take her partner, Valerie, to her sister's second wedding. She did it under the guise of wanting some company to travel to the event. Phyllis's parents knew that Valerie shared an apartment with Phyllis, but they had never been told of Phyllis's lesbianism. Phyllis knew her family would be outraged and reject her if they knew about this aspect of her life. Phyllis is a writer who has written extensively on subjects of interest to the homosexual community, and though many in the family had read some of the articles and probably suspected that Phyllis was gay, her parents either didn't know or were pretending not to know.

At the wedding reception, family and friends behaved warmly toward Phyllis and her *roommate*. If anyone had any idea of what the true relationship was between these women, nobody said or intimated anything. After dinner, Valerie, who smoked, went outside to have a cigarette. Phyllis joined her. While outside, in what they thought was a safe place out of view, they kissed on the lips. What Phyllis didn't know was that her father had gone out to his car to get some camera equipment. He saw his daughter and Valerie in their passionate embrace. On that day, he said nothing, but the following week, he met Phyllis for lunch and asked her if she was a homosexual. She said no, she wasn't. He then told her what he saw the day of her sister's wedding. In that unforeseen moment of confrontation, Phyllis finally decided to tell him the truth, though she had never planned to tell him anything. In fact, she said if she were ever to tell anyone in the family, she would have preferred to tell her sister and her mother and then let her mother decide what to do about revealing it to her father.

Her fears were justified. The admission proved too much for Phyllis's father, who, it turned out, had never really accepted Phyllis as a person because she lacked the feminine qualities he expected in a woman. Phyllis suspected that her father had been repressing a great deal of hostility toward her for years, since the days when Phyllis followed him around the yard in overalls, trying to emulate him as he performed such masculine chores as mowing the lawn, transplanting shrubs and spreading fertilizer. Once she told her father the truth, he said that he now understood why he always felt there was something wrong with her. Then he got up from the table and left the restaurant. He never turned back.

For the next week, Phyllis heard nothing from either of her parents. Her sister was away on her honeymoon, but even if she were available, Phyllis said she doubted her sister would have been much help because she was the type of person who went out of her way to avoid confrontations. A few days later, Phyllis's mother telephoned and asked Phyllis to come for dinner the following weekend. From the tone of her mother's voice, Phyllis could not tell if she knew anything or was innocently inviting Phyllis to dinner as she did almost every other weekend. Phyllis called her father to ask if he mentioned anything to her mother. He said that he hadn't, that it would break her mother's heart, and that if she wanted to come for dinner, he wouldn't be there.

This presented a terrible dilemma for Phyllis. She didn't know what to do, so she made an appointment to see a therapist, one who specialized in coming-out issues.

The therapist advised Phyllis to tell her mother the truth, especially since her father already knew. She went home that weekend and true to his word, her father was not there. He had decided to play golf with friends. Her mother seemed her usual vivacious self and had cooked Phyllis's favorite foods, including a baked apple cake to take home and share with Valerie.

"My memory of telling my mother is murky," Phyllis said, "I think because it was one of the most difficult things I've ever had to do. I knew my mother had dreams of me marrying, having the big wedding and babies—all of it. She was a worldly person, but so very conventional in every respect. She and my father were always close, more so than the parents of many of my friends. In fact, I often felt as if my sister and I were left out of their happiness. I felt it was me most of all who was left out. When I finally told my mother that Valerie was more than a roommate—she was my partner—I could see that my mother didn't grasp what I was saying, so I used the word, 'lesbian.' It struck my mother like a charge of electricity. She didn't fly into a rage because she's a controlled person, but I could see that she was shocked, hurt and sad. Still she said it was best that I had told her. Then, quite predictably, she said she expected me to keep my personal life to myself; in other words, as long as no one knew about it outside of her, she would keep my secret. That's when I told her that Dad knew. She gasped in shock. She wanted to know how he knew and when and why. I answered all her questions, including the incident at the wedding, the lunch with my father and his request that I not tell her. Uncharacteristically, she shouted, 'Why did you? Why did you tell me?' I explained that I had gone to a therapist who said it would be best if my mother knew, particularly since my father knew, and that it was an unfair burden on him to have to keep it from her.

"We didn't have much to say after dinner, and she never did remember to give me the apple cake for Valerie, and I didn't remind her. On the train back to the city, I felt cold and shaky. I didn't hear from my mother for several weeks, and, of course, there was no word from my father. My sister called me when she returned from her honeymoon. She told me Mom had said something to her, but my sister admitted it was no surprise to her—she had always suspected. I asked my sister if there was anything she wanted to ask me. She said she didn't. My relationship with my sister and my mother proceeded in a polite course, but at least it was somewhat of a relationship. Whatever warmth and spontaneity may have existed was now gone."

When asked about her father, Phyllis said that she had finally reconnected with him because of a letter she had written to both her mother and father. After receiving her letter, her family decided to see her, and to accept her and her partner. They continue to be cordial, but reserved. She shared that letter, and I include it here:

Dear Mom and Dad,

This is the subject you don't want to hear about, and the one I'd rather not discuss, but I think it's time for the kind of discussion I can't seem to have with you face-to-face.

First, and most importantly, I love you both. I always have. I've put a lot of thought into this letter, but it's tempered by what I feel in my heart for both of you.

Mom, you're willing to continue your relationship with me, but on terms that I find difficult to accept. When I told you I was gay, you basically said let's keep that to ourselves, ignore it and say no more about it. That's rejection of who I am, and through no choice of my own. I didn't choose to be gay. In fact I tried to ignore it for as long as I can remember. I don't know how it happened or why. No one really does, but it did happen. It's what I am. I can choose to act straight, but I can't be straight.

Dad, your decision to banish me from your life is so hurtful. I think you're feeling in some way responsible for what I am. You're probably asking yourself, "What did I do wrong?" I guess the worst I can say is that your inability to verbalize the words, "I love you" was deafening, but I don't know if that had anything to do with my being a lesbian. I doubt it. Well, probably some other things done were wrong, but I believe you and Mom did the best you knew how. You and Mom may be part of why I turned out this way, but not because you intended any wrong. I know you didn't. All I'm asking is a chance to continue to be your daughter, one you love and want to be with. I would be forever heartbroken if you shut me out of your life. Please don't do that to me, and to yourself. It won't help anything. I need my family, maybe more because I bear the burden of being different, than if I were heterosexual. I suppose you probably need time to think about what I've asked of you. I await your decision, and will always love you no matter what you decide.

Your devoted daughter who loves you,
Phyllis

Phyllis's story is most significant because it illustrates how her own strong need for her family prompted her to write the kind of letter that reunited her with her father. Though Phyllis believed that her father never fully accepted her even before he knew of her sexual orientation, she did not allow that to get in her way. That aside, she loved him as she did the rest of her family. Like most of us, she wanted the approval and encouragement of her family. The sensitive wording of her letter was the turning point that persuaded her father to reunite with her.

Letters are particularly useful in mending rifts. In a letter you can prepare exactly what you want to say without accusation or defense. If the tone is accusatory, it will probably fail its purpose of reconciliation. Most important, letters permit you to convey your entire message before having to respond to the other person's reactions. To accomplish its goal, the letter must have an honest but loving tone.

In the next story, Rick's videotape proved to be as successful as Phyllis's letter.

AGAINST THE WORD OF GOD

Rick had always loved his family, and they loved him, so it was particularly devastating for him to learn that some of the people who loved him could not accept him for what he is, a homosexual. Rick is 30 years old and now in close contact with his parents and his sister, but it wasn't always that way. Prior to coming out, Rick lived at home and worked for his father in the family business, a furniture moving company. Rick described his father as a "macho kind of man, one who liked watching ball games and drinking beer with the guys." Though Rick worked with his father and loved him, he was especially close to his mother. They did so many things together—shopped, cooked and traveled the yard-sale circuit looking for the antiques they both loved. He described his mother as a real homemaker, active in her church and a respected member of her suburban community. Rick's older sister had always been close to Rick. They were not only brother and sister; they were friends.

Rick couldn't remember when he first knew he was "gay," but was certain that his awareness occurred when he was quite young, still in grade school. He says he "liked being close to other boys—I felt attracted to them."

"My homosexuality was never a tendency or a phase or a choice. From the start, every instinct was directed toward it."

In high school, Rick dated girls and avoided any hint of his true preference. When he was twelve, he found an older boy in his neighborhood who encouraged him to perform oral sex on him, but at the same time, this boy steadfastly maintained that he would prefer a girl if he could have one. Rick knew the pleasure he experienced was the "wrong way to feel," so he hid his desires from everyone. He avoided the homosexual lifestyle but had occasional, anonymous encounters with men. At the age of 23, he met Ben, his partner, an older man who had been previously married with children. This prompted Rick to reconsider telling his family that he was gay. He said he always knew he would never say anything to them unless and until he met someone to share his life with.

"And then, I couldn't imagine how I would even begin to tell them," he said. "I dreaded hurting them and was afraid to defy them. But it finally took care of itself."

When he first met Ben, he wasn't sure Ben felt the same way he did, so he kept up the pretense of being straight while living at home. One Sunday evening after having spent a couple of days with Ben, he called to tell him how much he enjoyed the weekend and how he looked forward to being with him again. While he was on the telephone, Rick sensed that someone was there listening. He turned around to see his father's ashen face. Quickly, he said his good-byes to Ben and hung up the telephone.

"Who was that?" his father demanded, but he didn't wait for an answer. He fired off another question. "Are you queer?"

"I guess I am," Rick said, his voice barely audible.

"Speak up!" his father shouted. "Are you one of those queers?"

This time Rick stood up and said firmly, "Yes, I'm queer."

A loud noise from the kitchen broke the tension of the moment.

Rick glanced through the door to the kitchen, where he saw his mother standing beside a large roasting pan that had fallen from her hands. "She looked like a cobweb that would disappear if touched."

"Get out," Rick's father said. "Get out of this house right now!"

"Is that what you really want?" Rick asked.

His father nodded. His mother turned away. Rick asked her if that was what she wanted, too. In an almost muffled voice, she said that it was.

Rick telephoned Ben and told him what had happened. Ben told Rick to pack some clothes and come over to his house. After he had put his luggage in the car, Rick went to his mother and asked her again if she still wanted him to leave, and she nodded. He left and moved in with Ben. The next day, Rick called his sister. They met and talked, and she admitted she had always known Rick was gay, that it made no difference to her, that she loved him and would always love him. Her only concern was how society would judge him.

"We were family, my sister and I, not a family of secrets exactly, but one afraid to deal with the truth until this happened."

A week later, to Rick's astonishment, his father phoned him at Ben's house. He told Rick that he loved him, that Rick was his son and would always be his son. This was entirely unexpected, because Rick always thought his father would be the most unforgiving one in the family. Instead it turned out to be his mother who held fast to her position of having nothing more to do with her son. Rick's sister played a vital role in bridging the distance between Rick and his father, but she was unable to persuade their mother to relent and resume a relationship with Rick. His mother steadfastly maintained that homosexuality was "against the word of God."

For about a year, Rick continued to see his sister and father. In fact, Rick said, "My father and I began to talk, something we never really did before, and actually, we became closer than we had ever been. I met him once a week for lunch or breakfast, and occasionally, my father even telephoned just to chat, usually about the business, but after a time, that seemed to be his excuse for just calling to say hello."

The estrangement that persisted with his mother had a devastating effect on Rick because she had been so important to him throughout his life. "It was like losing a part of myself," he said. "I missed her and wanted desperately to see her, but neither my sister nor my father could budge her. I felt like an exile, banished forever from the person who gave me life and was now draining it from me a drop at a time."

Rick said having the love of his father, sister and his partner Ben was vital to his sanity in handling his mother's rejection. Sometimes he'd telephone his parents' house when he knew she'd be there alone—he would listen to her voice but not speak, then hang up until the next time.

About a year later, Rick noticed that a film entitled *Doing Time on Maple Drive* was going to air on television. It was about a young man who revealed his homosexuality to his family, and was at first thrown out of the house. Rick decided to tape the movie. It portrayed the agony and attempted suicide of a person wrestling with his own demons. Ultimately, the young man found peace with himself and with his family, but not before he experienced a tortured period of near insanity and a brush with death. And the family went through an awakening, a realization of not only the suffering they had put their son through, but the misery they had put themselves through by rejecting the child they loved.

Rick gave the video to his father and asked him to watch the movie with his mother, and to do it on a Sunday afternoon when they would both be relaxed. That Sunday evening, the phone rang, and it was Rick's mother calling to ask him if he had gone through that kind of pain while growing up. He told her he had had very similar feelings and experiences, and like the boy in the movie, had even once contemplated suicide. His mother broke down and cried, and said she was sorry that she hadn't understood what it was about, and that she wanted to meet Ben.

That was her way of saying, *I love you, Son, and accept you as you are*. Since that day, Rick and Ben have been close to both their families, including to Ben's married daughter. Rick and his mother have resumed their weekend excursions to yard sales. They are all together on holidays and often at other times throughout the year.

Predictable Outcomes

Real acceptance is powerful and healing and large enough to accommodate disappointment, grief, guilt, hurt, anxiety, joy, hope and truth. *When families close ranks, defend, forgive and embrace loved ones, everyone is a winner.* Parents may not like what their children are doing, but they love them nevertheless. That's even true when they cast them out.

What goes on in the minds of parents when their son or daughter reveals the deep, dark secret they've been keeping for years—that the sexual attraction they have is for members of their own sex? Once parents digest that startling information, they mourn the loss of the heterosexual identity of their child and their hopes, dreams and expectations for a traditional life for that child—along with the special and wonderful role of someday being a grandparent. Then they perceive themselves as having done something terribly wrong when raising their child. They hold themselves responsible for causing what to most parents is a sexual deviation in their beloved child. For parents who subscribe to certain orthodox views of the three major religions, homosexuality is more than just a sexual deviation—it is outright sinful behavior, a sin against God.

Is it any wonder that young people struggling with their same-sex attraction will conceal or even deny this aspect of themselves from family by presenting a false picture of who they really are? They say what others want to hear, conceal what they think others will disapprove of and *act* in a manner that is expected of them because they believe this will get them the most love. But then how can they trust that the love is real if they are creating an illusion of themselves instead of being who they really are? It would be analogous to an artist who received accolades for art that wasn't his own. When you genuinely love someone, you love the person he or she really is, but that doesn't alter the likely response of parents when they first hear of their child's homosexuality. Often the announcement of being gay or lesbian is a prescription for an estrangement. These are the steps that typically take place in the minds of parents:

- My son or daughter is homosexual.

- Being heterosexual is the only way to have a healthy, happy life.

- By approving of my child's homosexuality, I am giving him or her license to continue a homosexual lifestyle.

- If I withhold approval, maybe he or she will choose to be heterosexual.

- Therefore, I will not give my approval.

Though this thought process is typical, it's wise to remember that unless a parent has a deeply religious reason to reject homosexuality, most parents will ultimately accept their child's sexual orientation rather than lose that child. After all, *a parent's love is as unconditional as love ever gets.* And most of the time, it's best to be honest with the family even in the face of some dire consequences. If those consequences occur, it's worth every effort to persist in keeping contact with family. The door might be closed, but it's rarely locked.

Conversely, the love of an adult child for a parent is not always as pure and unselfish. Sometimes there are forces at work that prevent unconditional love and acceptance, particularly if the parent's homosexuality is both shocking and humiliating to the child. Take the case of Greg and his two sons.

COMING OUT THE WRONG WAY

Greg and Megan, both in their mid-40s, had been married for 18 years when he told her he wanted a divorce so that he could live his life "honestly." Megan was puzzled—what did her husband mean when he said he wanted to live his life honestly? Greg refused to elaborate. Megan was deeply devoted to Greg, despite his infrequent demonstrations of any sort of desire for her. When they were first married, he showed a normal sexual interest in her, and the marriage was happy, at least for Megan, and she thought her husband felt the same way.

Greg was a good father to his sons, Peter and Patrick. He coached Little League when the boys were young, and when they were teenagers, he took them to ball games and on fishing trips. Greg was a professor of business at a university, but he was also a wise investor and had made a lot of money over the years investing in the stock market. When Greg asked Megan for a divorce, he assured her that her standard of living would remain the same. He promised to pay for the boys' education and for further training for Megan if she wanted to resume her prior career as a real estate agent.

He also told Megan he wanted to sit down with the boys and tell them of his decision. Megan was insulted and enraged.

"Decision to what? Live honestly?" she asked. "What do you think that will mean to them?" Greg didn't respond. "They'll be just as confused as I am!" Megan shouted angrily, frustrated by his unwillingness to explain precisely why he wanted to break up their marriage. "Look, if there's another woman, just say it!"

Greg shook his head and said nothing.

"Then what?" Megan demanded. "What is it?"

Greg persisted in keeping silent about his reasons for leaving, but reiterated his intention to leave within the month. He told Megan he'd sleep in the guest room.

"Why bother? You never touch me anyway," Megan said bitterly.

The following week, Peter, the older of the two sons, overheard his parents quarreling about the divorce, which was how he learned of his father's decision to divorce his mother. Megan's suspicions had gotten the better of her—she had to find out if there was another woman. She enlisted Peter in her ill-conceived plan to follow Greg on a day when he called to say he would not be coming home until late that night. Megan borrowed her sister's car so that Greg would be less likely to notice that he was being followed. She and Peter followed Greg to a motel about 10 miles from town. When Greg got there, he went directly to a room, knocked and someone let him in, but Megan and Peter could not see who the person was, but there was no longer any doubt that there was someone else. Megan wondered—was it a student or the wife of a friend or another professor?

"Peter was furious," Megan said. "I should have pushed Peter away, and we should have left. I knew I had made a crazy, hasty decision to confront Greg with Peter present, but I was so angry and wanted Greg to be as humiliated as I was."

Megan knocked on the door of the motel room. When Greg called out, "Who is it?" Megan replied, "It's me. I need to talk to you right now."

Greg finally opened the door. Peter shoved his father aside and entered the room. A naked young man was lying on the bed. With a sound of disgust, Peter punched his father in the jaw.

"I was so stunned," Megan said, "when I saw that it was a man— it was as if my mind froze and refused to absorb the whole picture. Greg stumbled but didn't fall down. His nose was bleeding. He said nothing. Peter kept yelling over and over that his father was 'a fucking fag, a no-good fucking fag!' When we got back into the car, he started to cry and kept shouting 'No, no! How could he be so disgusting!'"

Megan felt pretty much the same way. "I felt repelled, physically sick with images of what Greg was doing with men and then coming home and touching me."

She acknowledged that she never should have taken Peter with her—regrets that more than anything she's ever done. "I never suspected Greg was homosexual all those years, and that made me feel so dumb and angry. For months afterwards, I wept as if Greg had died. I felt that I had failed the children for ever even marrying him, which I now know is an absurd reaction."

Megan said it has been five years since that ugly, violent scene, and Peter still refuses to see his father. Patrick also refuses to see him, and won't even discuss it with anyone—including Megan and Peter. Patrick acts as if Greg never existed. True to his word, Greg paid all their living expenses and college tuition. He has made repeated but unsuccessful efforts to see his sons.

Peter has seen a therapist, but Patrick refused to seek help. Peter told the therapist he was so ashamed of his father and that he dreaded anyone ever finding out that his father is a "fag." Therapy has not altered Peter's resentment of his father. Megan said Peter won't use any other word, not homosexual, not gay, just "fag," and he always prefaces it with a string of obscenities. Greg continues to contact Megan and has come to the house many times while their sons were away at school. Greg makes constant overtures toward reconciliation with his boys, but they have not been willing to see him. Greg was furious with Megan for having brought Peter with her that fateful day, but forgives her because he feels responsible for all that's happened. Megan fears the long-term effects on her two sons, especially Patrick, who refuses to see or talk to or talk about his father.

Ordinarily, "coming out" has been seen very much as an individual choice and experience, and one that is barely recognized by society at large. But "coming out" to a spouse and children is particularly problematic. Yet it happens throughout all strata of society, too often with devastating and long-term effects on the family as a whole. According to Megan, Greg regrets his delay in telling his family the truth because of what happened and the damage it has done. At the same time, Megan knows Greg considers that their divorce was a weight removed from his shoulders. He now lives with a man that Megan has never seen and doesn't want to see or know anything about. Greg is happy with his new life, but sad about losing his sons and disappointing Megan. For several years, Megan underwent tests for AIDS. Fortunately, she was not infected, and to her knowledge, neither was Greg.

For Megan and her two sons, the picture is in sharp contrast to Greg's. "I feel as if I'm a failure," she said. "I used to be sociable and basically a happy person, but not anymore. The boys are so ashamed. The only thing Patrick ever said was if it had been another *woman*, he might have eventually forgiven Greg, but because of what his father is, he'll never forgive or forget what he did to his family 'for his own selfish, disgusting needs.' In some ways, I think Patrick has lost all respect for me, too. He doesn't say it, but it's the way he acts. He never hugs or kisses me. He has a girlfriend now, and I think he plans to ask her to marry him. Peter has decided to go to law school. He dates, but no one special. I'm working again as a real estate agent, and that's all I do. I work all the time. Greg has tried to get us to go to some kind of support group, but we don't want to. We don't want to think about it anymore. Greg gets a lot of help from a support group for gay fathers, but nothing they have suggested to him has been effective toward a reconciliation with his sons. And nothing Greg says helps us."

Megan and her sons are indelibly scarred by the brutal way they found out about Greg's homosexuality. Taking her son with her to follow her husband was a foolishly vengeful act on her part, and all the more so when the "other woman" turned out to be the "other man."

"Every day I'm yelling in my gut," Megan said. "Sometimes I wish Greg would hear me and come running home to be with me and our sons as it used to be. Sometimes I wish he had never told me he wanted to leave and that he could have just kept his dirty little life to himself and pretended to be normal. I don't know if I could have been happier that way, but I do know the boys would have been better off if they never knew what their father really is."

Married, but Gay

Many marriages face the trauma of one partner coming out, but there are no statistics on the extent of the problem. In the famous Masters and Johnson study of human sexuality published in the 1970s, William Masters, a physician, and Virginia Johnson, a researcher, concluded that at least 25 percent of gay men are married and leading a double life. These men usually know what they are, but marry to dispel from their own minds the desires they must wrestle with.

Understandable as it may be that a gay person wanting to marry would not inform the prospective spouse of an attraction to the same sex, by concealing the truth the gay person is drafting a blueprint for disaster—as was the case with Greg and Megan. It's not unlike withholding any other information that could lead the other person to feel manipulated and deceived. The rage that the deceived partner might subsequently express is likely to be attributed to the disclosure. More likely, it comes from feeling duped and betrayed.

According to Dr. Fitzgerald, for Greg to be reunited with his sons two things must happen: first, the sons must have a change of heart about their father's homosexuality, which could happen as they mature and experience the vicissitudes of life; and second, Greg must make sure that the door remains open to his sons. To do that he will have to send them birthday cards every year, including not just a birthday wish but also a declaration of his love. There should be nothing more in the communication, and most emphatically no literature on the subject of homosexuality.

Orchestrating the split so that the relationships can endure after a divorce is difficult, at best, but it can be done and is often done successfully. The help of a professional accustomed to dealing with "coming out" issues is vital for maintaining the well-being of the rejected spouse and children. That point cannot be overemphasized. Too much depends on avoiding estrangements that are painful and debilitating for everyone.

Following is a true success story, and I assume the happy outcome is not only due to the mature handling of the situation, but also due to the fine character of the people involved.

COMING OUT THE RIGHT WAY

Marital breakup follows what social scientists call a natural progression; that is, most individuals pass through a series of predictable stages on the way to ending their marriages. They must make an emotional separation, work out legal arrangements, divide their economic assets, come to some agreement about how to continue their parenting responsibilities, renegotiate relations with their respective families and become reintroduced into the larger community as divorced, single persons. Add a few more items to that mix, such as a 25-year marriage between a Protestant minister and his religious wife, five children between the ages of 13 and 24, and the fact that the father is gay and wants to live the rest of his life as a gay man! Can these people continue to remain loving to one another after this marriage is dissolved? On its face it doesn't seem possible, but that's the astonishing part of this story, because they can remain loving to one another, and they have. Their success is due largely to the remarkable good nature of Larry, the gay father.

When Larry was the minister of a large congregation, he and his family appeared to be the perfect model of traditional American values, with five lovely children and no sign of trouble. In fact, there weren't any visible problems, not only outside the four walls of their home, but inside, too, unless you could *see* Larry's inner struggle with himself.

Like many gay men, Larry's appearance offers no hint of his sexual orientation. He is a tall, muscular, handsome, 50-year-old man with the soothing manner of a clergyman accustomed to listening to *other* people's problems. Larry has lived as a heterosexual all of his life. He speaks of his former wife in loving terms. "No man could ask for a more perfect wife, and she's beautiful, too—a good wife, a good mother, a good person. I can't say I was unhappy for most of the years of our marriage. It was a full life, one we shared together, and we always parented our children together."

Behind this very "straight" façade was a man struggling with his desires, his religious convictions, his moral obligations and his own need for serenity. The questions that came up as the interview progressed are probably the same ones that are occurring to you. What kind of sex life did he share with his wife? Did he ever cheat on her with men? If he had a rich, reasonably happy, heterosexual life for this many years, why disrupt the family and change that now? Why create an upheaval and revelation that could lead to a devastating estrangement?

Larry candidly answered all the questions. He and his wife had an active sexual relationship, and he felt a certain amount of enjoyment just providing pleasure for his wife because he loved her. And yes, he did cheat once with another married clergyman. He and Larry saw each other on three separate occasions, and then they both stopped the relationship without any discussion of their mutual inner torment. That brings us to the last question—why "come out" and disrupt the family now?

"I couldn't handle it anymore," he said. "I want a loving relationship with another man—not a feminine man. That's not what I want. If I wanted a woman, I had the best, a wonderful woman. I want to live with a man and have the freedom to have an intimate homosexual relationship with someone I love and who loves me.

The sexual attraction I have for men is much more intense. I just decided I couldn't go on with my marriage any longer."

When Larry finally discussed the dilemma with his wife, she was heartsick, but not hateful. For a year they tried to work things out. Both of them went to support groups; Larry attended a group for married men with children, and his wife attended a group for wives with gay husbands. Both Larry and his wife found the group discussions to be of no help to them—in fact, they considered the support groups to be detrimental to them. Many of the wives revealed how the men had abandoned their families, physically and financially, and this produced added anxiety for Larry's wife. Repeatedly, Larry assured her that he would never do that, and he didn't. Larry found the group of gay fathers to be in far worse trouble than he was. Most were handling their situations in a way that was destined to be unsuccessful. When a couple of the men chose to use the group to solicit for sex, Larry left the group and sought guidance from a gay Baptist minister who was ministering to a congregation that included many gay couples. The minister offered Larry the opportunity to come to terms with his own inner conflicts.

After a year of talking things out with his wife, and even contemplating a marital arrangement, they decided it would be best if they divorced. Once that decision was reached, with all five children present Larry revealed that he and their mother would be getting a divorce. He told them exactly why—that he was gay, that he had known it since he was 13 years old, that he could no longer live a lie, and that he wanted to have his own life, his true life. He assured his children that each of them was conceived in love, that he loved each of them and yes, he loved their mother and would never abandon any of them either emotionally or financially. Just as Larry was strong in his faith in God, so, too, were his wife and children. Instead of their religion being a reason to cast their father out, these children, secure with the knowledge that he had always been not only a man of fine character, but also a loving father, they accepted him in this time of extreme change. Though it was a painful and emotionally charged meeting, Larry left with the feeling that he had handled everything with honesty and compassion.

He thought the matter was settled, but then he began to notice that his children were avoiding him. After a couple of months of little contact with them, doubts began to set in about his decision to admit he was homosexual. He missed his family and became depressed. He persisted in trying to see them and repeatedly told them how much he loved them and missed them. These months were the most difficult ones Larry had ever faced in his life. He had given up his ministry, was living alone and had very little money. He wasn't sure he could stand much more of it. He literally begged his children to see him. One by one, the children began to respond and to reconnect with him. Eventually, Larry met someone—a man many years younger than he was. That didn't last very long. A couple of his children told him to find someone closer to his own age. Knowing they meant that he should find a mature man, he took that as a signal of their genuine acceptance of him as their father who happens to be gay.

Today, Larry finally has peace of mind, comfortable with his choices despite having to live frugally so that his children will have what they need, and he is dating a man that he cares about. When asked what he thought was the major reason his family relationships endured, Larry said, "I was always consistent with the children, always appropriate. I maintained constant contact with them even during times that were strained and tense for all of us. No matter what, I kept on seeing them and always letting them know how much I loved them. Neither my former wife nor I have ever had a bad word to say about the other. I suppose that was the key ingredient because if she had poisoned their minds, none of it would have worked. But that was not her, not ever. She is a remarkably fine and loving woman, and now remarried to a good man."

Larry allowed his head and his heart to guide his every move with his family because they were all so important to him, and he was intelligent enough to realize their understanding and acceptance was critical to his happiness and to theirs.

When Larry was in his most depressed state, he turned inward and searched for answers. Ultimately, he found his way through his lifelong faith in God. I asked him, "Could it be that same God others refer to when they reject homosexuality as 'an abomination'?"

"Yes," Larry said, "because there's only one God, but the God I know doesn't reject anyone who comes to him with love and faith."

A BISEXUAL MOTHER

Nell's story is the most unusual one of this chapter, because Nell's decision to enter into an alliance with another woman occurred after "a happy, normal, 20-year relationship" with her husband Sean. When Nell was a sophomore in college, she became involved in two sexual relationships at the same time, one with Sean, whom she later married, and another with Ann, one of her sorority sisters. Prior to the relationship with Ann, Nell had never had a lesbian alliance, nothing more than an adolescent crush on a girlfriend. She had had several dates with young men, in fact was popular with the opposite sex, and had been sexually attracted to them. Other than the usual teenage foreplay, Nell had no previous sexual intimacy until she met both Sean and Ann. Finding herself deeply in love with Sean, Nell ended the relationship with Ann and married Sean. About a year into their marriage, Sean found some letters Ann had written to Nell. From the content, he could tell there had been a sexual relationship between his wife and Ann. He was furious and finally, after a bitter argument, he extracted Nell's promise that there would never be anyone but him. Nell kept that promise for the duration of their 20-year marriage. They had two children, Troy and Elise. Nell described her marriage as "a basically happy one, one in which [she] lived the usual heterosexual role of wife and mother. I never really considered myself a lesbian."

The only continuous problem they had was Sean's distrust of Nell, and his suspicions extended both to men and women. This had the effect of isolating Nell, because Sean would not allow them to have the kind of social life most married people had with other couples. To fill the void, Nell began to work toward an advanced degree in psychology. Sean's ongoing distrust created an untenable situation and endless arguments, even though Nell was doing nothing to provoke Sean's continued suspicions. Finally, after a couple of years of growing detachment between Nell and her husband, and when their son was 17 and their daughter 13, they divorced, but in the interest of the children, the couple chose to live within walking distance of each other. This allowed a joint custody arrangement to work effectively, although their son chose to spend most of his time with Nell.

When loneliness set in, Nell took a critical step—she decided to try to locate Ann, her lesbian girlfriend from college. "There was a lot of unfinished business," Nell explained. She found Ann working as a psychologist and living in another state. Ann told Nell she was involved with a divorced woman with a small child, but she assured Nell the relationship was not important to her. She said she'd like to meet Nell in some mutually convenient place. They met and began to renew their relationship by seeing each other once or twice a month. Over time their relationship intensified. Nell said she had fallen in love with Ann, the same way she had fallen in love with Sean years before. While these meetings took place, Ann was trying to relocate to the city where Nell lived.

About a year after the divorce, Nell decided to visit her brother in Germany and to take Elise with her. While in Germany, Nell and her daughter shared a bedroom since it was the only guest room in her brother's house. Upon their return to the United States, Elise found out her mother was spending time with a woman named Ann. She told her father about it. He was livid and threatened to file a court action to obtain complete custody of Elise, alleging that Nell had abused Elise by sleeping with her in the same bed during their stay in Germany. Nell was beside herself with anxiety and depression over the prospect of losing her daughter. Her husband tried to enlist everyone to testify against Nell, including Nell's mother! With the exception of one sister-in-law and the daughter's soccer coach, who refused to say anything against Nell, everyone else sided with Sean and agreed to help him gain full custody of his daughter. Because the sister-in-law always found Nell to be a good mother to both her children, she steadfastly refused to assist Sean.

Nell's daughter, Elise, felt resentment toward her mother and stated her wish to be with her father. This was devastating to Nell. Not knowing where to turn, Nell went to see a therapist, a step she described as being one of the best decisions she made at the time. During the course of therapy, Nell asked her therapist, "What am I? Am I a lesbian? How was I able to love my husband and enjoy sex with him all those years?" The therapist told Nell she was just a human being attracted to a person rather than to a person's sex—a true bisexual.

Dealing with the anguish of losing her daughter was almost more than she could bear, but the therapist advised Nell to "expect nothing and accept what is," words Nell repeated to herself over and over again. "Therapy helped me to let go," Nell said. "I learned that a parent must hold its child in its hand like a bird—birds need some resistance to fly. You can't grab a child and hold it tight. Eventually, you must let go. It was just that I didn't want to let go that way—by losing custody of my daughter. But, on the advice of both my lawyer and my therapist, I gave up without a court battle. I didn't want my children and my parents to have to testify. By then Elise was 14, so there wasn't much I could do anyway."

Throughout the entire custody fight, Nell's mother sided with Sean and refused to have contact with Nell as long as she was involved with her "lesbian friend." Ultimately, Nell became estranged from both her daughter and her mother. "These losses," Nell said, "were unbearable except that I knew I could not give Ann up even though we were not yet living together."

Shortly after the custody battle, Sean remarried and moved with his daughter and his new wife to another state. For the next three years, Nell had little or no contact with her daughter. During this painful period, Nell kept a journal for her daughter. "I wrote my thoughts primarily for her. Somehow, I knew we'd be together again, so this journal was for her to read when that day arrived. I wanted to fill in the precious time we lost."

Conflict is an intense, intimate engagement between people, and particularly so when they are so closely related as mothers are to daughters. It signifies that those involved in the conflict feel strongly about their positions and are willing to risk fighting for what they believe by exposing themselves emotionally. Did Nell feel so committed to her alliance with her lesbian friend that she was willing to lose contact with her young daughter and with her mother, both of whom decided they wanted nothing more to do with Nell because of her relationship with Ann? The answer to that question would have to be yes, because Nell refused to end her affair with Ann, even with consequences as grave as they were. Each person was fighting for what she believed. As noted in chapter 2, there are some conflicts that don't lend themselves to compromise—the ones we call "irreconcilable." In such situations, one side or the other has to give up its position or the feud goes on.

During adolescence, emotional upheaval between daughters and mothers can assume wild proportions, and in Nell's case, these stormy episodes were compounded by divorce followed by a mother's lesbian relationship. Nell confessed to feelings of guilt, but nevertheless she stayed her course. She turned to work and to the comfort of her partner. During that same period, Nell had no contact with her mother. Both of these estrangements were gnawing at her. "I was close to the brink," Nell said.

After three years of no contact, Elise began to telephone her mother, complaining that she couldn't live with her father and his second wife. She described conditions as "too restricted." She asked Nell if she could stay with her, even though she knew her mother was then living with Ann. By that time, Nell's son had left for school, so his room was available to Elise. Elise's father warned her that if she ever moved in with her mother and "that woman," she would not be welcomed back into his home, "not ever." Despite his ultimatum, Elise chose to live with her mother. When Elise arrived at her mother's home, "she was really an unwilling family member." For those reasons, Nell insisted that she and her daughter see a family therapist, and reluctantly, Elise agreed.

"What made all the difference," Nell said, "was the therapist's approach. The therapist said, 'You're the mother, Nell, so you get to make mother decisions. You're the daughter, Elise, so you get to make daughter decisions.' That was the tone, and it worked. Eventually, Elise's anger subsided, and we were all able to live together peacefully."

Nell's estrangement with her mother was still going on. After five years of no communication, Nell received a phone call one day from her mother, inviting her to come with Elise to visit for the Christmas holidays. But Nell refused the invitation when she was told that Ann would not be welcome. At this point, Nell and her mother still had irreconcilable differences over the issue of Nell's lesbian lifestyle. Nell's sister-in-law intervened and persuaded Nell's mother to accept Ann rather than to permanently lose her daughter. The following year, quite unexpectedly, Nell received another invitation from her mother—this time the invitation included Ann. That Christmas was a very special one, because Nell was finally reunited with both her daughter and her mother.

Acceptance Is the Key

When a loved one, an adult, is involved in a long-term homosexual relationship with another consenting adult, and where it is not causing any harm to anyone else, it's best to accept not only the decision of the loved one, but also the relationship. Sexual orientation is a complicated, multifaceted process. It may be chromosomal or experiential, but the plain and simple truth is that no one can say what the cause is with any certainty. Who we are sexually attracted to is a mysterious phenomenon, and one over which we have no real choice. Have you ever tried to love the person your mother would have chosen for you? You know you can't make it happen. Remember when a family member shares his or her secret, that person just wants to be honest with the family about who he or she is rather than living a lie. We don't have to like the homosexual lifestyle, but it's unfair to assume the person is sick or abnormal. Each of us has to make our journey through life in the best way we know how. Yes, we may think the gay person is making his or her life more complicated and difficult, but then, whose life is simple nowadays? Remember, this person we love is not out there committing murder or abusing children or scamming the elderly, so why not accept that what the person is doing is simply loving someone else? Just how bad can that be? Perhaps we can find comfort in the fact that although our loved one's homosexuality—or bisexuality—doesn't make us happy, at least he or she chose honesty, and that is a profound act of trust. A scary secret was shared in the hopes that the family would love him or her enough to accept the truth. Acceptance is the key. Ultimately, Nell's mother and daughter did just that: they accepted Nell for who she is, and for that acceptance they now have each other—evidence that estrangements can be mended by the mere act of genuine acceptance.

OUT OF THE CLOSET, OUT OF THE FAMILY

Steve is an example of a gay person who is unable to find an easy fit inside his own skin. For Steve, not only was his loss of family a source of great unhappiness, but his own homosexuality was yet another source of discomfort. The classically indirect way Steve had of coming out to the family is an interesting aspect of this story because it is not unusual for homosexuals to leave gay literature in view to be "accidentally" discovered by family members rather than to confront the problem head-on. There's not much mystery in why this happens—the person cannot find the courage to confront the family with the fact of his or her homosexuality. Professionals who deal with "coming out" issues frown on this method and urge their clients to deal with the family in an honest and open way.

The way Steve's family learned of his sexual orientation was especially damaging to his relationship with his parents. While Steve was away at school, his parents were having their house painted. Steve's mother found a magazine in his room that dealt with gay activism. She called Steve at school hysterical with accusations and threats, not only because of what the magazine revealed but because Steve had always shared a room with his younger brother, and Steve's mother was horrified that her younger son might have been the one to discover the magazine. When Steve admitted he was gay and living with his lover, Alex, his mother told him if he continued to live that way, she would no longer pay his tuition and living expenses. Steve had a great gift and love for music and was attending Julliard, one of the country's finest music schools. When Steve refused to comply with her demands to evict his partner, his mother was true to her word.

At the end of the semester, Steve was forced to quit his musical education and get a job. He was not trained for any meaningful employment, so he took day-laborer jobs for about a year until he and Alex moved away to a city not too far from where his family lived. By the time they were settled in, his relationship with Alex ended. Now his loneliness began in earnest. Loneliness had always been a problem for Steve, who, for as long as he could remember, had difficulty making friends. He hated the gay bar scene and found that he didn't know how to make small talk or develop social friendships in either the gay or the straight world.

Steve learned to cope with his family's rejection, but the void that it left in his life, together with the difficulty of living as a homosexual, prompted him to seek therapy that went on for many years. He longed for contact with his family, especially his brother and sister. By this time, Steve was busily involved in a new career in computer programming and active in libertarian politics. These two pursuits filled his time for several years, but the lack of love and intimacy and even friendship made Steve realize he needed some company. He decided to share an apartment with a female coworker whom he liked and respected. He said it was not a romantic involvement. When that came to a natural end, Steve enlisted the help of a clinical psychologist who specialized in family communication.

The treatment, which included both individual and group therapy, encouraged Steve to reconnect with his family. During one of the group sessions, Steve realized he might have to go home to discover who he was and why he had so many problems interacting with people. One of the women in his group intervened for him and called his mother. By now, seven years had passed since Steve had had any contact with members of his family.

Steve described his mother as a fearsome woman given to dramatic mood swings, and his father as a passive man who did whatever was necessary to keep his mother's rages to a minimum. When Steve returned home for a reunion with the family, he was received as if nothing had ever happened. No one discussed his leaving or the reason for it. He learned that his brother and sister were never told anything about his sudden departure from the family, and also that his father tried to find him, but was unable to because Steve had his phone listed first in Alex's name and then in his female roommate's name.

His father missed him, but his mother made no mention of him through the years of his absence. In fact, he found out that she admitted to having only two children—a denial of Steve's very existence.

At the time of his return, his parents were actively engaged in what Steve described as "cultlike seminars." His parents would check into a facility where they would live on almost no sleep with the purpose of discovering themselves. Steve decided to attend the sessions with them. He recalled the name of the program was something like "Lifespring." Personally, he didn't find the sessions helpful, except that he could see a change in his mother—she had mellowed, he said. The reunion with his brother and sister was most important to him and, to this day, he remains close to both of them even though he moved back to the city where he had been living prior to reconnecting with the family. In more recent years, and before the death of both of his parents, Steve and his family visited back and forth. He felt that they had finally come to full acceptance of him as their son who happened to be gay.

Steve would advise anyone cast off from the family because of a homosexual lifestyle to be patient. "People change, even parents who once eliminated you from their life. What they once couldn't tolerate, given time they will tolerate rather than to lose a loved one." When asked what he would suggest someone do to endure the pain of a breach with family for all those years, he said, "Stay active and busy. I became a marathon runner, a political activist, and I poured myself into the challenge of a new career. I also found an enormous comfort from therapy and the guidance back to my family. Now I'm able to rediscover my music. I couldn't find my way in music until I found my way back to family, especially to my brother and sister."

SOMETIMES GAY ISN'T HAPPY

Cheri had been struggling with both family rejection and her gay orientation for a long time before finding the strength to confront her own addictive personality. More than most people, those who are substance abusers need the support of family and friends.

When Cheri was 15 her mother died, leaving a husband and four children to fend for themselves. Cheri was the youngest child, and the one most affected by her mother's premature death, which Cheri thinks was alcohol-related.

Cheri admits she became rebellious and flaunted her homosexuality to the family, particularly to her father, when at age 21 she first announced that she was a lesbian. Her girlfriend was actually sitting on her lap when she told her father she was gay. Considering the way she handled the situation, it is to his credit that he maintained his dignity and kept his outrage to himself. Basically, what he told her was that he was sad about the news of her lesbianism, but he loved her and would try to adjust to it.

Ultimately, Cheri's father, along with the other members of her family, came to accept Cheri and her way of life. But there was one exception—Jack, the older brother who was closest to her while growing up. Jack's continued rejection is the cause of Cheri's ongoing sorrow. Cheri explained that Jack also had a drug and drinking problem, but found his road to recovery through a deep commitment to his religious faith, which, Cheri acknowledges, is the obstacle that keeps him from accepting her.

"Not only does he believe I'm a sinner, but also a destroyer of families. I wish I could make him understand I don't want to destroy the family; rather what I want is to be included in his family, which is also my family."

Cheri went on to explain how difficult it had been for her to cope with the rejection by the family prior to their change of heart. She turned to drugs and alcohol, not only to drown her sadness, but to help her overcome the frustrations of living within her own skin. About five years ago, she went into a recovery program and credits the program with saving her life. Now she considers her brother Jack's rejection as unfinished business. She is thinking of taking some initiative to mend her relationship with him, but can't seem to figure out how to overcome his religious objections to her way of life. For him to fully accept her, she would have to promise to refrain from any homosexual activity, and this is something she cannot agree to. She's hoping that as he lives his life he will become less intolerant.

"If and when that day comes, perhaps then we will reunite. He can accept a murderer who has repented, but he can't accept me—his own sister—the one closest to him all the years of our growing up. That hurts me."

People can easily be stuck between their attitudes about homosexuality and their love for a homosexual member of their family. For Cheri, the alienation that exists with Jack has become an impossible barrier for her to overcome. Having support from the rest of the family has been critically important to her recovery. The best she can hope for now is that Jack will eventually come around. Even if he doesn't respond, Cheri intends to continue sending him e-mails and letters and gifts, so that when Jack does come to terms with his own conscience, he'll know that Cheri is there waiting to reunite with him.

As much as Cheri flaunted her homosexuality to her family, she was still deeply hurt at their rejection of her. Substance abuse was her unhealthy means of coping, and it almost destroyed her. The recovery program has saved her life, and at the same time she is able to maintain a hopeful attitude about reconciling with the brother who continues to reject her.

❈ HELPFUL GUIDELINES ❈

Accept who you are. Before you can deal with the pain of estrangement, it's important to accept the person you are so that you can have the strength to work toward reconciliation or toward coping with the loss.

When "coming out" to the family, expect a period of adjustment. Although parents often react in a less than ideal fashion after learning of their child's same-sex attractions, most will eventually arrive at tolerance or acceptance of their son's or daughter's sexual orientation. This process is not an easy one, and a period of uncertainty, disruption and, in more stormy cases, confusion and anger is often created within the family.

Persist in keeping contact with family. This guideline applies both to the gay or lesbian person as well as to the members of his or her family. No one benefits from an estrangement because of a person's sexual orientation—neither the family nor the child. If there's one thing that bears repeating, it's the notion that persistent efforts to keep in touch with loved ones will ultimately pay off. Even if you can't mend the relationship, you will always know you at least tried.

Tolerate the family's period of denial. After the initial shock at the disclosure, parents often deny the reality of their child's sexual orientation. Denial provides a buffer zone—a time to regain equilibrium. At a certain subconscious level, the parents know the truth, but refuse to believe it and choose to dismiss it as "a phase" in their child's life. Give the family time to digest what to them is hard to even swallow.

Use a therapist who specializes in coming-out issues where spouse and children are involved. This is one of the most important guidelines offered in this chapter. The shock of learning a parent is gay can be permanently damaging, especially to the child of that gay person, and it's no parade for the spouse either. Don't allow the situation to be discovered by family. Use an experienced therapist every step of the way, most of all to avoid hurting the family, and also to help maintain an enduring relationship with children in the years ahead.

Don't measure the family's love by their initial reaction. The family's love may be obscured for a time by the anger they express at the shocking news. Give them time and help in understanding what took you a long time to understand about yourself. And don't hold them to a standard of accepting homosexuality as equal to heterosexuality, because our entire culture has not yet done that. Remember, when a family fears that their homosexual relative may be harshly treated in an unsympathetic world, they may urge outward conformity even if inward conformity is impossible. There may even be an element of shame involved. Don't walk away from them. Try to understand how difficult it is for them to cope with the unexpected. It took you time. Give them time.

Locate and use educational and support resources. The gay man or lesbian should use all that is available to move the family toward understanding and acceptance. The family should willingly go to support groups (not for lectures, but for real support) and read educational materials to help themselves understand the gay family member. Good support groups will usually help the parents to not feel guilty, humiliated or frightened by their child's sexual orientation. One of the most useful support groups, Parents and Friends of Lesbians and Gays ("PFLAG"), has an Internet Web site: *www.pflag.org.*

Don't leave homosexual literature around to be discovered so that you can avoid the issue. If you're planning to let the family know about your sexual orientation, it's best to be forthright with them, but gently make your announcement with expressions of love and concern for the fears that are sure to be expressed.

Don't flaunt your same-sex attraction in your family's face. That would be cruel and completely counterproductive. Though you believe this is a time when the family should be reassuring *you*, it is also a time for you to be reassuring them that you're still the same person and you need them now more than ever.

Show that you value your gay or lesbian relative. There is a wonderful feeling we can give to each other by both expressing and showing how much we value one another. If your relative is gay and has a partner, the way to show that you value your relative and want his or her happiness is by accepting his or her partner, welcoming this person into your life. The gay couple may not be able to marry, but the long-term relationship they have is as meaningful to them as a heterosexual marriage.

Be loving to the gay family member. Remember that the person who is struggling to reveal his or her homosexuality to family is as much in need of loving as a lost and frightened child would be.

Keep a cool head. This guideline is for parents, siblings and the gay child. Even if the news is shocking (and usually it isn't), don't say things that you will later regret, such as, "I can never love you again." Why? Because, first of all, it isn't true, and, second, it may forever impair the parent-child bond that you will want to have once the initial reaction is over. And for the gay relative who is told to leave, don't say, "You'll never see me again," or "I hate you," because, most likely, neither statement is true.

Learn to say the words, "You are my child, and I love you no matter what." Even if your initial reaction was negative, even if you have been estranged from the gay family member, you can repair that rift by using these simple words. There may be a part of you that never quite comes to terms with your relative's homosexuality, but do your best to overcome your disappointment, at least to the extent of suppressing it. Rejoice in your ability to maintain a close relationship with your loved one, because that is more important than all the confused emotions you have had to experience. There's no confusion about families loving and caring for each other.

Chapter 6

GRAVE CONSEQUENCES

Death, Greed and Inheritance

A son can bear with composure the death of his father, but the loss of his inheritance might drive him to despair.

~ Machiavelli, *The Prince*

*The single most important thing to know about Americans…
is that [they] think death is optional.*

~ Jane Walmsley, *Brit-Think, Ameri-Think*

Family rifts over inheritance are not only rampant in our culture, but they are the most difficult and stubborn to mend. They often lead to permanent family estrangements.

A year after her mother died, Eleanor can finally talk about what she calls "the war of the banjo clock," when Eleanor and her brother, Albert, battled for months over the clock that he felt should belong to him because it hung in the hall next to his bedroom. Eleanor argued that the clock's location near her brother's bedroom gave him no proprietary interest in the clock. Instead, she believed that as the only daughter, she should have her mother's special possessions. Eventually, they sold the clock in an estate sale and split the proceeds, leaving a brother and sister angry with themselves and with each other because the clock had sentimental value that money couldn't replace. Familial fights like Eleanor's and Albert's are ripping apart many a once-close clan.

A Cornell University study predicted that the largest intergenerational transfer of wealth in history—approximately $12 trillion—began taking place in the mid-1990s and will continue until around 2020 as the frugal Depression generation dies off and leaves its money, French provincial bedroom suites, ranch houses, carnival glass collections, Hubbell figurines and moldering photographs to its baby-boom offspring, a generation weaned on credit cards, margin accounts, dot.com dreams and divorces.

It doesn't matter whether it's a big estate or just a few personal possessions, says Gary Zweifel, an Atlanta estate lawyer. "Wills dispose of property, but they are also documents with an emotional component. Heirs tend to view these documents as expressions of love or the lack of it. Money is a way to quantify love. I've seen families come apart over an ashtray!" Anticipating and receiving an inheritance exaggerates both the loving and hating aspects of family relationships, particularly between siblings. And it is a doubly sensitive issue when what is being inherited is valuable and tangible: the "cottage" at Martha's Vineyard, the Meissen collection, even the cultured pearls from Aunt Bea or Mom's full-length mink coat.

In a recent survey conducted by Scudder's American Association of Retired Persons investment program ("the Scudder Survey"), one in three baby boomers says there's been feuding in his or her family for years over the distribution of family assets.

Federal Reserve Board data suggests there will be 3.4 million bequests by the year 2015. With one-third of baby boomers admitting to disagreements and "irreconcilable differences" over matters of inheritance, we can readily anticipate a proportionate increase in the number of disputes and estrangements. And bear in mind, people don't have to be rich in order to leave a respectable inheritance for their heirs. Among homeowners 65 and older, more than 80 percent have paid off mortgages, own cars and have bank accounts. On average, each beneficiary can expect to inherit $95,000, according to New York University economist Edward Wolff. Most transfers will come from smaller estates that usually consist of the family home place, its contents and some cash.

Usually parents struggle to maintain equality and fairness when preparing their wills, but despite their best efforts, friction between siblings, even the ones who normally get along, often intensifies over the distribution of their parents' estate. Each family has its own dynamic. For example, leaving everything for the children to share equally would appear to be the ideal way of avoiding acrimony among offspring, but that isn't always true. Perhaps there's only one Royal Worcester urn that's been in the family for three generations. Who gets it? Or which of the three siblings gets the fine old American tall-case clock that still chimes? And what about the old family photograph album lovingly compiled for four generations or the stamp collection that Dad worked on till the wee hours of the morning? When people fail to specifically bequeath personal possessions, feuds that lead to estrangements are almost inevitable, as are the feuds over issues of fairness.

In the course of our lives, we slide from dependency to independence and back to dependency again. We depended on our parents for everything and took for granted whatever we received. Then we left the nest, sometimes peacefully, sometimes with a vengeance, but we made the move and became independent, and before we ourselves become dependent once again, we're faced with a responsibility we didn't anticipate. As Dr. Joy Browne says in *Nobody's Perfect*, "Our parents dare to get old and childlike, and needy and demanding. We then have to be in charge, becoming the very parental figure we resisted in them years before; and they horrifyingly and cunningly adopt the whiny, stubborn obtuseness that served us so well with them." If we do what's honorable and decent and loving, we provide care and supervision for them that will make their lives comfortable for whatever time they have left.

Our mobile society scatters children all over the country. Therefore, most will not share in caring for an ailing parent. When one daughter has devoted years to taking care of an elderly parent and the other daughter has visited only on holidays, is it reasonable for the caretaker to get the same monetary inheritance as the daughter who did nothing? Isn't it only fair that the one who took on the difficult, sometimes burdensome, responsibilities should expect more?

A TALE OF TWO SISTERS

Mrs. Turner died three years ago and left her entire estate to her married daughters, Bonnie and Joan, to be shared equally between them—a formula for a harmonious outcome, right? Wrong! Bonnie and Joan haven't spoken since the reading of their mother's will.

Bonnie lived a few miles away from where her mother lived. When Mr. Turner died, Mrs. Turner was left financially well off, but for the last two years of her life, she needed close supervision and frequent medical attention. In short, she needed to be cared for. Bonnie was there whenever her mother needed her. Joan lived in another state and came to visit occasionally on Mother's Day, sometimes for Thanksgiving, sometimes for Christmas. When Joan and her family arrived, they usually stayed in a nearby hotel so that they "wouldn't be a bother to anyone." Bonnie knew it was the other way around—so that no one would be a bother to them.

Mrs. Turner continued to live in the big, old family home with its four large corner bedrooms, two of them unused, and the large dining room where the family gathered for holiday dinners. During Christmas and Thanksgiving, it was always Bonnie who made all the dinner arrangements, did the shopping, cooking, serving and clean-up afterwards, plus taking care of her own family and her mother on the days when Mrs. Turner's live-in housekeeper was off. When Joan came to town, she spent most of her time visiting with old friends. She never seemed to notice how hard Bonnie worked to make the holidays a happy, traditional family event. On the few occasions when Bonnie asked Joan for help, Joan always managed to have some previous engagement. Joan was never mean, but she certainly was insensitive to her sister's role as caretaker.

When the will was read, stipulating that Mrs. Turner's estate be divided equally between the two daughters, Joan told the lawyer that she would trust him to see that her half was given to her as promptly as possible. And she immediately laid claim to the family silver—since she already had the same pattern—and the 18th-century secretary in the living room, as well as the Pembroke tables that graced the camel-backed sofa.

"That's grossly unfair!" Bonnie's husband's angry voice cut through the solemnity of the meeting, silencing everyone. "Joan, you don't see anything wrong here?"

Joan shrugged and shook her head. "No. What do you think is wrong?"

Bonnie's husband was livid. "Bonnie has spent the last 10 years since your father died taking care of your mother. You've done nothing to help your mother or your sister during all that time. Getting half of the estate is much more than you deserve, but dictating what personal items you should have is adding insult to injury."

"I agree," Bonnie said to her sister. "Joan, you've never really helped me with Mother. What's more, you've never even said thanks for all I've done. Why should you just take whatever you want?"

Joan's husband glared. "Don't try to give Joan a guilt trip. This is nothing more than greed." He stood up and steered his wife out of the room.

These two sisters have not spoken a word to each other since that day. Acting on his wife's behalf, Bonnie's husband hired a lawyer to prevent Joan from removing any of the personal items from the family home. Despite Bonnie's justifiable anger toward

Joan, she is heartsick about first losing her mother and now having a painful estrangement from her sister.

Bonnie wonders if she should have spoken to her mother about the unfairness of Joan's neglect and her own entitlement to a larger portion of the estate, but she never brought up the issue because she didn't want to add any stress to her mother's already fragile condition. She also questions whether the fight over a few pieces of furniture and some silver is worth losing her only sibling. Because Bonnie knows her husband would be furious with her if she were to drop the matter, she is conflicted by the situation. Her husband has made it abundantly clear that he would never have anything to do with Joan unless she dropped her demands for specific personal items in the estate.

Mrs. Turner probably thought she was being fair by stipulating that her daughters share equally, and she didn't know how to give Bonnie a little more without upsetting her other daughter. Had she consulted an experienced estate planner, she might have learned that she could have provided extra compensation for Bonnie's greater sacrifice without creating a rift between the sisters.

Rightfully, Bonnie placed no blame on her mother because she knew her intentions were good. But now Bonnie is separated from her sister. Because she still very much wants to have a relationship with Joan, there is a chance that, with time, the estrangement will mend; that is, if the brothers-in-law can be persuaded to back off.

Forgive or Forsake

Instead of angry shouting and accusations by Bonnie's husband, Bonnie should have said, "Joan, I love and respect you and want you to have your share of Mom's things, but you know I've taken care of Mom all these years. This is not a question of blame or resentment and I'm not trying to give you a guilt trip. Since the estate is being divided equally, don't you think I should at least have the *first* choice over some of Mom's personal things?" Given Joan's selfishness and insensitivity for so many years, it's doubtful that

Bonnie's plea would make Joan change course, but it's worth a try. Almost anything that will hold family relationships together is a worthwhile effort.

Equal Is Not Always Fair

The Bonnie and Joan story is an excellent illustration of why equal is not always fair in matters of inheritance. Because this is such a contentious area among siblings and so likely to cause estrangements that never mend, the best approach is for the family to anticipate the problem and compensate the caretaker over and above what the other siblings inherit from that parent's estate.

There are two ways a parent can make provision for the caretaker:

(1) Insurance Policy. An insurance policy on the parent's life can be taken out with the proceeds going to the caretaker as the beneficiary. By permitting the caretaker to own the policy, the proceeds are not a part of the parent's estate. As such, there would be no requirement to mention its existence in the parent's estate tax return, in which case other siblings would not have to know about the arrangement. As a practical matter, the premium payments might be too high on a new policy because of the parent's advanced age and physical condition. Another point worth noting: there is an added risk that the insurance company could avoid payment of the proceeds if the elderly parent were to die within three years from the date the policy was taken out. This three-year rule is based on a legal principle that the policy was taken out "in contemplation of death." So unless this insurance plan could be initiated earlier in the parent's life, it would be better to transfer ownership of an existing policy if there is one rather than take on the burden of inordinately high premium payments. If it's too late to take out a new policy and there is no existing one, there is another way that additional compensation can be arranged.

(2) Employment Contract. Gary Zwiefel recommends that the parent enter into a *written employment contract* with the child who is providing all the care. Most children would not want their parent to have to pay them for this care, so this arrangement needs to be carefully explained as the parent's means of providing more for the son or daughter who's doing all the work than for the other siblings who didn't make the same sacrifice. This employment contract can be set off as a credit against the parent's estate on behalf of the caretaker and paid off the top before other distributions are made and without any deduction from the caretaker's equal share.

In the absence of either of these alternative solutions, what can be done to rectify the problems for Bonnie and Joan now that the will is a fait accompli? Most states have mediators available for family disputes. First, both sisters should ask their husbands to stay out of the controversy. Second, Bonnie should try to persuade Joan to go before a mediator where they would relate what occurred, and putting all animosities aside, agree to abide by whatever personal items the mediator allocates to each of them. This would be their best course for mending the estrangement.

In the interest of equality, many lawyers recommend dividing assets equally among children, but that may not be the best answer for all situations. Some experienced planners know that fairness is often sacrificed for equality. The typical lawyer's view is to divide the assets in equal shares, but that avoids the question of needs and priorities. According to Gary Zweifel, if there's a huge difference in the needs of children, those differences should be taken into account when the wills are drawn. What if there were three children—one is a teacher married to another teacher, the second is a dot.com gazillionaire and the third one has special medical needs requiring lifelong care? There's an obvious difference between "fair" and "equal" treatment. It's preferable to treat children fairly based on their needs, even if that promotes some initial discord. A statement in the will of the parents' reasons for how they are dividing their property helps to eliminate doubt that the parents had anything but good intentions. This could go a long way toward a better understanding among the heirs.

The Tug of War over Possessions

Unfortunately, sibling rivalry is alive and unwell in many families. These rivalries are a major source of inheritance battles and are only worsened by the element of surprise. While money can be neatly divided, household possessions are often ignored by the terms of the will. Sometimes the document will contain vague wording like "in equal shares as my children shall select." While those words sound appropriate, they are often a formula for heir wars. Most elderly parents are unlikely to discuss estate planning unless their children broach the subject or health problems arise. But failing to discuss the matter—specifically who will receive certain heirlooms—can easily lead to family warfare. How can these conflicts be avoided? Many estate lawyers now encourage parents to invite their children to choose items they may want and give Mom and Dad the opportunity to settle any disputes while they are still alive. When parents resist the prospect of discussing their wills with their children for fear of making them angry, smart lawyers in the know will often tell those clients, "Let them be mad at you, not each other."

To be absolutely certain that specific items go to the intended beneficiary, the items can, of course, be listed in the will, but that's not the prudent thing to do. The reason is simple: it will give the IRS a road map to assets and drive up probate costs. Instead of taking those risks, estate lawyers advise clients to include language in their will directing the executor to divide items among heirs "in accordance with my wishes." The wishes are expressed in a nonbinding memo stating who gets what; then several copies are made for the executor, the heirs and the lawyer who will probably probate the will. But what if the heirs refuse to agree to the nonbinding memo? One lawyer, forewarned that two brothers had wives who would never agree to anything, decided to include a provision in the will that said, "If the heirs cannot agree to a division within six months, all property will be sold, and the proceeds donated to the Union Mission." You can bet all differences were worked out in a timely manner!

No one answer is right for everyone, because each family is unique. We must always remember that we're dealing with heightened emotions and family sentiments at the time of death. Grief-stricken people often don't deal with issues in a completely rational manner. Children can't be counted on to work things out among themselves, even though they may be able to do so under normal circumstances. It's best to provide clear and detailed instructions. The fewer the uncertainties, the less chance for the greedy grabbers in the family to get what they think should be theirs.

MORE WARFARE

After Helen's 90-year-old mother died, dividing her financial assets was the easy part. Her will dictated her estate be shared equally by her three daughters. Yet when it came to cleaning out the family home, the middle-aged sisters battled over everything from pots and pans to photo albums and jewelry. When Helen said she wanted a photo album that included pictures of her high school graduation, her older sister, Marie, lambasted her for stealing her memories. "But the pictures are mostly of me," Helen said. "The other album has more of you."

"You can both have the albums," said Lola, the youngest sister. "I'm taking the piano."

"Why should you get the piano?" Helen asked. "My daughter plays piano and she's the only child in the family who does."

Lola stood firm, reminding her sisters that the piano was bought for *her* after the other two sisters went off to college. The furniture, including the piano, had to go in storage until the antagonism between the women had abated. "Lots of cobwebs and ghosts come out at a time like that," said Helen. "Instead of grieving and consoling each other, we went back to being the way we were as kids—accusing, arguing and insulting one another."

Three years later, they were still paying storage fees and still not talking. Helen claimed she was the only one who was upset by the estrangement, but she was also discouraged about making another move toward reconciliation because she had tried twice to bring her two sisters together, and they had refused. In desperation, Helen spoke to her minister about the situation. He suggested that they draw lots to see who makes the first selection, then the second and finally the third, then rotate with the second one going first, the third one going second and the first going third. To Helen's surprise, the sisters agreed to try the minister's recommendation. By the end of the second day, the three were looking at old photos, trying on old clothes and laughing with each other. They made enough copies of the photographs so that they each had their own album. It didn't matter that it wasn't the original photograph; it was the image that mattered.

Feuds like this can be avoided if the battles are fought before Mom and Dad pass away. The sisters should have gone through their parents' home, labeling the items each of them wanted, and if there was a dispute, the parents could have settled it. Had the mother of Martin and Sam made similar provisions, these two brothers would still be talking today.

CAIN AND ABEL REVISITED

Martin was two years older than his brother Sam, and for as long as Sam could remember, Martin was his hero. The brothers attended the same schools and both were star athletes in high school and in college. Shortly after each was married, they returned to live in the same city where they grew up. Their mother and father lived close by. When their father died, he left his entire estate to their mother, Mrs. B. Martin's wife, Lynn, had grown up nearby and had a long, close relationship with Martin's mother. Sam's wife, Betty, who came from another part of the country, felt like the outsider in her husband's family. She resented the closeness her sister-in-law enjoyed with their mother-in-law.

When Mrs. B's health began to deteriorate, Lynn became the caretaker, a role she took on willingly. Betty rarely spent any time with her mother-in-law. Mrs. B loved Lynn, and during her lifetime she gave Lynn several pieces of her fine jewelry, including a gold monogrammed pin.

After another 10 years, Mrs. B died. She left everything to her sons, "share and share alike," but she made no arrangements for the division of the household items—including fine silver, china, paintings, antique furniture, Oriental rugs and a host of other less valuable items. The distribution went smoothly. On the day of the funeral, Lynn wore the beautiful gold pin on her navy blue suit. Though Betty didn't recognize the pin as belonging to Mrs. B, her husband Sam did.

After the funeral when they returned to the house Sam confronted Lynn. "How did you get that pin?"

"Your mother gave it to me several years ago, and she gave me other pieces, too, including her pearls."

"That's a lie," Sam shouted. "You stole my mother's jewelry."

This encounter established the hateful tone of the relationship between both brothers and their wives even before the final distribution of property had taken place.

Some families take the high road. After a period of grief, a friendly discussion might take place where requests are made and a fair give-and-take occurs. But many families are like Sam and Martin's, and the battle lines are often drawn over trinkets. These disagreements stem from guilt, power, jealousy, obligation, entitlement and physical possession.

How did these two brothers, who had always been close, become bitter enemies in the competition for their mother's jewelry? It's not unusual for a family member who took care of an ailing parent prior to death to expect to have first pick of personal possessions, but in this case Lynn didn't do that. The items of jewelry were *given* to Lynn by her mother-in-law, although neither of them ever mentioned the gifts to Sam and Betty. When Martin tried to explain this to Sam, his brother continued to call Lynn a thief.

It became impossible for the two brothers to agree to anything. The closeness they had once felt for each other was gone. In its place was anger and distrust. Eventually, Sam and Betty moved to another city.

Martin has suffered immeasurably from the loss of contact with the brother he still loves. "I would do anything to patch this up," he says. "I've even offered to let Betty have whatever jewelry my mother gave to Lynn, all the pieces if that's what she wants, but so far we've heard nothing from them." As Martin told this story, he choked up and his eyes welled with tears. Lynn sat beside him and held his hand. She blames herself for the split between her husband and his brother, though she really did nothing wrong by accepting the gifts. The problem arose because Sam and his wife did not believe these items were gifts, and nothing Martin said could convince them otherwise.

Martin went to see a family counselor who arranged for the brothers to meet in his office. At first, it seemed that Martin and Sam were going to be able to work it out, but when Sam's wife heard of the meeting, she "blew a gasket," according to Sam. Now the brothers are unhappily estranged, though both want to resume their relationship. Unless Sam is willing to stand up to his wife, who forbids contact with Martin and Lynn, it's doubtful the brothers will be able to repair the relationship, particularly with regard to their wives.

Here is another situation aggravated by the in-law factor; in this case, a controversy over substantial real estate has been going on for more than 20 years.

POLITICS, POWER AND GREED

We are all a rich weave of love and hate, kindness and meanness, generosity and stinginess. From birth to death we play out our most volatile emotions within the family. We love and hate the same people. We embrace them and cast them off. But these contradictions, these ambivalent feelings are difficult to handle, and it is particularly so when innocent family members are caught in the crossfire.

When Hank married Marlene, they were the golden couple. Hank's family was politically prominent, rich and powerful. Marlene was the cute blond country girl who found her prince. The wedding was a major event. Hank's older brother, Royce, served as his best man, and the prominent daddy, Mr. Smith, seized the moment for all the good local and national media coverage he could muster. After three years, Hank and Marlene had two little boys and the promise of a happy future.

Everything seemed to be heading in the right direction until that icy day in February when an 18-wheeler careened into a car in which the one inhabitant, Hank, was driving home to the city from the country farm. The car exploded, and the young father was dead.

This tragedy was the beginning of family dissension over Hank's enormous inheritance of his paternal grandfather's wealth, which upon Hank's death automatically went to Hank's widow and their two young sons. The estate consisted largely of Hank's undivided interest in real estate, including timberland, shopping centers and other strategically located undeveloped land that he shared with his father, Mr. Smith, and his brother Royce.

Before Hank's body was laid to rest, the family began to plot how they could get the property away from Marlene. Not only was Marlene acting on her own behalf, but also as a fiduciary on behalf of her two minor sons. Royce tried to buy the real estate from Marlene. She wasn't selling—certainly not at the cut-rate price that was being offered. What was formerly a campaign to reclaim the real estate had now become the family crusade, led primarily by the ruthless brother Royce and Mrs. Smith, his crafty mother, Marlene's mother-in-law.

Throughout the state where the land was located, no one wanted to buck the powerful Smith family. And what about the two young grandsons who not only lost their father, but now were losing the devotion of their father's family and possibly their rightful inheritance? Mr. Smith, the nationally prominent father-in-law, stepped in to defuse the friction that was developing within his family. On the rationale that the two young boys would ultimately inherit the land back from their grandparents, and to provide some badly needed cash to pay estate taxes, Mr. Smith persuaded Marlene to sell some of the land at a higher price than Royce offered. This bought Marlene some time to repair her relationship with her influential father-in-law and to find her own lawyer, a task that turned out to be unusually difficult because of the broad-based power of the Smith family and their far-reaching tentacles.

"By agreeing to the sale, I had prevented my children from being alienated from their grandfather," Marlene explained. "Not only did I genuinely like my father-in-law, but I needed him. I was a public schoolteacher. There was no way I could go out and earn enough to support myself and my two babies. I knew my father-in-law liked me and would try to prevent Royce from taking everything away from us."

The repaired relationship with Marlene's deceased husband's family went on for several years. But it didn't last. Behind the scenes, Royce continued his strategy to acquire the land by having a local court partition the undivided interests. Marlene wound up with her acreage landlocked and inaccessible to the roads needed for timber removal.

Another obstacle was soon thrown in Marlene's face. She could no longer turn to her father-in-law because he and her mother-in-law had divorced. And he had remarried a much younger woman who was now maneuvering for her own interests in the family property.

"The fix was in," Marlene said. "Even with the courts and the lawyers, there wasn't much I could do. Especially now that there was a new, young wife in the picture. My children were teenagers by then, and all of a sudden they were cast out of the family like infectious diseases. My father-in-law's new wife was the keeper of the gate, and that gate was locked to my boys. They've been the real victims, the ones who lost first the love of their father and, ultimately, a devoted relationship with their grandfather. By then we were completely estranged from my husband's family. And my own sister and brothers weren't there for us either. They said I'd become too 'high and mighty' by marrying Hank. It wasn't true, but that's the way they perceived it. So, we were really estranged from two families."

During these years, Marlene suffered both emotionally and physically. She had nowhere to turn except to her sons, who were also feeling the pain of being ostracized from family. "I often wondered if I should've just given up the property," Marlene said, "but that really wasn't an option because I was the guardian of my sons' inheritance. I never could understand why my husband's family would have wanted to deprive their own flesh and blood of their rightful inheritance. As the years went on, it was really Royce and his grown sons who carried on the vendetta. When the timber had to be cut, they would come down to the area, accuse us of trespassing and threaten us with assault weapons. I had an easement over their property for the removal of the timber, but Royce refused to acknowledge the easement and tried to do anything he could to interfere and make it difficult for me. I've had to hire security guards to protect us. Because they own and control the county, I can't even get the sheriff to stop them."

Marlene has suffered from periodic bouts of depression, which has placed a huge burden on her two sons, who have, under the circumstances, shouldered the responsibility reasonably well. Marlene has had the support of friends, but she laments, "Even friends tire of hearing about the family hostilities." Instead of finding a new focus, Marlene has spent the last 20 years agonizing, fighting and litigating to preserve what she and her sons inherited from her deceased husband. Her life consists of seeing accountants, lawyers and the inside of courtrooms, all for the purpose of warding off the onslaught of Royce, his sons and their battery of lawyers. Because of her age and failing health, the grandmother has eased out of the situation. Mr. Smith's health has also deteriorated to the point where he is unable to manage his own affairs. Marlene and her sons are now at the mercy of the reprobate brother-in-law.

This is one of those fractured family relationships that stem from meanness, greed and an abuse of power. Because much of the timber acreage Marlene holds is landlocked and surrounded by Royce's property, it has been devalued and can't be sold for what it should be worth. It's also doubtful that this estrangement will ever mend—bitterness and resentments run too deep and have gone on for too long, escalating over the years.

AUNT NAN'S BEACH HOUSE

We'd all like to inherit a beach house, but what if it's only a part ownership that has to be shared with brothers, sisters, cousins and assorted spouses? Scheduling visits for dozens of relatives is the least of it. As the property gets older, the cost of maintaining it increases. Getting everyone to agree on the sharing of the expenses can be more difficult than getting the heirs to agree to different vacation time slots. And just imagine how many people may be involved as the first generation of beneficiaries die and leave their shares to their children. If it's difficult to get brothers and sisters to agree, think of what it would be like down the line with second and third cousins.

When a place holds nostalgic memories of childhood, emotions can get out of hand. After Aunt Nan died, Doris, her brother Stu and her cousins Lois and Ruth each inherited an undivided one-fourth interest in Aunt Nan's beach house. The first time they visited the house after Aunt Nan's death, they talked about all the good times they shared with their aunt and with each other. But at that same time trouble began. Doris suggested that they replace the carpeting on the stairs, buy new kitchen appliances and a new sofa and chairs for the living room, and enlarge the screened-in porch.

Her brother glared at Doris and told her to stop taking over. One cousin said she agreed with Doris on the things that needed to be done. That's when Stu let the others know that he wanted to sell the property and had no intention of putting *any* money into it.

"I'll never sell it," Doris said adamantly.

The cousins agreed with Doris. They loved the place and wanted to keep it up and use it. Stu's wife's family had a bigger summer place in a nearby town, which is why he wanted nothing but his share of the proceeds from the sale of the house. He expected his sister to side with him, but even if she had, the cousins were opposed to a sale. Doris and her brother had been at odds in the past over other matters, but still Doris loved Stu and didn't want to lose her relationship with him. She offered to buy his interest, but he felt she hadn't offered him enough money. They agreed to hire an appraiser to place a fair market value on Stu's one-fourth interest in the beach house. He found an appraiser who placed a value on his fractional interest that was considerably less than what he thought it was worth, and even less than Doris's offer. Despite his sister's efforts to maintain a good relationship with him, Stu was angry with her and with the appraiser. Doris generously reiterated her original offer, but Stu continued to refuse it. Instead, he made it difficult for the others to do anything with the property because, true to his word, he would not pay his share for improvements and maintenance, arguing that he wasn't going to use the house so why should he pay anything toward its upkeep. Doris believed her brother was being an obstructionist just to force a sale. Before long, the whole family was mad at Stu for being so difficult. Over the years, everyone but Stu used the beach house and paid for its upkeep. The battles continued over Stu's failure to pay his share.

Finally, Stu cut himself off from his sister. Even though Doris knew her brother was being impossible, she was still heartbroken about losing contact with her only sibling.

"I felt there was nothing I could do," Doris said, "short of paying for my share and his share of upkeep expenses. But I was willing to do it if only my brother would've stopped being a horse's ass."

As the years went on, contact between Doris and Stu was almost nonexistent except for weddings and funerals. And then tragedy struck—Stu's wife was diagnosed with cancer. Suddenly, priorities changed. Doris went to Stu and gave him a shoulder to cry on and offered to drive her sister-in-law to chemotherapy treatments whenever Stu was at work. Sheepishly, Stu and his wife accepted Doris's kindness. Doris never mentioned the beach house or, for that matter, anything that might revive old grievances and resentments from the past. This went on for almost a year, and during that time Stu and Doris patched up their differences. Eventually, Stu asked Doris if he could sell her his interest in the beach house, not at the amount she first offered to pay but at the lesser amount—the price the appraiser said it was worth with an adjustment for inflation. When Doris accepted his offer, Stu hugged her and said, "I'm sorry for being such a horse's ass. You said I was one, and you were right."

Being the Bigger Person

Despite the rancor that had built up over the years, Doris never lost sight of what she wanted—a loving, harmonious relationship with her brother and his family. When she had an opportunity to give of herself at a time when her brother and his wife needed help, Doris was there without recrimination. She offered unconditional love and support to Stu and his wife. What moved her brother off his intractable position was Doris's gesture toward conciliation. Stu showed his gratitude by bowing out of his share of the property at the price quoted by the appraiser. Doris's desire to reconnect played an overriding part in her decision to take the first step. Unfortunately, not many people are so unselfish as Doris, even though such generosity often works to end the estrangement.

Mediate Instead of Mutilate

Of course, the better course is always to try to avoid disputes of this magnitude altogether, by structuring ownership and responsibilities in a family beach house to suit the individual family members involved. But the sad reality is that, in many cases, such disputes are inevitable. Whenever heirs are given undivided interests in real estate, they are forced to become business partners—something they may not wish to be or have the skill or temperament for. But if it's too late, and they are fighting over the family property, the key is to acknowledge the problems and address them right away, usually through an objective third party such as a mediator or an arbitrator.

The Academy of Family Mediators was started in 1981, because the legal community recognized the need for mediation in family disputes over property. By contacting the local bar association, families can usually locate the right kind of mediator to resolve these problems before the family has broken apart. Mediation is not binding on family members, which means if there is dissatisfaction with the decision of the mediator, the parties can still seek a court judgment.

Arbitration is another recourse. A third party, an arbitrator, decides who is right after hearing arguments and seeing evidence from both sides. Arbitration *is* binding on the family members, which means they can no longer seek redress in the courts. The decision of the arbitrator is the same as a court judgment or a jury verdict, but the procedure is not only less expensive but usually less adversarial.

Home Sweet Home

Disposing of the beach house had its own set of problems, but what about the family homestead? This isn't just an economic decision—children may have emotional attachments to the property—and it is often impossible or impractical to divide the property itself among the children.

Sometimes a child with a physical or mental disability, who is still living in the home when the parents die, needs to continue to live there, even if it is a valuable piece of property and even if there are other siblings. The parents' will can leave a "life estate" to that child, meaning the residence becomes trust property for the child's lifetime, with final distribution of the property—usually a sale and division of the proceeds—to occur sometime in the future. Until that happens there is the risk of disputes between the life tenant and other siblings. Just as with Aunt Nan's beach house, the question of who pays for expensive home repairs can be a source of conflict and resentment. The best course is to grant the trustee the right to settle any disagreements so that family members don't have to go to court and become enemies. And what if the house is the most valuable item in the estate? Should one child be entitled to have it, causing the others to feel deprived of their fair share? Since every family's circumstance is unique, no single answer is right for everyone. But if the disabled child has the greatest need, or there's a child who has always lived there and taken care of the aging parents, then it's sometimes necessary to abandon the idea of treating all the children equally. Whatever the decision, it's best that the will provide detailed noncontestable instructions, in order to prevent arguments, hard feelings and harmful estrangements.

If you think the questions of real estate, household items and the disposition of jewelry are tough ones, imagine what it would be like to provide for "the other woman" when no one is supposed to know she even exists.

INCONVENIENT WOMEN

When Derrick died, his wife, Kate, and his teenage children found out about his long-term adulterous relationship with another woman. That was difficult enough, but even worse was learning that Derrick's parents and his two brothers knew about the relationship and tried to hide it from Kate by trying to persuade the lawyer, who was filing the estate tax return, not to disclose the life insurance proceeds left to the "other woman."

Derrick's family, particularly his mother, Mrs. Moore, has now been estranged from her daughter-in-law and her two teenage grandchildren for three years because Kate is so angry about the "complicity" of her in-laws that she will not allow them to see the children.

Because of the estrangement from her grandchildren, the grandmother suffered months of serious depression. Even with the support of her family and friends, she has not coped well with the estrangement. She feels that Kate has been particularly punitive toward her because she never condoned her son's illicit relationship. In fact, she repeatedly tried to discourage it and hide it from her daughter-in-law, not to protect her son, but to protect his marriage to Kate and any embarrassment to the children.

"My daughter-in-law insists we betrayed her," Mrs. Moore says. "I've tried to explain why I kept it from her, but she sees that as support for Derrick's affair. That was never my intention. I've attempted to talk to the children, but Kate has them so brainwashed they refuse to even meet with me."

Mrs. Moore explained how everyone has tried to reason with Kate, even Kate's own parents, but to no avail—Kate has dug in her heels and won't budge.

Mrs. Moore continues to send gifts and cards for birthdays and holidays, but she receives no response. She has even learned how to use a computer so that she can send e-mails to her grandchildren. Recently, one grandchild, now away at college, responded by sending an electronic birthday card to her grandmother.

"It's the first step," Mrs. Moore said. "Maybe it will be the beginning of a thaw. I hope so. It proves I was right not to give up."

Ironically, Derrick's infidelity would not have come to light were it not for the broad scope of the IRS, which requires that all life insurance policies be listed on the estate tax return, whether or not the proceeds are taxable. Others more famous, powerful and richer than Derrick, and who can afford to hire the best estate lawyers, have tried unsuccessfully to provide for mistresses as well as illegitimate heirs. Longtime TV personality and traveling journalist Charles Kuralt, department store magnate Alfred Bloomingdale and former New York governor Nelson Rockefeller all embarrassed their families by trying to provide inheritances for the "other woman" in each of their lives.

A *Forbes* magazine article (June 1998) cautions people who provide anonymously for a lover or an illegitimate child that it's practically an impossible task. The Kuralt and Bloomingdale situations are cited. "Why don't people like Kuralt and Bloomingdale leave things in better order when they die? The short answer is it's hard to, given legal and tax requirements. A lover's largesse often leaves a paper trail that could turn a discreet arrangement into a scandal."

Upon the deaths of Kuralt and Bloomingdale, their mistresses sued the estates to collect what they believed they were entitled to. Six years after Kuralt married his second wife, he met Patricia Shannon and began an affair with her that lasted for over 30 years. In a handwritten codicil to his will, Kuralt left Shannon a Montana house and acreage valued at $600,000. Kuralt's second wife, Suzanna "Petie" Kuralt, is still fighting Shannon's claim in state district court in Montana. The feud has turned ugly. Court papers reveal that Petie Kuralt had an antique desk, an Oriental rug and a valuable painting removed from the Montana house. Shannon is demanding they be returned. Charles Kuralt had a successful career of telling homespun stories with happy endings. His own life didn't have one.

Bloomingdale had an affair with a much younger woman named Vicki Morgan, who claimed he had promised her "lifetime" financial support. When his widow, Betsy Bloomingdale, cut off support payments to her husband's paramour, Morgan sued his estate for $11 million. The court denied her palimony claim, but a sympathetic jury awarded $200,000 to *her* 15-year-old son. Although Bloomingdale had no legal obligation to support Morgan's son, he obviously did contribute to his support voluntarily, which accounts for the jury's decision.

Not only is there a great risk in trying to provide for a mistress through inheritance, but there's also the risk of dying in her bed! Nelson Rockefeller died of a heart attack at age 70 while in the arms of his 25-year-old assistant, Megan Marshak. In his will, Rockefeller forgave a substantial loan he had made to Marshak. The question arises: Why didn't he simply give her the money during his lifetime and spare his family the added insult of seeing Megan Marshak's name in the will? And if he hadn't mentioned her, he probably could have escaped the long arm of the IRS, although that's not certain, because even a lifetime gift would have meant filing a gift tax return, which then would have had to be repeated in the estate tax return. What Rockefeller did do was defer the day of reckoning, obviously to hide it from his wife, Happy Rockefeller, who we can safely assume was not very happy about any of this, even if her husband's philandering days were over.

We can only speculate about the family feuds and estrangements that may have arisen from these situations. How many other family members knew about these infidelities and may have aided or abetted them, for the same reason as Derrick's family did, to prevent a scandal and protect wives and children from humiliation?

All of which begs the question: How can anonymous provisions be made for a mistress without the spouse knowing about it? An irrevocable trust prepared by a different lawyer, other than the one who is probating the will and filing the estate tax return, might work.

But even that would not be a foolproof strategy. There is still the tax requirement that the trust be mentioned in the estate tax return, which then must be signed by the surviving spouse. In effect, the surviving spouse would still have to pay taxes on her rival's reward.

The safest course is to provide for the mistress or illegitimate heir prior to death. Cash gifts of no more than $10,000 per year could be given without discovery and without the need to file a gift tax return. Employment arrangements where the mistress is put on the payroll to perform secretarial services have also been known to work. However, I'm only mentioning these two possibilities because avoiding this type of inheritance pitfall flows naturally from a discussion of same, but it is definitely far afield from the purpose of writing this book.

NO ONE'S ENTITLED TO AN INHERITANCE

Many elderly parents are not joking when they put the popular bumper sticker on their cars that reads: "We're Spending Our Children's Inheritance." But the real threat to anxious heirs comes not from gilded wheelchairs and Renaissance Cruises but from medical bills.

Estelle's father had a long-term debilitating illness before he died. He had to dip deeply into his savings to pay the astronomical cost of prescriptive medication for the last five years of his life. After his death, Estelle, a divorced mother of two and a registered nurse, moved back home to take care of her aging and ailing mother. The house was large, but in dire need of repairs that had been neglected for many years. Estelle's married brother, Joseph, lived nearby, but he rarely visited or even offered to relieve Estelle of some of the caretaking responsibilities.

"My brother wouldn't even come over to stay with our mother when I had to attend my son's graduation. That whole time was especially hard for me. I was still working because I needed to pay for my youngest daughter's college tuition, plus I had to pay for the upkeep of my mother's house. I couldn't even get Joseph to do some minor chores around the house—for example, changing filters on the heating unit. He wouldn't do anything."

After a few years, Estelle's mother, without anyone's knowledge, not even Estelle's, quitclaimed ownership of the house to Estelle. Five years later, her mother died. When Joseph found out that Estelle owned the house and that there was nothing much left of their mother's estate, he went to court to have the house transfer set aside, claiming his mother was a victim of Estelle's undue influence—coerced into quitclaiming the house to Estelle, and for that reason the transfer should be nullified. He also reported the transfer to the IRS in the belief that the transfer of the house to his sister constituted a taxable gift. This was a truly mean-spirited act of betrayal.

"Can you imagine that?" Estelle asked. "He thought he was catching me in some kind of tax fraud, his own sister. As it happened, whatever needed to be done to comply with the IRS was done. My mother's lawyer handled the whole thing."

Estelle and Joseph have been estranged for almost 10 years. During this time, Estelle has tried on several occasions to reconnect with her brother. He refuses every one of her overtures. At this point, Estelle wonders why she even bothered to try to mend the estrangement, and yet she has a strong, sentimental attachment to Joseph. "Without him, I have no one to talk to who shared the same things with me growing up. There's no one to reminisce with. Sometimes, it really gets to me."

Estelle is doubtful she'll ever be able to persuade her brother to get over his irrational anger and his feeling of being "shortchanged." Estelle says, "He really believes because I was the daughter, it was my responsibility to care for our mother, but how, in his own mind, that could relieve him of all responsibility is beyond me."

When one wonders why Estelle wants to patch up the relationship with a brother who behaved so deplorably, she quickly refers to their history as explanation.

"I remind myself that it wasn't easy for Joseph. He was born in Germany and my parents had to live in constant fear until they were able to escape to Palestine, where I was born. Joseph had a hard time adjusting to our new country. He used to wake up with nightmares. That's why I try to overlook what he did. He's my brother. I still love him. And now I'm sorry I didn't make more of an effort to keep the relationship alive. I've decided it's not too late. I'm going to write a letter to him, not accusing him of anything, just telling him some of my memories of childhood that we shared and how much I miss him.

"I remember when we were living in what is now Israel, and my brother and I slept in the same tiny bedroom. I would hear animals howling outside my window—coyotes or wolves, I thought. I was scared they'd jump through our open windows and eat me. Joseph built shutters for the bedroom window that he would close when the howling began. How can I forget that? When we came to America, both my parents had to work. My brother had to take care of me. So, of course, I love him. I want us to be close again, even though he did some terrible things to me. I can forgive him."

Reward the Caretaker

As so often happens when there are two or more adult children, only one of them shoulders the full responsibility of caring for the elderly parent or parents. Is that person entitled to receive more of an inheritance than the others? Not *entitled,* but more deserving perhaps? In fact, rarely do parents give more to the child who tends to them in their declining years. Thus, the one who took care of Mom and Dad will most assuredly feel cheated by receiving the same (equal) inheritance as their sibling or siblings. That may be a bitter pill to swallow, but in the long run it's wiser to accept whatever inheritance there is and not lose the connection with family.

Nothing drives siblings apart more than rivalry for their parents' love, but second only to that, nothing drives them apart more than rivalry for their parents' money. According to the Scudder Survey, of those who reported conflicts over inheritance, 69 percent clashed over money, 42 percent over possessions. Attorneys who practice in the field of estate law find these types of estrangements have the lowest chance of mending, so the best course is to try to prevent them from happening in the first place. A good estate lawyer can usually work something out that minimizes the risk of family estrangements over the disposition of property. If it's worth saving a family from potential breakup, then it's worth paying for a few hours of expert advice.

❧ HELPFUL GUIDELINES ❧

Don't allow rifts to fester and destroy relationships. It may take an act of extraordinary courage to write or call the relative you haven't seen in months or years and say, "I miss you and want to see you." If the letter is ignored or you get a cold response on the telephone, give it some time, then write or call again. Most people will respond in time. Just remember, we can't wallpaper our coffins with money.

Parents can minimize sibling feuds. Sibling rivalry, a major source of inheritance fights, is worsened by surprising revelations. Where parents sense this problem exists, it would be wise to discuss inheritance matters with their children rather than have them find out what allocations were made at the reading of the will. It's better to try and work it out and even fight it out with parents than with each other once the parents are gone.

Put it in writing. Money can be divided. Possessions are usually one of a kind. A nonbinding letter of instruction with specific bequests of personal possessions will usually avoid the bitter squabbles and estrangements that are so frequent among the heirs.

It's more important to be fair than equal. When preparing wills and trusts, remember that there is no obligation to leave all the heirs an equal portion of an estate—or any portion at all. If one child has been a decent and good person to the family and another has ignored the family, why should there be any obligation to treat them equally? It sends the wrong message to the child who has been close and loving. Also the financial circumstances and special needs of heirs should be a serious consideration in dividing an estate.

Forgiveness is a powerful elixir. Someone once said we only become adults when we learn to forgive our parents. We can extend that maxim to the rest of the family. Forgiveness takes time, but it not only heals the rift, it also heals the people involved. Keeping grudges in your head is damaging, and they don't pay rent, so why should we give them a free place to stay?

Men should shoulder their share of responsibility. Brothers should not assume that their sisters will happily take on the entire burden of caring for elderly parents while the brothers share equally in the estate.

Acknowledge the caretaker(s). If one of the siblings takes on the majority of the care, the other siblings should make sure that person is acknowledged and supported emotionally and financially, even to the point of voluntarily giving up a portion of the inheritance to compensate the person who made the sacrifice.

Keep inherited money separate. Don't put your inheritance in a joint bank account with your spouse, because if you do, and if you get a divorce, that spouse will probably wind up with half of your inheritance.

Be ready to share. If a relationship has been severed because of an unfair distribution of an inheritance for whatever reason, and you really want the relationship to mend, it will mean relinquishing a part of the inheritance to the other person. When money is involved, estrangements are not going to mend unless the estate is fairly divided no matter what the will provides. Unfortunately, most people won't part with a single thing just to keep relationships alive.

Providing for "the other woman" can be a hateful legacy to the family. If you feel you must take care of that other woman, then for goodness sake, do it while you're alive and make no mention of it in the will. Be sure to do it in a way that it will not have to be reported on the estate tax return, the one your spouse has to sign.

Spend your children's inheritance so that you can die broke and avoid all of these problems!

Chapter 7

~~~

MIXED DOUBLES

Interracial, Interfaith and Intercultural Marriages

Foolish men and the dead alone never change their opinions.

~ James Russell Lowell

*Getting others to come to our way of thinking, we must go over to theirs,
for it's necessary to follow before we can lead.*

~ William Hazlitt

For love … is the blood of life, the power of reunion in the separated.

~ Paul Tillich

Interracial or interfaith marriage is an extraordinarily complex, painfully edgy subject that asks families wholeheartedly to accept what for many is their worst nightmare—having their child, who embodies their values, marrying someone of another race or religion.

You may recall interfaith marriages are as old as the Bible. In the Book of Ruth, we find that Naomi, whose husband and two sons have died, decides to leave the land of Moab and head for Judah, where her family and fellow Jews reside. Naomi offers her widowed, gentile daughter-in-law, Ruth, the choice of staying in Moab among her people and starting a new life there or going to Judah with her. But Ruth clings to Naomi and, in these oft-quoted words, says, "Where you go, I will go; where you lodge I will lodge, your people shall be my people and your God my God."

In that period after the Jews had returned from Babylonian exile, Nehemiah reminded his people that no Moabite or Ammonite was to be part of the Hebrew people, and these gentile wives of Jewish men were to be sent away, along with their "half-breed" children. It is in that context that we can understand how ancient is the notion of interfaith marriage, and that the message of the Bible is to include and embrace those of another faith.

When families of one race or religion are asked to merge with families of a different race or religion, they are in effect being asked to accept that their own racial characteristics or religious beliefs may be *submerged* or possibly even eliminated from succeeding generations.

In some stories, there is evidence of progress, moments of truth and reconciliation, small epiphanies when one side comes to understand the thoughts and feelings of the other, and both come to understand that for the sake of not losing their children and grandchildren, they must all come together. In others, the divisions are too wide to bridge. And sometimes these divisions are triggered by broken promises.

One new mother went to church to pray, and when she came home her mind was made up. Her child would be baptized even though she signed a document promising her husband to raise their children as Jews. Now, with the families completely estranged, her husband is contemplating divorce with the intention of seeking custody of his son.

Without deliberately trying, the people involved in these stories provide an uncomfortably candid dialogue about racial or religious bigotry that Americans normally shrink from. These situations hardly depict an ideal world, but they do depict men and women struggling to cope with the pain of estrangement from their families for having done nothing more than falling in love with someone of another race or religion. They reveal strong feelings, profound thoughts and, in a heartening number of stories, resilient spirits in coming to grips with a subject that is still one of the most abiding of family life.

FAMILIES AREN'T COLORBLIND

When a son or daughter brings a prospective spouse into the home, racial difference can be like a spark to an oxygen tent. Remember that breakthrough movie from 1967, *Guess Who's Coming to Dinner?* Not much has changed since then. People who mistakenly think their parents are tolerant and understanding may be in for a real shock when that tolerance and understanding is put to the ultimate test: acceptance of their child's marriage to someone of a different race.

Candace, a white woman, and her family had always been close. While she was attending Yale University, she met Charles, a black fellow student.

"Telling my parents was a long, strained process. I knew Charles for two years before we decided that we wanted to get married. When they first met him on one of their visits to the university, they began to get the idea we were romantically involved. That's when they started working on me, and saying things like, 'You don't understand what you're doing. Marriage is hard enough. You don't have to make it more difficult, and what about the burden on children?'"

When Candace told her family she was going to marry Charles, her father, a partner in a prestigious New York law firm, said, "What's the matter? You can't get a white man?" Candace told her father she loved Charles. Her father replied, "You think I'm going to have Charles and his black friends around your sisters? Not a chance! You marry Charles, you won't be a part of this family anymore!"

Her mother broke down, crying, and shouting, "You don't care about us. We've done everything for you, and this is how you repay us."

Candace used to speak to her parents every few days. After that scene, she stopped calling them and refused their phone calls. Candace and Charles eloped.

"We were always such a close family," Candace said. "My older brother was very protective of my parents and very angry with me for the pain I caused them. We were both brought up to please our parents and make them proud. It was bred into our bones. They couldn't understand what could have made me defy them. That's the way they viewed my marriage to Charles. I can't say my family doesn't matter, because they do. I will always love them in spite of their reaction to my marriage. But I'm not willing to give Charles up, so we have a standoff."

It should come as no surprise that white parents of an interracial couple can be this dismissive, insulting and incredulous that a child of theirs would marry a black person. In a recent study of white women married to black men, almost all said their white parents were initially hostile about the mixed relationship. Despite the fact that racial intermarriage has long been a source of anxiety and antagonism in America, the numbers of couples marrying out of their race has been growing steadily. If we look at the Census statistics from 1960 to 1990, the number of black-white couples has quadrupled and the number of white-Asian couples has grown tenfold. The 1990 Census data showed 8 percent of black men and 4 percent of black women between the ages of 25 and 34 were married to someone of another race. For whites in that age group, 4 percent of men and 3 percent of women were married to someone of another race. Over the last two decades, the number of interracial marriages in the U. S. has escalated from 310,000 to 1.1 million. The recent 1998 Current Population Survey (based on Census data) reveals what is happening in populous, trendsetting California: nearly one of every 12 whites is marrying an Asian or Hispanic person. The 2000 Census data can be expected to reveal a rise in all of these percentages.

What has not changed is the normal desire of parents of each of the various races to see their children marry people of their own persuasion. Families want someone who is like them, who looks like them, who has similar values and experiences, and most importantly, who will fit snugly like a jigsaw puzzle piece into their family. When a person marries someone of the same race, the same religion, the same socioeconomic level—even someone from the same neighborhood—there is no guarantee of compatibility, but with these similarities in place, it is more likely that the families will get along with each other. If the families blend well, the couple is more likely to remain united. When a person marries outside his or her race, these normal desires are thwarted, and the very consequences families fear are likely to occur—conflict and alienation.

The most frequent marriages among the races are black men marrying white women and Asian women marrying white men. It should come as no surprise that these matches are most resented by black women and Asian men. For example, undoubtedly the most disastrous mistake Marcia Clark made in prosecuting O. J. Simpson was to calmly allow Johnny Cochran to pack the jury with black women. Clark smugly assumed that all female jurors would be so horrified at Simpson's alleged brutality and murder of his wife, they would automatically identify with Nicole Simpson, her white race notwithstanding. Clark ignored pretrial research indicating that black women saw Nicole as the enemy—one of those beautiful blondes who steal successful black men from their first black wives—and enemies deserve whatever they get.

Black women's resentment of intermarriage is now a subject of daytime talk shows and hit movies like *Waiting to Exhale*. By the same token, the black man's family is as likely to alienate his white wife as the white wife's family is to alienate her black husband. Black women are motivated by a desire to marry within a culture, but they're having a difficult time finding mates. Over the past four decades many black women who fought alongside their male counterparts for civil rights and economic justice have been disturbed by one of the unintended by-products of their accomplishments: increasing rates of interracial marriage between black men and white women. Two thirds of African-American intermarriages involve black men and white women. With increasing rates of more educated and affluent black men marrying out of the black community and the high rates of young, poorly educated black men who are unemployed or entangled in the criminal justice system, it's no wonder that black women react so negatively to the loss of eligible men for them to marry. Asian men are also angry, but they don't go on talk shows or write books about their resentment of Asian women marrying white men; they just complain about it on Internet chat rooms where they refer to these Asian women as "self-hating Asians." If ever an area of family life was rife with estrangements, interracial marriage is surely it.

Sociologists and others doing research on the subject of interracial marriage maintain the most serious objections usually come from white Christian fathers, a finding borne out by several of the following stories.

RAINBOW COALITIONS

Grant and Melanie, who have been married for over 20 years, met in college. When Melanie told her parents she was dating a premed student, they were delighted until they found out Grant was an African American.

"Why would you put yourself through the anguish this will cause?" asked Melanie's mother. "We've never had any contact with black people, and we're not comfortable with any of this."

"My father was brutal about it," Melanie recalls. "'What are you going to do when he leaves you with black babies?' he asked me."

Four months later, the couple wed with only Grant's family in attendance. "It still bothers me that my parents weren't there. It makes you wonder how to continue loving people who cause so much pain." Melanie pauses. "Except that I knew I was causing them a lot of pain, too."

Over the next few years, Melanie learned some hard truths— i.e., that both races maintain certain beliefs among themselves about interracial relationships. The black culture believes: (a) a black man belongs with a black woman, (b) a black woman will treat a black man better than a white woman, and (c) children will be viewed by everyone as black and should have a black mother. Within the white culture, people believe: (a) black men marry white women as status symbols or to get ahead, (b) the interracial marriage will fail, (c) there is something psychologically wrong with a white woman who marries a black man, and (d) white women who marry black men must hate their parents.

According to Melanie, those beliefs, maintained by both hers and Grant's family, really added another layer of problems in their marriage. The rejection Melanie experienced by her parents was especially difficult because she had always been close to her family, a salient fact that contradicted some of the beliefs her white family held about her and her reasons for marrying a black man. She didn't hate her parents. Quite the opposite—she loved them. The break in the relationship caused her to feel extremely isolated, not only from her family, but also from her white culture. This feeling of alienation resulted in problems with her husband early in the marriage. Melanie soon found herself depressed and increasingly unresponsive to her husband and his family.

When Melanie and Grant had their first child—a girl—they sent an announcement with photographs to Melanie's parents. Her mother called to ask if she could come and visit her new granddaughter. At that point, Melanie's father was still resisting contact. But the birth announcement and the intervention by Melanie's sister finally prompted him to change his mind about Grant. Slowly but surely, Melanie's parents became more accepting of the marriage.

"My mother wanted to be involved with her grandchild," Melanie said. "The more time they spent with us, the more they began to see Grant as a good husband and a good father. Grant really shot down most of their racist beliefs about black men."

Though Grant has forgiven his in-laws, his family still harbors deep resentments against Melanie's parents for scorning their son. However, for the sake of the child, everyone has tried to make the best of a highly volatile situation.

During the period when the families were estranged, Melanie received support and counsel from other interracial couples who had had similar experiences. Those who also had estrangements from their families, and had been able to mend them, advised Melanie to give her parents time to get accustomed to the situation. And Grant was urged to keep a forgiving attitude in his heart.

Though Melanie's family appears to get along with Grant, Melanie knows there's a difference in the way they interact with her husband and how they normally behave with each other. If someone begins to discuss any subject that includes black and white issues, a certain tension starts to build.

"My dad was furious when O. J. Simpson was acquitted," Melanie said, "but when Grant was around, as soon as the subject was mentioned on TV, Dad would turn off the set. One day I asked him why he did that. He told me he didn't want to get into an argument with Grant. I asked why he thought there would be an argument. His answer was just what Grant thought were my father's feelings—that all blacks think alike and wanted Simpson to get off, because even if he did do it, the only two people he killed were white. When I told my father that Grant believed Simpson committed the crime and should have been found guilty, my father was really surprised."

Melanie gave other examples of her family's behavior that raised questions in her mind about just how much they *really accepted* Grant.

Whenever Melanie wanted to join them at church, her mother said they didn't attend church regularly anymore, but what she really meant was that they didn't attend whenever Melanie, Grant and their child arranged to visit on a Sunday. Her mother no longer invited other relatives for Thanksgiving dinner with them if Melanie and Grant were going to be there. When Melanie questioned why her mother was deliberately doing that, the answer, Melanie thought, was a lame excuse—that she was not physically able to handle a large crowd anymore.

Melanie's father paid very little attention to his granddaughter. "It's as if he doesn't really think of my daughter as his grand-daughter. People will talk about who everyone looks like the family. When my sister had a baby, relatives eagerly discussed whom they thought the baby looked like, but that kind of conversation never comes up about my daughter. I don't believe that my parents think of her as *my* daughter, so how can she be their granddaughter or anyone's niece or cousin. The sad thing is that Grant's family acts the same way."

Melanie explained that if she and Grant want to continue having contact with their respective families, they must accept their attitudes and behavior and hope that, eventually, both sets of parents will become "colorblind." Melanie related that her most difficult relationship is with Grant's youngest sister, who considers black men marrying white women to be a blatant slap in the face of their black sisters.

"How will we ever be friends?" Melanie asked. "Grant's sister may think of it as black men slapping the faces of black women, but in reality her anger is directed at me, not at her brother."

Melanie believes that black and white women who marry outside their race have the common experience of no longer being fully accepted by members of their respective races—and therefore of needing their families more than ever.

WILL I EVER SEE HER AGAIN?

Not all situations are capable of mending. When Tess, a white woman in her late 40s, married Alex, a black dentist, Tess's 20-year-old daughter, Cindy, was appalled. She wanted nothing further to do with her mother. In fact, Cindy moved closer to her father, who happened to live in the state where her mother's extended family lived. For several years, Tess tried to communicate with her daughter, but Cindy refused all overtures. Tess continued to have good relationships with her elderly mother and her sister, both of whom were living near Cindy, and they tried to persuade Cindy to reconnect with her mother, but their efforts were in vain. Tess never knew her daughter was so racially prejudiced—Cindy never gave any indication of her deep-seated intolerance—but according to Tess's sister, the interracial marriage was clearly the reason Cindy moved out of Tess's home and cut off all contact with her. This total estrangement went on for several years.

Then Tess was diagnosed with lymphoma. Tess's sister—and Cindy's favorite aunt—tried to persuade Cindy to visit her mother, but she refused. Tess suffered through a long bout of chemotherapy and radiation, all the while longing to see her only child. The strain and depression of the illness was compounded by the estrangement. Alex did everything he could to make Tess comfortable and took her wherever she needed to go to receive the best treatment. Finally, her cancer went into remission, but Tess knows it could return and metastasize again.

"I can't help but believe I was a sitting duck for cancer because of all the stress of losing my daughter. I never stop agonizing about it. I've missed her so much, but I have to accept that the situation is hopeless. If she couldn't even come back long enough to say good-bye to me, because I was really dying at that time—the doctors had given me six months—then I know I've lost her for good. I try not to think about it anymore, because I need to have strength and optimism if I'm going to fight this cancer."

When asked if there was anything she would have done differently, Tess shook her head. "You mean would I have married Alex if I knew it meant losing my daughter? The answer is yes—I'd marry him again. He's a loving, supportive, wonderful man."

Shades and Highlights

In his 1984 book, *The Psychology of Blacks,* Joseph White offers an African-American perspective on the importance of the extended black family. "Wherever blacks appear in numbers of two or more . . . they form a quasi-family network . . . get together, get down, rap, and party. White folks don't know what to make of this thing. The ideal of sharing, closeness, and interdependence expressed in socio-familial groups is so deeply ingrained in the fabric of the [African]-American ethos that it is not likely to give way to the nuclear family with its stress and isolation, competition, and independence."

The conservative white view of a traditional nuclear family includes a mother, father and children in each house while ignoring that that particular description fits a surprisingly small minority of American families. Often the nonwhite family consists of at least three generations living under the same roof or in close proximity to each other—brothers and sisters, aunts and uncles, and grandparents and cousins. Joseph White points out some of the advantages of the extended family with its members able to "experience life in retrospect and prospect in a mutually supportive atmosphere." The salient points he makes about the extended black family are also applicable to most Hispanic and Asian families in America.

With three generations in close contact with each other, in African-American, Hispanic and Asian families there is a stronger bonding between all ages and a more caring atmosphere. Their elderly relatives are taken care of instead of being farmed out to nursing homes as is so often the case in white families. How many old people in nursing homes die feeling useless, abandoned and forgotten? With the generations together, the old can see the life cycle recreated just as the young can see it unfold ahead of them. Children who miss the day-to-day experience with their elders may perceive them as cranky, senile old crones instead of a wonderful link to their own past history. In most nonwhite families, the children learn to appreciate and admire people their grandparents' age because they see them all the time. And perhaps most important of all, the absence of an elderly relative in a child's life deprives that child of learning firsthand how to cope with loss—and with death as a natural part of life.

Often interracial couples are offered no options because family members completely alienate them from their lives. This was the case with Tess and her daughter, Cindy, and is also true in the following story.

LOVE WAS NOT A MANY-SPLENDORED THING

As soon as engineer Chang's family found out he was planning to marry Daphne, a Caucasian woman, they began a campaign to remove him from what they considered an impending disaster and to convince him to go to work in his uncle's construction company in Hong Kong. Chang says, "I had visions of getting off the plane and being drugged just long enough to get me married off to some nice Chinese girl who would giggle and serve me Moo Goo Gai Pan."

In fact, both Chang's and Daphne's families disapproved of the marriage. The couple eloped anyway. For the last two years, they have not seen anyone in their respective families though they live in the same city where they both grew up and where their families still live. Chang is often depressed about the loss of his family, but he never talks about it. Daphne feels just the opposite.

"I obsess about it," she says. "I can't stop talking about how angry I am that my own parents would cast me out of their lives just because I fell in love with and married a Chinese-American man."

Both Chang and Daphne have decided to work for the next several years and delay having a child. She is rather fatalistic about this choice.

"The truth is that we both wonder if we'll stay married, but we never say the word 'divorce.' We do love each other, yet there are so many differences we hadn't recognized before. Chang doesn't express his emotions, so I rarely know what he's thinking. He wants me to cook Chinese food, but I'm not much of a cook, and it's hard to get food to taste ethnic unless you use their seasonings. And right now I don't have the time to learn. I work a very long week."

When Daphne spoke about differences in food culture, she recalled how another American woman she knew who had married a Chinese man had to undergo a kind of initiation rite into her husband's culture. The woman's mother-in-law took her to ethnic food stores to select just the right vegetables and spices, taught her how to use a wok, to use a cleaver and chopsticks as cooking utensils—a type of kitchen apprenticeship.

"That's how they really got to know each other," Daphne said. "But that's also when the problems really began. Once they got to know each other, the Chinese mother and American daughter-in-law discovered that they couldn't stand each other. Maybe the family rejection in our case is a good thing. At least I don't have to put up with his family on a regular basis."

Daphne's cavalier attitude about the estrangement from her husband's family came through loud and clear, but it was an altogether different matter with respect to her own family. At first reticent to express her feelings about them, Daphne finally admitted she desperately missed her mother and her younger sister, and that it was her father who had been the most vocal in his prejudice toward her Asian husband.

"My mother probably would have come around, but she never overrides my father. He's bigoted about everyone—even Catholics and Jews, so how could I expect him to accept a son-in-law from another race? Dad's from a small southern town and never even saw anyone but Baptists, white and black, until he was in military service. He literally believes no one but Christians are going to heaven. I asked him, what about the millions of Buddhists and Moslems and Hindus and Jews? Yes, they're all going to hell is what he believes."

Daphne is deeply and genuinely saddened by the loss of contact with her family. When asked how she intended to deal with the estrangement, she said she'd try to see her mother without her father knowing about it. Her advice to others contemplating marriage to someone of a different race was to think long and hard before making this decision. "If you think you can live without that person," Daphne says, "then you should break up the relationship and find someone of your own race. Marriage is hard enough—so why make it harder?"

Daphne appears to regret her marriage to Chang and dismissed any suggestion of seeking help from other family members, friends, therapists or clergy. "There's no point to it," she said. "Nothing will do any good with my father, and I don't want to complicate things even further by trying to connect with my husband's family. I guess I don't much care if I ever see them."

As for Chang's feelings of loss of his family, Daphne says, "He'll just have to deal with it as best he can. I have enough to handle."

At the time of this interview, the prospects for the future of this marriage seemed dismal, and within six months Daphne and Chang had filed for divorce.

A poignant recent story in a popular magazine article showed how even the most enlightened of parents can erect a wall between themselves and their child married to someone of another race.

Tshi tshi, 28 years old, was born in Korea but grew up living all over the world since her father was being sent from one United Nations assignment to another. Despite their travels and cosmopolitan lifestyle and their constant contact with people of all races, her parents rejected Tshi tshi when she married Tom, a WASP from Connecticut. They boycotted the wedding and have been estranged from their daughter since that time. Unfortunately, this story—like Tess and Cindy's—still has no happy resolution. And together with the one that follows, these sad circumstances indicate that the world still has much to learn about accepting and adapting to interracial and intercultural marriages.

INTERCULTURAL, INTERFAITH, ENTER TROUBLE

"To any Western woman contemplating marriage to an Iranian Muslim, I would say don't do it." Those were the first words uttered by Angela in describing her interfaith and intercultural marriage to Kahlil. For five years Angela was married to Kahlil, an educated, well-traveled man in the hotel business. "Though we're finally divorced and I'm back home in a different state with my child, I dread what could still happen to us, mainly that Kahlil could kidnap our son and take him back to Iran." Her fear of reprisals is warranted because of Kahlil's prior behavior. He had been an abusive husband and has been stalking his child since the divorce became final three years ago.

Angela was 22 years old and Kahlil was 35 when they met while working at the same hotel. During a one-year romantic courtship, Kahlil seemed to be an enlightened gentleman with a great love for his family, particularly his mother. Angela took that as a sign of someone who had enormous respect for women, unlike the stereotypical Middle Eastern man she'd read about. But Angela's family, who were Christians, refused to accept Kahlil because he was a Muslim. Her parents tried to warn Angela of the dangers of marrying someone who was neither of her faith nor an American citizen. Her family knew of another instance where a friend's daughter who had married an Arab Muslim had been a victim of his physical abuse, and then after she divorced him suffered the loss of her two children when her ex-husband kidnapped them and took them to Saudi Arabia. Angela's family thought Kahlil "had a little too much charm," and never trusted nor accepted him.

Angela married Kahlil against her parents' wishes. Neither family attended the wedding. As soon as they knew of the marriage, Angela's entire family cut off all contact with her. Angela said she and Kahlil were happy, but as soon as she gave birth to their son, Yousef, Kahlil turned cold and indifferent to her. In time, his verbal abuse became physical; every time Angela disagreed with her husband, he'd respond by slapping her.

Angela longed for the support and comfort of her family, but realized they had warned her of these potential problems and would probably say, "I told you so," if she asked for their help. Kahlil began to ignore Angela and bring only Muslim friends to their house. Then, over Angela's objections, they moved to a small house in a rural area, more than an hour's drive away from the city where they had lived and where Kahlil continued to work. He told her it was a better place to raise their son and that he would sell her car and buy a newer, more reliable and safer one for highway travel. After Angela's car was sold, Kahlil never did buy another car for her. It soon became obvious that his plan all along was to deprive her of access to anyone but him. Angela and their baby son were virtually Kahlil's prisoners, cut off from everyone except for a couple of friends Angela had made at work. When Kahlil found long-distance calls on the telephone bill, he forbade his wife from using the phone except to call him or the local supermarket that made deliveries.

"I was living a Kafkaesque nightmare," Angela says. "I decided I had to have my family's help. When I called home, knowing the long-distance number would show up on our bill, my father answered and told me, 'You made your bed, now lie in it.' I begged him to help me. He told me to get a divorce. Of course I had no money for a lawyer and no way to even get to a lawyer's office. I was trapped. Finally, I told the man who delivered groceries what was happening and that I needed help. Not having any of my family to be there for me was probably the worst of it. I felt so abandoned and depressed. I began to neglect myself. I had no appetite, but I had to cook because Kahlil would have beat me if there was no dinner when he came home, sometimes as late as midnight, sometimes not at all. The more I neglected myself, the more Kahlil abused me, verbally and physically."

After Angela had asked the deliveryman to help her, he began to notice her bruises and decided to drive her and her son to her parents' home 100 miles away. Her shocked mother immediately welcomed Angela with love and the promise of the support she needed. After a few days, her father and the rest of the family came around. Kahlil decided to fight for custody of their son, but with the help of the deliveryman's testimony, Angela won full custody of the child. Because the court recognized the risk of a kidnapping by the father who had threatened to go back to Iran with his son, the decree required supervised visitation in the presence of Angela and other members of her family.

Angela's marriage to Kahlil was such an obvious mistake that it hardly seems worthwhile to discuss ways of overcoming the problems within the marriage. The family's decision to abandon their daughter was reprehensible, particularly her father's reply to her plea for help. Still, the lesson to be learned by all of us is that *home is where they have to take you in*, and they almost always do. Friends can be wonderful, the best, but there aren't too many friends who will open the door and let you and your children move in bag and baggage for some indeterminate time.

A World of Differences

A major challenge to interfaith marriage consists in the couples who lack understanding, both of the cultural context and meaning of each other's behavior and the behavior of their respective families. Conflicts are inevitable in interfaith marriages, as they are in most marriages, except a little more so. But as recently demonstrated by the 27-year marriage of well-known and highly regarded media personalities Cokie and Steve Roberts, love and respect for each other's religious heritage can result in enormous success. As an interfaith couple—he's Jewish, she's Catholic—the Robertses have been able to create a blended culture—interconnection, routines and rituals—that foster both the expression of their individuality and the resolution of problems. Another significant aspect of their strong marriage is the closeness they have been able to maintain with their respective families. Without that support, it is extremely difficult for either party to maintain his or her religious identity.

The number of interfaith marriages, particularly between Jews and Christians, has been growing steadily for the last 50 years. For the first half of the 20th century, there was no more than one in 10 Jews marrying Christians. According to the American Jewish Committee, that number doubled by 1960, doubled again by the 1970s, and in the 1990s, slightly more than 50 percent of Jews married Christians. One out of three American Jews lives in an interfaith household. The comparable figures for other interfaith marriages are 21 percent for Catholics, 30 percent for Mormons and 40 percent for Muslims (*Newsweek*, Dec. 15, 1997). According to a recent survey, among Japanese Americans, 65 percent marry people who have no Japanese heritage; Native Americans have upped that number to 70 percent.

In *Love and Tradition: Marriage between Jews and Non-Jews,* E. Mayer shows the extent to which parental opposition is a problem for interfaith couples: 43 percent of Jewish parents and 30 percent of Christian parents openly oppose their children's unions.

An extended family that disapproves of the marriage will not be available to provide support when trouble surfaces in the marriage. The commitment of the Jewish extended family to its Jewish identity, the tendency of the Jewish family to be very close-knit and, most importantly, the fact that Jewish religious celebration is inextricably woven into family rituals may put added pressure, stress and confusion onto the marriage. This layered dynamic may in itself be a source of conflict that prevents the couple from creating a blend of cultures.

Why is there so much family objection and estrangement when a Jew marries a non-Jew? Because the stakes are higher for Jews. The traditional Jewish stricture against intermarriage grew out of the experience of Jews who have had a much longer history of persecution and genocide than any other single group, including blacks. Jews still, for all their prominence in American life, comprise less than 3 percent of the population. When half of them marry someone outside the faith, says Elliott Abrams, the president of the Ethics and Public Policy Center in Washington, D.C., and former assistant secretary of state, "We're looking at a very dismal prospect" for the survival of the Jewish people.

While such statistics account for much of the Jewish family's disapproval of interfaith marriages, it should be noted that the objections to a Jewish-Christian marriage often come from the Christian family.

FORSAKEN BY FAMILY

Steve and Becky live in a predominantly white, blue-collar, mostly Irish, Eastern European and Christian neighborhood where there is pride of property and active involvement in community affairs.

Two years ago, when the newlyweds moved into the area, they became acutely aware of the neighborhood customs—well-tended gardens, lavish outdoor Christmas decorations and regular church attendance. Steve didn't want Becky's Jewishness, the flicker of Shabbat candles on Friday nights, a Chanukah menorah in the window, or the absence of a Christmas wreath, to advertise their difference to the neighbors.

For the three years of his relationship and marriage to Becky, Steve had no contact with his family because they flatly refused to accept his marrying a non-Christian.

"We saw our marriage as a challenge from the start," Steve said. "We knew it would take work and some loss, particularly for me. Strangely, Becky's religion has been both an enriching and an uneasy change for me. We celebrate Chanukah as well as Christmas. We have a tree but no wreath, and we observe Passover as well as Easter. When we first met, Becky told me of the deep feelings she has about her religion and how much she wants to pass it on to our children when we had them. There was never any surprise. We've both been honest with each other."

"That's not entirely true," Becky said. "You have problems with my faith."

Steve explained that it wasn't her faith that he had problems with, but what he referred to as her "Jewish obsession"—that Jews have suffered, they are the "chosen people" and that not observing the religion makes Becky feel guilty. She believes she has to carry out every ritual or it would be a betrayal of those Jews who were persecuted and died because of their religion. Steve admires and cares about Becky's family. He described them as spiritual people who question life, society and even some of their own religious practices.

"They're intellectual and charitable and interesting, but much too clannish. They confine their friendships primarily to other Jews."

When Steve was asked to explain how he felt about losing contact with his own family, he emotionally expressed his sense of loss in terms of the imbalance in their lives—i.e., spending time with Becky's family for every Jewish holiday and having no one over for Christmas.

"I do have a background and culture of my own," Steve said, "but one that I'm exiled from. I guess it's not really a culture the way Judaism is. Christianity is a religion, and one I don't completely believe in. That's why I have a hard time making my case. Without my family to take part in the celebration of Christmas, it's not much of a holiday. Becky doesn't do anything but decorate the tree after I put it up."

Becky made it perfectly clear that she would do whatever Steve asked to help mend the rift with his family.

"But there's nothing she can do," he said. "They told me if I married Becky that I would no longer be a part of their family. Even my brother won't see us for fear of making my parents angry at him."

When asked if he knew precisely what it was that caused his family to have such strong feelings about Becky's faith that they would cast their own son out of their lives, Steve shook his head.

"They're anti-Semitic," Becky said. "It's not complicated. They're Catholic and they all went to Catholic schools where they learned the old catechism that taught them to hate Jews—that we killed Christ. You think the Pope's recent pronouncements will erase their bigotry. I doubt it."

Steve nodded. "That's probably true. I've tried to persuade them to get to know Becky, but they've refused. Some of our friends say that if we have a child, they may change their minds. I guess we'll have to wait and see. But even if they did change their minds, how can I expect Becky to be comfortable with people who have treated her the way they have? Her family has been so good to me that it makes me ashamed of my own family. But that doesn't alter the fact that I always feel this void. I miss my family. I really do."

It's Your Move
How can Steve and Becky open the door to a relationship with

Steve's family? Where can they begin? It will be up to Steve to make the first move toward reconciliation. He will have to find some means of reaching their better nature, perhaps by writing them a long letter explaining how he misses them and how not having them in his life has created an unbearable void. If there is an aunt or uncle whom he can talk to, that person might be able to intervene on Steve's behalf. If that doesn't work, Steve should try calling his mother and appealing to the love she felt for him and that surely must still be there. As has been demonstrated in so many of the mended relationships, *persistence is key*.

Clergy Epiphany

According to theologian Martin Marty, who grew up in the 1940s in a small Nebraska town, "If a Catholic married a Lutheran, they had to move out of town, because the hassles were just too much. Today, mixed marriage is not a big deal among most American Christians." Before Vatican II (1962–65) in which Pope John XXIII eased restrictions, Catholics weren't allowed even to attend the wedding of a friend or relative if they were marrying in a non-Catholic church or in a synagogue.

Nowadays, even if a staunch Catholic marries an Episcopalian or a Presbyterian, families will sigh with relief that at least their child isn't marrying someone addicted to drugs, alcohol or gambling. Several clergy interviewed for this chapter had similar opinions and said they would perform a wedding ceremony for interfaith couples. One Methodist clergyman, whose daughter married a Catholic, said he was happy about the union because his son-in-law is a good person, husband and father. That was all that mattered to him. When asked if he would feel the same way if she had married a Jew or a Muslim, he said that might be more difficult because the husband, not being a Christian, might pose more problems, baptism of children being one of them. "I guess I would find it easier to accept her marriage to someone of the Jewish faith than a Muslim, because Judaism shares a history with Christianity." Then he laughed and said, "And Jesus was a Jew."

Staunchly conservative sects such as Old Colony Mennonites, Seventh Day Adventists, Jehovah's Witnesses and born-again Christians can be expected to be less tolerant of intermarriage, particularly with non-Christians. This trend toward more acceptance of interfaith marriage is bound to be helpful in minimizing the strife and grief families used to experience.

Attitudes about interracial marriages are changing, too, but not as quickly as about interfaith marriages. The right to love and live with the person we choose is fundamental to the concept of freedom. But laws that made it a crime to marry, live with or have sex with someone of a different race restricted that freedom throughout much of the country for more than three centuries. A little over 30 years ago, when Thurgood Marshall was only months away from his historic appointment as the first black man to the Supreme Court, he suffered the humiliation of not being able to move into the Virginia house he and his wife planned to purchase because they could not lawfully live together in the state of Virginia: he was black and his wife was Asian.

Fortunately for the Marshalls, in 1967 the Supreme Court struck down the anti–interracial-marriage laws in Virginia and 18 other states. Two states—South Carolina and Alabama—actually kept this invalid prohibition inscribed in their constitutions well into the 1990s. Is it a dead issue now? One would think so, but in June 1999, the Alabama legislature approved a similar referendum, and its sponsor, Representative Alvin Holmes, is still struggling to get it on the ballot.

Can we gloss over this obsession with interracial sex as a product of Confederate hysteria? No, not if we look at some of the Northern abolitionists like Harriet Beecher Stowe and the madcap Horace Greeley, who did much to inflame Southerners about the question of interracial sexual liaisons.

In 1957, when Josh, a white Jew, married Melinda, a black Baptist whose mother was white, they had to have the ceremony in New York City, because the state where they lived had a law barring interracial marriages. Once married, the couple had to live in a basement because no one would rent an apartment to them close to the university they both attended. Over the years, they had a son and a daughter, both of whom were raised in the Jewish faith.

A generation later, their son married a white Episcopalian with a rabbi and a priest officiating at their wedding ceremony. None of the bride's relatives, except her mother, was in attendance. Her father raged, "I can't believe anyone would expect me to accept my daughter marrying a black man, and a Jewish one at that." Several years later, the daughter gave birth to a blue-eyed son and her father and the rest of the family came to the infant's Jewish circumcision ceremony.

According to a *New York Times* article, "In the 1980s and 1990s, America has had the greatest variety of hybrid households in the history of the world." As more and more couples wedge through religious, ethnic and racial barriers to embark on a life together, families are being forced to rethink and redefine themselves. Despite the rhetoric of cultural separateness and ethnic pride, never before have so many families struggled so hard—sometimes successfully, sometimes not—to deal with this sort of upheaval in their traditions and values.

❧ HELPFUL GUIDELINES ❧

Time is a good shock absorber. Families need time to adjust to what they may consider a betrayal of all the values they hold dear and worked hard to instill in their offspring. Don't be too quick to condemn others' reactions to your relationship, especially those of family members.

Tolerance is a two-way street. To reconnect with family, you need to develop the kind of tolerance you want them to have for you and your chosen spouse. If they sense that you are trying to understand their concerns, it can go a long way toward helping them to try to understand yours. It means accepting the family with all their flaws, which is not to say we have to accept the flaws themselves. To most families, a child marrying someone of another race, culture or religion is not cause for celebration, but rather something to be tolerated, and a kind of declaration that the son or daughter has chosen not to accept the family's culture and religious heritage.

Get help from a knowledgeable outsider. These interracial, interfaith or intercultural marriages often need a knowledgeable outsider to help family members get beyond seeing each other in stereotypical, two-dimensional ways and to help pave a road of understanding between the generations. Many families are understandably anxious about allowing an outsider into the intimacy of their own family life. The objectivity of a professional third party can be curative. But sometimes aunts and uncles or grandparents can be useful intermediaries. Some grandparents are more rigid than their children; but others may have mellowed with the years. Often grandparents are more flexible with their grandchildren than they were with their own children. One grandmother said, "If God hadn't intended for the races to mix, he wouldn't have made body parts that fit."

Know your limitations. Recognize you are limited in your ability to solve the problems of others, and that there are no certainties that others will want to live according to your values. But if you acknowledge your own shortcomings, it would be only fair to let others be less than perfect and love them regardless.

It's a shock to learn that the love of parents is not unconditional, but they, too, have been shocked. All those years of believing your parents loved you unconditionally now have come to an abrupt end. The conditions are evident when they cast you aside because you've married someone of another race, culture or religion. This rude awakening will come at a time when you need family the most, because intolerance is still so prevalent in our society. This is the time to be patient and hold your own resentments at bay. Don't retreat in anger before the situation is truly hopeless. Take risks and persist with family. They are so important in a cold and often rejecting world.

Know your strengths and weaknesses. If you're a person who craves acceptance by others, than you need to reexamine whether you're strong enough to withstand the widespread rejection you're likely to experience from a world that has not fully accepted interracial marriage. I limit this guideline to interracial marriages because skin shows on the outside, and there is still a greater intolerance as a result.

Clarify your own family connection first. Creating a shared sense of cultural and religious identity is a complex task. In order to help your partner blend with your family, it's important that you first sort out your own past and develop a better understanding of what is culturally and religiously important to you. That will give you a better view of your partner's sense of identity and a foundation to create your new family identity.

How to heal. Look at all points of view, force a connection, let others help and don't expect miracles.

Chapter 8

DIVIDED WE STAND

RUPTURES OVER THE FAMILY BUSINESS

Money is a good servant, but a bad master.
~ A FRENCH PROVERB

The 51 percent owner of a family-owned chain of beauty salons arrived at an emotional and traumatic breakup with the other actively involved 49 percent owner of the business. The other party was her mother. After years of arguing about business matters, the daughter finally asked her mother to name her price for her share of the company stock, and she paid the price to get her out. The mother had started the first salon and grew it into a thriving business. She was irate with her daughter for what she considered a forced and humiliating exit from the business, but still she loved her daughter and went through a year of despair, during which time she poured herself into volunteer work at her church.

They didn't talk or see each other for the next three years until the daughter had a baby. The estranged mother called her daughter up to tell her that she had no intention of being deprived of contact with her first grandchild.

"You can keep me out of the business," she said, "but you can't keep me away from my grandchild. We don't have to talk, but I'm coming over to see that baby."

The beauty salon business was booming and the daughter, who missed her mother and hated what had happened, needed her mother's help more than ever, not with the business that they could never agree on, but with the care of her new baby. That suited the new grandmother and served as a basis for a restored family relationship that had no connection with the beauty salon business.

This is an atypical success story, because most family business fights go on for a long time, usually until the business goes under or is dissolved, and even then the rancor continues. No area of family relationships is more afflicted with estrangements than the one where family members are involved in running a business together. The tattered relationships in family businesses are growing because the number of such enterprises is increasing.

According to the year 2000 statistics put out by the United States Department of Commerce, more than 75 percent of all businesses in the United States are family owned or controlled, and they generate over 60 percent of the U.S. gross national product.

And don't assume that all family businesses are small. Are you surprised to learn that more than a third of the Fortune 500 companies are family controlled, and many of them have wrenching family feuds?

HEIR SPLITTING

Craig Warren, the eldest son and member of a billion-dollar family business (paper products) talks about his childhood. "My brother and I were constantly vying for Dad's approval, which he never gave. I'm almost 40, and my father has never said, 'I love you.' He's never said it to anyone that I know of. He never expresses any emotions, not even to my mother."

Craig is suing his father and the family's billion-dollar company because he claims he was cheated when his father chose his younger brother to succeed him after Craig had spent 10 years working in the company for "a pittance." Craig believes his earlier failed marriages and a bout with alcoholism turned his father and brother against him. Craig is particularly bitter because for the last five years, his life has been on the right track, but his family refuses to see his progress. He believes they have used his past to cheat him out of his fair share. Craig doesn't want to reconcile his estrangement from his family. All he wants is his "rightful place as head of the company."

When family business estrangements fail to mend, it's often because the family members express no willingness to reconcile. Thus the emphasis of this chapter is on preventing the problems in the first place. Invariably, the relationships between competing family members become so damaged by feuds over the business that the sense of a common heritage normally felt among family members is gone. Seeing how the problems began and evolved should help in understanding what needs to be done to prevent them.

Trust Busters

More than in any other facet of family life, trust is critical to harmonious family relationships in business. Without trust, there is no assurance that a person will receive what he or she deserves without having to threaten, manipulate or retaliate. With trust, there is freedom to "give" without fear or worry and with the comfort of knowing the rewards will be commensurate to what is given. In the following story, there were two serious problems—a lack of trust, a widespread problem with too many family businesses, and a failure of the founder to provide for succession.

HEIR TODAY, GONE TOMORROW

For the last four years, Philip and his wife and children have not seen any of his three brothers, Jay, Michael, and Matt, or their families or his ailing mother, Mrs. Jones. For the past six years, the Jones family has been embroiled in civil and criminal litigation. Matt, the brother who had been closest to Philip, pleaded guilty four years ago to embezzling $800,000 from the family business— the manufacture of cleaning solvents. Matt returned most of the money and served six months in prison. Mrs. Jones sued all four of her sons for cutting her out of her fair share of the business.

"That dispute was eventually settled out of court," said Philip, the youngest brother. "When my father died, all hell broke loose. His death paved the way for these bitter court struggles over the business that he founded by selling cleaning supplies door to door."

Last year, a court made a ruling aimed at resolving the ownership controversy. The decision has done nothing, however, to put an end to the animosity among the brothers and the mother who are now split into three sharply divided camps.

"As the youngest," Philip said, "I was forced out of the business because my oldest brother Jay had to have total control. He tried to set me up and make it look like I was involved in the embezzlement with Matt. He made a deal with Michael to implicate me. I had nothing to do with the embezzlement and certainly no money from it, but I had no way of proving my innocence, so I walked out of the business rather than put my wife and children through the ordeal of another court fight. Michael and Jay now run the business, my mother and Matt have been squeezed out, and I had to walk away."

While not all battles are as heated as the one among the Jones family, experts say it is common for families to fight over control of a business after the death of the founder. Only a third of family businesses survive into the second generation because of ownership disputes.

Philip said that he didn't know if he and his family would ever be together again. "We're thinking of moving away," Philip said. "Right now, it's hard on my kids. They used to be close to their cousins. They never see them anymore. On holidays, we were usually together at my parents' home. Now, my mother is virtually alone. Her lawsuit was justified, because Jay and Michael really did engineer a plan to squeeze her out. Originally, I sided with my mother, but my wife can't forgive her for including my name in the suit as one of the defendants. No one has heard from Matt since he got out of prison. He and his family moved three thousand miles away. I'm still not sure if he really had any intention to embezzle or was just doing what he could to protect his interest in the business from Jay and Michael. Matt knew they were plotting to take over. My brothers were ruthless. I guess they deserve each other."

Philip and his mother are the only people in this family who are unhappy about the estrangement. Mrs. Jones has expressed enormous regret for not being able to hold her family together and for bringing the lawsuit against her four sons. At the interview, Philip said he was willing to forgive his mother, because he knew her lawyers and accountants convinced her to sue her children. But in order to reconnect with his mother, he will have to contend with his wife's strong objections against having anything more to do with the family. Still, he's determined to patch things up with his mother even if it means doing so without his wife's knowledge. As for the rest of the family, Philip has little hope they'll ever get back together.

Sibling Succession

Business consultants who deal exclusively with family businesses say 70 percent of these enterprises fail within five years of the death of the founder because there was no plan for transition. Often the founder of a business is skilled in the operational aspects of the business, but just as often he or she may not be sophisticated in, nor attentive to, record-keeping, corporate structure and form, financial arrangements and raising capital for expansion. A group of relatives who are part of the business may have developed those skills, but without a plan that defines who will be in charge of what, those skills may not be enough to maintain and grow the business.

Parents have a fantasy of wanting their children to share equally in their family business, but it rarely works out that way. If a father wants to leave his business to his four children, he might instruct his lawyer to draw up papers providing each child with 25 percent of the business. A good lawyer will stop the father long enough to ask these questions: How many of the children actually work in the business? Do they normally get along? Who will be in charge? If any of the children are not working in the business, how will the ones who are working there handle advice from those who aren't? And, how will compensation be arranged for the ones who are doing the work as compared to the ones who aren't? And how have you arranged for your own support (and your wife's) from the business?

Any parent who has more than one child who expects to take the helm of the business one day should assume there will be bitter fights for control unless a plan is put in place well in advance of that day.

According to experts in family business planning, exit and succession strategies are essential. You have to know where the business is headed to know what skills and experience are needed of the successor generation and where each of them would best serve.

The problems can be agonizing as parents wonder how they can select one of their children to be the next president. Can the others accept the decision as fair? Normally, favoring one child over another is resisted by parents—and rightly so. But business needs a single chief, and that means choosing one child over the other for a job with more status, more pay and more responsibility. For most families, that, in and of itself, is a blueprint for terrible trouble. The parents want to believe that if they don't face the issue of succession, it will somehow solve itself or go away. If the business can be comfortably divided into separate and roughly equal parts, it can be a happy solution as well as a means of avoiding the predictable conflict that leads to estrangements. Unfortunately, that solution is rarely available. Few businesses divide easily and profitably.

One family-business consultant graphically related a problem he tried to solve. The business was created after World War II, and the founder was at retirement age, but he didn't want to face the issue of succession because he felt signing papers transferring ownership to his two sons was akin to signing his own death certificate. His wife colluded in not wanting her husband to retire. She said she "married him for life, not for lunch." And she was especially worried about his "take-charge" personality once he had nothing else to do but stay home with her. The sons, who got along well, were grown men, and needed the freedom to take over. They could no longer tolerate being treated like the father's two kids. They had reached an impasse, but what could they do? Tell their father, "We quit, and, by the way, what time do you want us to be there for Thanksgiving dinner?"

The two sons brought the consultant in to help work through the succession problem. The consultant treated the matter as a process of control being gradually, over a five-year period, relinquished by the father to the sons. Once the father could see the transfer was neither abrupt nor immediate, he signed the necessary papers. A family rupture was averted. The incremental transfer of control was the basis for this family's success.

ONE BUSINESS INDIVISIBLE . . .

Another family feud over succession and control of a specialty food business has persisted for years. In the end, the only thing left of the Benedetto family business was the name, Benedetto's Food Emporiums, and even that was sold to an outside company. With so many third-generation members of the family available to take over the business, how and why did the upscale food stores wind up out of the family's control? That was the question asked repeatedly by all of the suppliers and customers of the business. One member of the family described the saga as a Byzantine soap opera of a once-proud immigrant family, but one that was plagued by rivalries, even fistfights, conflicts over control, and lawsuits. Mr. Benedetto, the founder of the business, had three sons, Nino, Tony and John. Nino was the father's favorite and heir apparent, but he had no interest in the business and chose to become an actor. That left the other two brothers to vie for top position.

Tony was next in line, but initially he chose a different route. He married a woman whose father had a business that was thriving. Tony went into his father-in-law's business where he worked for 10 years, but when it became clear that Tony would always remain just a well-paid employee, he decided to quit and return to his family's food business.

John was the only one of the three brothers who had worked tirelessly for years with Benedetto's Food Emporiums. "I could see the writing on the wall," John said. "What I had been working hard to build and expand was now in jeopardy of being taken away from me by Tony. We all knew Tony was never going to be made an owner of his father-in-law's business, not with his lousy personality. When Tony gave notice he was leaving, his father-in-law said, 'So what are you going to do? Go back with your father and sell pickles?'"

To solve the problem, the elder Benedetto opened a fourth store in this thriving metropolitan city and turned the management over to Tony. This plan seemed to be working. Tony turned the store into the most profitable one of all, but because his overly aggressive personality was abrasive to customers and suppliers, he had to use outside help to run the day-to-day operations. Moreover, as the store thrived, success went to Tony's head. He tried taking over all four stores in the city.

During that time, the elder Benedetto died. He left the business in equal shares to his wife and their three sons. Tony persuaded his actor brother, Nino, and his mother to stay out of the business in return for "a nice salary." That left John and Tony to squabble over control. John suggested that they divide the business into two corporations, with Tony having two of the stores and John the other two. But Tony wouldn't hear of it. He complained that the salaries for Nino and their mother would have to come from the profits of all four stores, and therefore the stores would have to remain under one corporate umbrella. Tony also argued that by buying supplies— food as well as kitchen equipment—for all four stores, instead of each brother negotiating separately, they could cut the operating costs considerably.

When John persisted in wanting to distance himself from Tony and his predatory personality, Tony began a new campaign for control. He persuaded his brother Nino to sell him his 25 percent interest. This provided Tony with 50 percent ownership of the business. John owned 25 percent, and their mother owned the remaining 25 percent. For the next several years, the two brothers worked hard, but not harmoniously, to build and expand the business. They were so successful that in each of the neighborhoods where they had Benedetto stores, they were able to drive most of their major competitors out of business.

During that same period, however, Tony continually harassed and humiliated John, insisting, for example, that "Without Dad or me, this business would have folded years ago." Over time, these insults destroyed the relationships between their respective wives and children. One day when John had taken just about enough, he grabbed Tony and threatened to "smash [his] mouth in" if one more word was uttered. Tony uttered that one word and the two brothers began pounding at each other until the police were called in to break up the fight. Their mother was heartbroken and decided to use the power of her 25 percent interest to persuade Tony to agree to divide up the business. But before that deal could be consummated, the ever-spiteful Tony sold his 50 percent interest to an outside competitor for a sum far in excess of what his share of the business was worth, considering that it was not a controlling interest. This jeopardized the family's control. When it became evident that the nature of the business had changed, John and his mother sold their interests and reaped a huge profit. The families were now completely divided, with Tony and his family having nothing to do with the elderly Mrs. Benedetto, John and John's family. This estrangement has been going on for the last three years. Only the family name remains on the awnings of the stores, and only one person is struggling with the pain of the estrangement—the elderly mother. Unfortunately, her advanced age and declining health leaves her too weak to deal with the painful loss of a son and her grandchildren.

If the founding father of the business had brought in some expert consultants to evaluate and put into effect an appropriate plan for succession, rather than leaving the brothers to battle for control, this unfortunate estrangement might have been avoided.

IN-LAWS MAY BE OUTLAWS

The Black family had been in the business of selling discounted drapery and upholstery fabrics since the 1950s. Marianne Black, present owner and daughter of the founder, was earning what she called "a nice living" in the mid-1970s. Marianne's son, Ralph, had no interest in the business so it was easy for the mother to pass control to her daughter, Carol. After Carol had been running the business for nine years, Ralph asked if there was a place in the company for his CPA wife, Lenore. Though Marianne no longer owned the business, she continued to go into the shop and help out from time to time. Against Carol's better judgment, Marianne persuaded her daughter that it would be good to have someone involved in the business who was knowledgeable about financial matters, and then they wouldn't have to constantly pay bookkeepers and accountants to handle all the paperwork.

Reluctantly, Carol gave the go-ahead to bring her sister-in-law into the business, not as a part owner, but as a salaried employee. Lenore not only had a head for numbers, she also had many ideas for expanding the customer base.

The problem began at a family dinner when Marianne's son Ralph remarked that the business was booming since Lenore began working there.

"Everybody acknowledged how helpful Lenore had been to the business," Carol said. "What we didn't anticipate was Ralph's next request. He wanted me to make Lenore a full partner, taking what he said would have been his 'rightful share.' Mind you, Ralph never worked in the business, not one day of his life."

The mother, realizing that the family was on the brink of a feud, persuaded Carol to think about giving Lenore a small percentage of the business.

"I liked Lenore well enough," Carol said, "but I have a daughter who may want to take over the business one day. And my brother shouldn't step in at this late date to make demands for his wife. I'm the one who's been working for nine years, six days a week. Why should I relinquish my complete ownership just to accommodate my brother and my mother, who only wants peace in the family, even if it means taking away what should be mine? Ralph's doing very well in real estate; he doesn't consider the family business to be important. He couldn't care less about my situation. All he cares about is his wife and what she wants. Besides, we've been paying Lenore a generous salary—she's been fully compensated for her work. In fact, it was costing us more to have Lenore there than if we'd been paying to outsource the financial part of the business."

Eventually, the mother was able to see that Carol's position was valid, so she decided to exclude herself from the discussions. When Carol refused to budge, the family began growing increasingly hostile to one another. Lenore quit her job with the company and refused to have anything further to do with her sister-in-law.

That all happened more than five years ago. Today, the brother and sister and their respective families have nothing to do with each other. The mother, who has made numerous efforts to bring the family together, is caught in the middle. She is deeply troubled by the rift. Even a family-business expert couldn't offer a resolution for this situation.

Ties That Don't Bind

So many entrepreneurial ventures start as mom-and-pop operations but fail to establish guidelines for bringing family members into the business. Founders can be blind to the perils that lurk when they impose the concept of "one big happy family" on their companies. They never imagine that the family can come apart over the business they've created with their ideas and hard work. One of the most difficult tasks is that of integrating in-laws into the business. Believing in-laws will be grateful to benefit from an employment opportunity is naïve. Regardless of whether or not the in-law is making an equal contribution, he or she will now raise the banner that says "I'm family. I want my equal share."

What happened in the case of the Black family is typical. According to the literature, such ruptures are usually initiated, driven or fueled by in-laws brought into the business, by the cousin generation when they inherit ownership interests, and even by the sibling generation.

Marrying into a profitable business is an example of success through accident, as opposed to success based on performance and moving up through the ranks. Children and grandchildren of business builders are also heirs to a family fortune in a similar way, because their success is also not contingent on hard work and merit but derives from the accident of birth. The problems associated with inherited wealth are testimony to the fact that unearned rewards can also lead to unfortunate events such as business failure and family estrangement. But it is far easier to rationalize unearned success that you attribute to your bloodline since it is, after all, a part of you. Having to share the rewards with someone who simply married into the family is much more difficult for other family members to accept, particularly when their own shares in the business are diluted in the process.

Family members who control the business often rebuff suggestions of in-laws looking to establish their worth. Unfortunately and unfairly, they will even rebuff in-law suggestions that result in increased profits, and then they go on to deny fair compensation for that beneficial input. What better way is there to create the kind of family dissension that results in estrangements?

As with all problems that arise in family business, planning ahead to avoid potential disputes is far less costly than losing part of your family or spending huge amounts of cash on therapy after the fact. Every family with a successful company needs to assume that, at some time in the future, they will find themselves with a family member suggesting that an in-law be allowed to join the business.

When that happens, the best way to handle it is to open all doors, call in all IOUs, or engage in good, old-fashioned horse trading to help that in-law find work any place but within the business. That will give the in-law an opportunity to show his or her competence, and even owe the spouse's family for opening doors with another company.

If that fails, a job should be offered that has a limited scope and fixed criteria for continued employment. For example, it might be stipulated that the in-law has to make a particular division profitable in two years or leave the company. Also it should be made clear that if the in-law behaves in a manner that would get any other employee fired, he or she should expect the same treatment. This might not sound like a formula for cozy family relations, but the risk of estrangement is so great, it's better for one of the senior family members to set boundaries right at the beginning even if it means risking some hard feelings for a time. And this alternative applies only if you're pressured to take an in-law into the business.

WOMEN'S RIGHTS

What happens when there are male and female relatives and the family business is left to all of them on an equal basis, but only the men are included in the management and operations? Be fore-warned, good things don't happen when this arrangement is made. An electrical supply business—let's call it Peterson's Supplies—was left to three brothers. For a long time, the company thrived and expanded. One of the three brothers was a bachelor. When he died, he left his share to his two brothers. One of the remaining two brothers brought his son Bruce into the business. When another brother died, leaving a widow and two daughters, Stephanie and Beryl, the problems began. At that point, the ownership interest consisted of the one surviving brother, who had always been the least effective in handling the business, his son Bruce, his brother's widow and his two daughters. Bruce was the only person involved in managing the business, and it was his responsibility to compensate all the other heirs from the profits. All the owners were also on the board of directors of the incorporated business.

Bruce had a background in accounting. For a few years, the business continued to earn a profit, but then the profits began steadily declining. At one point, Bruce had an opportunity to sell the business to a large national competitor, but without divulging the offer to the board, he declined it because it would have had the effect of putting him out of a job.

When the mother of Stephanie and Beryl died, their lawyer informed them that their mother's estate owed a substantial amount of estate taxes and that the money to pay those taxes wasn't in her account. The daughters discovered that their cousin Bruce had been dipping into their mother's share of the profits to keep the failing business afloat. It soon became evident that Bruce had been taking the money without their mother's full understanding of what was going on. The problem of declining profits was not simply a matter of bad management, but of increased competition from national conglomerates selling the same products at substantially discounted prices. When Bruce was confronted with the truth, he offered a lame excuse that had no credibility. Stephanie and Beryl broke off all contact with him and his father. Prior to this devastating revelation about Bruce's deception, Stephanie, Beryl and Bruce had been more like close siblings than cousins. Ultimately, the business was dissolved with no receivables—only debts remained.

This family estrangement occurred almost 10 years ago. No one in the family has had any contact with each other except Stephanie and Beryl and even their relationship has deteriorated because of resentments and ongoing arguments over the way the problems should have been handled.

Though the female members of this family had a right to share in the profits, historically they had never participated in the operational side of the business. Furthermore, throughout the decline of the business, they had no information about what was going on until it was too late to do anything about it.

Silent Partners

The Petersons' situation illustrates the tension that develops as a family starts to outgrow a business with declining profits. Disagreement naturally evolves over what to do with the primary source and repository of the family's common income. The board, in its responsibility to the shareholders (who were one and the same as the directors) should have acted to protect the company's assets by considering the competitor's offer to buy the business. Sadly and perhaps fraudulently, too, Bruce—the one remaining relative who was actively involved in the business—withheld that vital information from the other nonparticipating owners—the female members of the family. To their detriment, these women never took part in the business except to receive their proportionate share of the profits and, apparently, they never even took an active role as board members.

This is a perfect example of why unsophisticated, silent owners should utilize the services of an outside accountant to regularly update them about the financial status of the family business.

SHE RULES

Not all women who inherit ownership interests in a family business remain passive. Since joining her family's company in the early 1990s, Jackie had clashed with her brother Steve over her role in the business. Aggressively demanding a much greater say in company decisions, the newly ordained MBA chafed at her job as head of market research while her older brother called the shots as president and chief executive officer of the cosmetic manufacturing company founded by their father.

Finally, 30-year-old Jackie prevailed: in a surprise announcement two years ago, her brother resigned, leaving his sister to take on the entire responsibility of the business. Their mother, who inherited the majority of the shares from her husband, functioned actively as chairman of the board. The big change came about because Jackie knew how to influence the person who really held the reins of power and control—her mother.

Exactly what persuaded Steve to walk out of the business is still uncertain, but when he did, the company lost a key person. The only reasonable explanation is the gang-up against Steve by the mother and sister, who together own 80 percent of the business. During his tenure at the helm, Steve had executed a sharp turn-around at the struggling company, which had posted annual losses for three prior years. By slashing production costs and pumping up the company products in broader markets, Steve had been the driving force behind the company's success. Whether the company can continue its comeback without Steve is a question that should concern Jackie, but she is so inflated with her own power and importance that she's unable to see the potential problems, not the least of which is the estrangement with her only sibling. And even if the company prospers after this dramatic turn of events, the mother has also lost contact with her son. Though the mother regrets the breach with her son, she has done nothing to mend it because that would mean a rift with her daughter. As the facts unfolded, what came to light was the troublesome relationship the family had with Steve's wife. Steve's wife was very close to her own family and had virtually ignored Steve's family for many years. The mother had only seen her son's children once or twice a year even though they lived in the same city. Neither the mother nor Jackie could recall anything they had ever done to alienate Steve's wife. According to Jackie, her brother had once told her his wife was close to her own family and that was all she needed. When Jackie asked him how he could justify cutting his mother and sister out of the lives of his children, Steve said to do otherwise would mean continuous friction with his wife. Now that Steve has been cut out of the business, it seems unlikely that the estrangement will mend anytime in the near future, if at all.

On the Edge

The strong wills and personalities that make family businesses successful are also the root causes of family strife. Too much of this dissension has been allowed to grow out of control and has wound up in litigation. Alternative dispute resolution such as mediation or arbitration should be considered in these matters, just as in the matters of inheritance addressed in detail in chapter 6.

Of course, the better solution is always to try to avoid disputes that wind up in court, by structuring the ownership and responsibilities in a family business to suit the abilities and personalities of the family members involved. But the sad reality is that in most situations, disputes are inevitable, not only from the business aspects alone, but also from personality conflicts. When they do occur, the key is to acknowledge and address them right away, usually through intervention by objective third-party professionals, including therapists and family business consultants. The sooner family members can act on a problem, the better the chances of avoiding the knockdown–drag-out family feuds that not only can destroy the business, but the family as well.

❧ HELPFUL GUIDELINES ❧

Put family first. Though it may seem naïve to suggest that family members who are involved in a family business put family relationships first, it's still worth aspiring to this ideal.

The founder should know what he or she wants to do with the company. If there is a likelihood that the family business will prove to be a terminal disease for the family, other strategies should be considered, such as a sale of the business or hiring an outsider to take over the reins (with a generous compensation plan). Of course, the family members will continue to reap the rewards on the basis of the ownership shares. This would be similar to hiring a property management company to manage an estate that consists of real property.

Plan ahead. Plan at least five years out. Involve all members of the family and board members in the process. If possible, take advantage of outside help from accountants, lawyers or professional family business consultants.

Force family members to get experience. If family members want to join the business, require them to get extensive work experience in another business enterprise first.

Use skilled family business consultants. An experienced and objective third person can soften the friction by creating a non-threatening environment in which to discuss each family member's fears and expectations. A family retreat (led by professionals) is an excellent occasion to create the family mission and values statements, and decide on next steps. Often, the mere fact of assembling the family reminds them of their shared history and family ethic. It can go a long way in preventing and solving problems.

Create family councils for resolving problems as they occur. Have regular meetings with all the family members involved in the business as well as in-laws who are indirectly involved in the business. Let everyone know what business decisions are being made so there are no mysteries to prompt paranoid machinations about who is getting what.

Structure and formalize the business. If the business is unstructured, change to a professional approach so that a formal policy and process is in place to support the next generation.

Plan for succession. Not only should there be a plan for succession, but it should contemplate a gradual process. A contingency succession plan will ensure that the owner (founder) is in the catbird seat when the transition occurs. The process should include the following: (1) Identify and prepare successors to both ownership and management positions. (2) Designate those family members who will own interests but not take an active management role. (3) Let key employees know just what will happen and who will be affected when a transition finally occurs so that important people will be discouraged from jumping ship. (4) Provide for a financial framework to facilitate a change in ownership. A well-structured insurance program with life and disability insurance can provide the purchase wherewithal for the eventual successors and the deserved financial rewards for the seller and his family. (5) A will and/or trusts, an estate plan, buy/sell agreements, and shareholder agreements should be in place to allow the transition to occur smoothly.

Use alternative dispute resolutions when the feud can't be avoided. Mediation and arbitration are means of conflict resolution that may very well prevent family estrangements. Legal costs are reduced and the decisions can be arrived at in a less formal, more family-like atmosphere. Be aware that mediation is non-binding on the participants; arbitration is binding.

Chapter 9

―⇒⋗⋖―

MAKING THE BEST OF IT

COPING AND MENDING STRATEGIES

We ourselves are the embodied continuance
Of those who did not live into our time
And others will be and are our immortality on earth.

~ JORGE LUIS BORGES

If we could read the secret history of our enemies, we should find
in each man's life sorrow and suffering enough to disarm all hostility.

~ HENRY WADSWORTH LONGFELLOW

Get over it! The thought behind those words is so intrinsically American. Don't waste your time obsessing about some past affront or disagreement. In her book *Life, Liberty and the Pursuit of Happiness,* Peggy Noonan repeats some advice given to her by a friend: "When you worry—you're paying a deposit on trouble that may not be delivered." We are a people who build on the past, dwell in the moment and look optimistically to the future. That's the American way.

Unlike so many Asians and Europeans, who worship their ancestors and resist change, Americans worship celebrities, welcome change and are forever seeking new innovation. So let's be American on the subject of yesterday's hurts. Get over the resentments and move forward. It does no good to dwell on every little slight that comes our way. Most importantly, we have to heal the big hurts that pierce us deeply, make us angry and make us *hate*. Only with hesitation do I use the word "hate." But it *is* hatred that people often feel when they are deeply hurt by a loved one, or by someone who can affect our relationship with a loved one.

Don't fade out of the lives of loved ones, and don't let them fade from your life. We need all the love we can get, and so do our children. The more family, the more loving experiences, the more support, the more comfort. And yes, more aggravation at times, and even more hurts, but that's a price worth paying for all the good that comes from family.

This chapter will explore:

* What's good about family?

* What's bad about estrangements?

* Why we need to get beyond blame and hatred to forgiveness?

* How to reconnect with people we love—and sometimes even with people we used to love or people we may never love but who our spouse loves or our son or daughter loves?

* What are the patterns of successful reconciliation that appear repeatedly in the stories of all the chapters—presented as guideposts for a successful journey forward?

* What are the best coping mechanisms when there are no other alternatives?

WHAT'S GOOD ABOUT FAMILY?

Families are the most ancient of institutions. Family is defined here in its broadest sense as it relates to human beings. Since humans crossed the earth's surface in search of food and shelter, the family has played the most continuous nurturing role for the survival of its young. Oh yes, we've heard stories, both real and fiction, where babies are abandoned and an adult female of one of the higher species of the animal kingdom has reared the baby and saved its life. But that's an anomaly—it's within the bosom of family that a child is nurtured to adulthood. Unlike many animal babies who can be self-sufficient at birth, human babies are born helpless and totally dependent on the family usually until puberty. So, one of the first good things about family is procreation and survival of the young. But family doesn't stop giving refuge to its members for as long as they all inhabit the earth.

Family is home, and that's where we go when we're in need and there's nowhere else to turn—and that can happen at any time in our lives. When we're sick and need care, family provides it. When we're traveling and run out of money, we call someone in our family to wire enough cash to get us back home. When a young parent has to rush an injured child to the hospital, a family member living nearby will take care of the other children. When there's a divorce or a serious illness or a death, the family comes to the aid of those most stricken. When a child has a dance or music recital, the family comes to beam and applaud and celebrate. When a child makes the basketball team or becomes a cheerleader or wins a spelling bee or graduates from school, or gets into a fine college or wins any award of accomplishment, the family is there to rejoice and bestow praise. When we've suffered disappointment, the faces of those we love are there to give us a feeling of comfort and security. When a new baby is born, family members commemorate the occasion, just as they do when there's a baptism or a "bris" or a confirmation or a bar mitzvah—or a wedding. They gather to share in the happiness of those they love, those who are a part of them. We don't feel comfortable bragging about our children to outsiders, but to grandparents it's not bragging. The pleasure they experience is genuine and enduring and meaningful. From one generation to another we convey the history of our unique little organization, and we define ourselves and learn what special attributes are passed on through the genes. We find out where the dimples come from or the widow's peak or that wonderful cleft in the chin, or which side of the family passed down musical or artistic talent. Or maybe we need to find out who among the blood kin is the best match to donate a kidney or a small part of a liver or marrow for a blood marrow transplant.

When we travel alone far from home, memories of family togetherness give us a sense of well-being. If we become disabled or suffer the infirmities of age, it is the love of family that we need most. When Mom and Dad die, no matter what our age, technically we become orphans. That's when brothers and sisters become so important because unlike anyone else, even our spouse, our siblings share a common history and can relive or reexamine memories of the past. Maybe you have a particular phobia or neurosis and want to find out what in your past may have caused it. Who else but a close family member can tell you that some little friend scared you with a snake or why your mother was gone for such a long time when you were three or four years old? Maybe an older sibling will know why you have a fear of tunnels? Or what caused that funny scar on your leg?

For the last 30 or 40 years—far too long—we have allowed ourselves to become a nation of victims who need a steady diet of self-esteem because of our childhood deprivation. That same message has been reinforced on radio and TV daytime talk shows, where we can see people spill their guts, blaming everyone for any of their deficiencies, but especially their families. Every type of adult problem is attributed to poor parenting and dysfunctional families. That overused word "dysfunctional" has become so broadly defined, there's hardly a family that doesn't have several major symptoms of dysfunction. One message being conveyed by many mental health professionals is that if people are having difficulties or are in emotional pain, their parents must have failed them. Yes, of course, there have been and will continue to be truly damaging parents, the ones who sexually molested their children or deprived them of basic necessities or were alcoholic or drug addicted for years, but most families have not damaged their children in these horrific ways. On the contrary, in navigating the costs and complexities of rearing families, most parents learned the necessity of a moral compass. They gave life, guidance for proper behavior, values and the tools to become independent. They taught us to be fully human, cautious about danger, confident about our own capacities, and they provided a safety net for hard times. In his book *The Uses of Enchantment,* Dr. Bruno Bettelheim says, "We expect everything to go smoothly and easily, and think that something is wrong if we run into a problem. That's the worst view a family can have."

No one can ever replace our parents and all that they did for us. There is a debt we can never repay. By the same token, in the early part of their lives children have given us the joy of pure love, the pleasure of holding their soft, silken skin and seeing ecstatic smiles when we peer into the crib. And who else but a completely trusting child can reach for our hand and make our hearts soar? These are joys we can never forget. This is what family is all about, and this is what it needs to continue to be about.

WHAT'S BAD ABOUT ESTRANGEMENT?

Not to be in contact with your parents or with your children is a profound loss because our families are so deeply bound to the sense of who we are in this enormous, chaotic world. Now that we know how important genes are in defining our physiological identities, and yes, even our personalities, how can we walk away from the people whose genes are propagated in us and in our children, genes that will go on and on, ad infinitum? We feel heartsick about our families when they cannot acknowledge us, love us and support us. If they don't, who will? No matter how far we travel in distance or success, no matter how old we are, our family belongs to us and we belong to it.

The general consensus among mental health professionals is that family will inevitably come back to haunt us—in our relationships with spouses, children, in-laws, friends and colleagues. There's a whole school of thought now that walking away from family to escape problems may very well mean that we will face more problems than the ones we left behind. Dr. Joy Browne, Dr. Mary Pipher and Monica McGoldrick, all well-respected therapists, support the notion that we must go home again to figure out who we are so that we can go forward to a full and productive life and be the best at whatever we choose to be. Sadly, many outwardly successful people are incapable of maintaining healthy relationships with members of their own families. They're unable to see through flimsy walls of self-defense into the hearts of the people who really love them and would do anything for them, far more so than many of the people they cultivate in their daily professional and social lives.

Pat Conroy in *The Prince of Tides* understands the profound consciousness of family. When Conroy's alter ego, Tom Wingo, witnesses the reconciliation of his sister and their estranged father, Tom feels "a fierce interior music of blood and wildness and identity. It was the beauty and fear of kinship, the ineffable ties of family, that sounded a blazing terror and an awestruck love inside of me."

Why do we have so much trouble being open and loving and intimate with our parents and brothers and sisters once we marry? Why do we ignore their joys and problems while we obsess about something as ordinary as our child beginning to crawl or cut teeth? Why can't we pick up the telephone and tell a sibling how much we miss her or just reminisce about happy childhood times spent together? Why is it that so many adult children, if they communicate at all, are locked into superficial and boring conversation with their close family members?

In the complex weave of the family, many people feel little pleasure in their connection to parents. Too few of us get to know our parents as people, let alone as individuals who may lead exciting and accomplished lives. One son, who calls his mother once or twice a year, spent 30 minutes telling her everything he was doing both at work and at home with his wife and two children. As he was starting to wrap up the conversation and say good-bye, his mother, a respected stage actress, told him that she had just been offered a leading role in a Broadway play. He said, "That's nice. I have to run now. Bye."

Often we're occupied or preoccupied fending off what we perceive as parental intrusiveness or busy wishing for them to be other than what they are. For some it's impossible to mature beyond those childhood experiences of helplessness and intimidation. Too often family visits become endurance contests, obligations. And children have enormous power to hurt parents. *In All God's Children Have Traveling Shoes,* Maya Angelou writes: "The thorn from the buds one has planted, nourished and pruned, pricks most deeply and draws more blood." What a child says pierces into parents' deepest feelings about themselves. Unwittingly, children's words can convey the terrible message that parents don't mean much to them anymore. Parents don't expect to be repaid for all they've done, but they do expect to be loved, respected and wanted. One point worth noting here: in almost all the stories in this book, the adult child disconnected only when there was no longer a financial dependence on the family. Prior to that time, the adult child either didn't seem to perceive egregious wrongs or didn't consider they were bad enough to cut off ties and risk losing financial support.

Estrangements between siblings based on rivalry and conflict are all too frequent. If two brothers stop speaking for a long period, each is likely to experience a profound void. They may look like each other, have the same speech patterns and gestures, and have a shared history that belongs only to them. What a regrettable loss!

In her autobiography, *Me,* Katharine Hepburn says of her brothers and sisters: "They are so much a part of me that I simply know I could not have been me without them." The sibling relationship is demonstrably important. According to one study of successful men (the Harvard classes of 1938–44), the one best forecast of emotional health at age sixty-five was having had a close relationship with a sibling while in college. The researchers found this singular relationship more predictive than childhood closeness to parents, emotional problems in childhood or parental divorce. Curiously, that sibling relationship was even more of a predictor than the subjects' marriages or careers.

Siblings, if reasonably close in age, share more of each other's lives contextually than anyone else, parents, spouses and children included. When both parents die, siblings are entirely on their own for the first time. Whether or not they see each other is now their choice. If one sibling is still harboring resentments because of what he or she perceives as disparate treatment, or if there are in-law problems, these issues may take on a life force of their own. If there is a disconnection, it is at this time that it can become a serious estrangement, for there's no one left to bring them together. With 51 percent of marriages ending in divorce, it's best to fast forward to that time in your life when your sibling may be all you've got left of family.

Grandparents and great-grandparents are extraordinarily beneficial to young children. When an estrangement has the rippling effect of separating the grandparents from their grandchildren, everyone's a loser. How many of us can recall the special times we spent with grandparents who gave us their undivided love and attention? The relationship between grandparents and grandchildren is one of pure love and joy. Grandparents see no faults. The patience and moderation grandparents often express are so needed in young lives. By encouraging and promoting this family relationship, parents can bring a gentler influence to their children. There is something to be learned from observing a grandparent who can accept and adapt to his or her shrinking world, and who can find great satisfaction in a contemplative, slower life. One family who had a borderline retarded child blessed the grandmother who had more patience with that child than anyone else ever had. From grandparents, children will get a sense of where they come from and the security of having other people besides their parents to love and nurture and protect them. Also, children learn to relate well to the elderly because of their contact with grandparents.

A grandmother can bring the right perspective to many situations. When one young mother grew anxious because her son was taking longer than usual to toilet train, her mother sang just the right note. "Don't worry," she said. "Have you ever known a groom to walk down the aisle wearing diapers?"

And grandparents are repositories of family history and colorful, funny anecdotes about many relatives that would otherwise be lost in time. In her article "The Importance of Grandparents," Lillian Africano shows how her own mother, "gave [the children] the kind of unhurried, unharried time that I could rarely manage. During weekend visits, when I'd be enjoying an extra hour or two of precious sleep, Mama would cook the children a wonderfully elaborate breakfast and entertain them with tales of my childhood indiscretions."

The grandchild-grandparent connection helps children better understand that their parents were once children, too, and had many of the same fears, faults and insecurities as they do. So think a long time before alienating grandparents from their grandchildren, and think of how much easier it is for us to grow old when we have access to the elder members of our family. For grandparents to have the company of their children and their grandchildren is key to enhancing the quality of their senior years and allows them to leave an important legacy to a future generation.

A GIFT TO YOURSELF

When a resentment of a wrong or a hurt or an injustice persists in your mind, it becomes toxic and corrupts not just your life but the lives of everyone close to you. Resentment escalates into grudges, then to rage and hatred, then to damaged and often completely ruined relationships. The only way to get over resentment is to forgive the person who caused it, but the act of forgiving is difficult because it always occurs within a tangled knot of emotions. What can make it somewhat easier is to view forgiveness as a necessary gift to yourself.

Forgiveness for a wrong that you didn't deserve is tough work. In fact, it almost seems unnatural and weak to forgive someone against whom you would prefer to seek revenge. Our innate sense of fairness tells us wrongdoers should pay for the harm they cause. Then how do we persuade ourselves that we should forgive and let the wrong go unpunished? In the matter of estrangement from loved ones, the question is not that hard to answer: we don't really want to inflict harmful punishment to the person we love even though we've been hurt by that person. But if I forgive, will it set me up for more hurt? Because the act of forgiveness means the person is being welcomed back into your life, you have to assess the risk that you may be hurt or rejected again. Is the wrong forgivable? Forgiveness does not mean re-arming an abusive person to take advantage of you—know that you can always walk away if serious problems resurface.

That moves us to another very important question: Do I want to heal myself by forgiving, or do I want to go on obsessing about the hurt I cannot forget? A hurt that is extremely personal, perhaps mean-spirited and unfair, is often more difficult to forgive than an unintentional deprivation or some slight indignity.

Let's define an unintentional deprivation or slight indignity. Our lives are cluttered with people who sting us but mean no real harm. Often family members hurt one another because they can't control themselves—a son who shouts hurtful words in anger, a parent who's never there because he or she is a workaholic, a father who can't express his love, a mother who can't offer praise, a daughter who wants more than the family can afford and puts them down for their lack of means. Parents are often hurt by children who take their love and generosity for granted. Parents hurt children by neglecting, abusing or shortchanging them in some way. Siblings hurt each other by disloyalty, rivalry or abuse. And yet none of these are unforgivable hurts.

There is no hurt quite so painful as an estrangement from the people who are closest to you. Frequently, people betrayed or abused by a close family member are afraid to admit their pain for fear they may recognize feelings of profound resentment, even hatred for the person or persons they most dearly want to love. Maybe you're a son whose mother helped a vengeful ex-wife alienate your children from you because your mother didn't approve of your divorce and remarriage to another woman. You want to love your mother, but instead you hate her for collaborating with a former wife who wants nothing more than to destroy you by using your children as leverage against you.

And it becomes even more difficult when this "hatred" is not conflicted by love. For example, when the person causing the estrangement is an in-law or a step-relative, one you've never loved, but one so powerful and controlling in the life of your mother or father, son or daughter, sister or brother, then forgiveness is just as important, yet much harder to achieve.

When people alienate themselves from family, there are often complex feelings that may include hatred. Hate is a parasite that feeds on our healthy organs even when it coexists with love. Unlike aggressive hatred where a person actively and passionately moves toward harming another person or wishing them harm, passive hatred withholds wishing someone well and resents their good fortune. With family, it is often a passive hatred that develops—an ingrown malevolence that prevents us from reveling in that family member's happiness. This is a common occurrence when rivalry develops between siblings. Later in life, one sibling is unable to enjoy another sibling's success. Sometimes this extends to another generation when siblings compete with each other through their children's achievements. Instead of cheering a nephew's admission to an Ivy League college, the competing aunt or uncle silently resents the child's good fortune. That's evidence of more than petty jealousy or rivalry—it's passive hatred brewing beneath the surface.

What circumstances are painful enough to promote this subterranean hatred that can ultimately lead to the most painful of hurts—estrangement? A son loves a father but grows to hate him after the parents' divorce and the father marries, has another family and loses touch with this son. A son loves the mother who nurtured him but grows to hate her for not accepting his spouse. A daughter loves the mother who gave her life, but hates her for being drunk all the time. A sister loves her brother but he marries, moves away and never contacts her. How could he do this to her, when they had always been close? She hates him for abandoning her. These situations, along with the problems of homosexual "coming out" issues and interracial or interfaith marriages, are all complex enough to create feelings of hatred.

With a close family member, hate often coexists with love. In fact, the hate we feel for the person we also love or used to love is the most crippling hatred we can experience. It has the potential of crippling everyone in its path—the hater and the hated. Feeling anger is one thing; feeling hatred is another. Hate needs treatment. Anger is often healthy and prompts us to act toward correcting a situation. Anger wants to make things better. Hatred wants to worsen a situation. Hate wants to destroy, and it often not only destroys a relationship, but also the one who hates. Usually, we hate those who are close to us; rarely do we hate strangers. Only close family members or friends are capable of causing the kind of profound hurt that leads to feelings of hatred, which in turn becomes a sickness that burrows into your heart, into your head, into your soul. *There's only one safe medicine for hatred, and that's forgiveness.* Hating a wrong is one thing—hating a person is quite another. Hating the person has a life of its own long after the wrongdoing has passed. How does the anger over the wrongdoing turn to hatred of the person who committed the hurt? We glue our emotions to the time when we were hurt—an hour, a week, a year or longer. We give a special attention to that hurt—we grant it immortality. It becomes like a backpack that goes everywhere with us. It invades our sleep, our moments of pleasure and our concentration. Maybe the hurts were inevitable, but suffering from them is optional. The runaway train that carries hurts from the past propels us toward a life-threatening collision and needs to be stopped in its tracks. Forgiveness works like a brake. Forgiveness eliminates that suffering. It is a gift we owe to ourselves.

You may have known fear, shame, abuse, scorn, even violence. Sometimes you may perceive what isn't there, or you may be exaggerating the hurt. Whether real or fantasy or an exaggeration, however, it gives us the burden of torment and guilt to carry with us in whatever we do. The past doesn't have to be our future. We can transcend the circumstances of the past. It can work for us or against us. If we allow it to haunt us through obsessive lists of grievances, we are disturbing our own present moments of joy or serenity. We would be fools to spend precious moments of our life replaying the hurt or hurts inflicted on us. Ultimately, it can even destroy our healthy and wonderful relationships.

If you harbor grudges and guilt from past events, if you're missing people in your life who are now alienated from you, if you dread the guilt you'll feel from the death of an estranged loved one, if you're bitter about past relationships, if you wish you could set the record straight, then *it's time to think about forgiveness and reconciling with a person you still love.*

CONNECTIVE TISSUE

Examine the estranged relationship. An essential part of the peace-making process requires that you take another look at the past and bring it into focus. Maybe there were hurts, but what about all the periods of love and caring and unselfish devotion? What about the happy times, the sharing of news around a holiday dinner table, the celebrations of happy events, vacation trips and special gifts because the other person knew what you wanted. Making peace with the past means letting go of the hatred that festers inside you. Letting go of the hatred doesn't mean denying the past and the wrong that was done to you or even discrediting it. It means releasing it, resolving it and putting it in perspective. The act of forgiveness is really a curative—it's a liposuction quick fix. It sucks out what's ugly and shouldn't be there—toxic, fatty hatred.

But how am I supposed to forgive someone who has committed a terrible wrong against me? I can't do that, you say. Yes, you can. When we're hurt, often our pain blinds us. If we are able to understand some of what was going on inside the person who hurt us, we might see what motivated him or her to take the step that hurt us. We might even see how our own behavior prompted the cruel words or actions.

Looking at the person who hurt you, not as some evildoer, but as a total human being who has a life apart from this conflict, is a good first step in building some connective tissue. Perhaps your anger is directed at a working mother whom you can envision diapering her baby, reading a bedtime story to her older child, dropping her children off at daycare on her way to work and worrying about not having enough time to spend with them. If the person who hurt you is a father, think of him mowing the lawn, washing the car, waking up early in the morning to be with his children before he rushes off to his office. If the person is a young single woman or man who has a career, think of their hardworking efforts to succeed in business, their sometimes lonely single lifestyle, dating and worrying about finding the right man or woman to marry and, at the same time, greatly aware of all the risks that are out there in the dating world. In other words, realize whoever hurt you is not a two-dimensional person. It's someone with a full life, responsibilities, joys, problems and worries—someone who probably pauses now and then to think of you, wondering what went wrong and wishing it could be the way it used to be.

Last year Lucy went home for her mother's funeral. Her father had died when she and her brother were young children. For the first time in years, she spent days with her older brother, Jeff, who was so grief-stricken over the death of their mother that he had lost his arrogant and condescending attitude toward Lucy. As children growing up they had been close, but once they were teenagers they began to argue about matters of no real importance. Lucy became wallpaper the minute Jeff walked into the room. Once, when he read some intimate letters that a boyfriend had written to Lucy, he threw them at her and called her a "slut" right in front of their mother. At that moment, Lucy hated him as much as she had ever hated anyone. Time passed and the hatred subsided. When she went away to college, she would call Jeff, but he was always too busy to talk and would brush her off. She'd send him birthday cards and sometimes gifts, but he never reciprocated. When she moved out of state, he never telephoned or wrote her a single letter. This alienation went on for many years.

According to Dr. Jim Fitzgerald, a psychologist who counsels families, at least a third of siblings describe their relationship as detached or antagonistic, and of that third many are estranged from each other even if they haven't declared war. Often, they have little in common with each other and use words like "hurtful" and "competitive" in discussing their childhood relationship. The quickness with which old rivalries reduce these adults to children again prevents them from seeing one another in a new and different light.

They push each other's hot buttons without the slightest understanding of why or how they recast themselves in their former childhood roles that never worked in the first place. When they try to describe their feelings, they resort to a variety of defensive strategies, like diminishing the relationship by emphasizing the importance of spouses and friends instead.

Since both Lucy and her brother are single, they now have no one but each other. Lucy wants to reconnect with him, but to do that she must forgive him for the years of hurt and neglect. Though she's ready to do that, she doesn't know how to begin.

As we forgive people, we begin to see the deeper truth of them as they really are. Like most of us, they have their weaknesses and fears as well as their strengths. Hatred makes us want to see them as cold and cruel and frightening. To overcome that myopic view, we have to go back in time and remember the camaraderie that was once there. If it was there, it can be there again. It's there to build on. Sometimes, just speaking candidly to the person about your desire to forgive and repair the relationship can be enough to lift the curtain so that you can both see each other in a kinder light.

And then proceed with an icebreaker. Remind him or her of a happier time—something that was fun or was shared by only the two of you or reinforced the bond you both had or was a comic memory of an event or a relative.

Forgiveness is like a work in progress. Start with a small step, then another one. It creates its own momentum, strengthens and builds on its own strength. The more you interact in a loving way, the easier it is to forgive the past. The whole person begins to appear just like a photograph being developed in a dark room.

You think this would be tough for Lucy? Try forgiving the stepmother who you believe took your father away. Or the daughter-in-law who turned your son against his family. Or the mother who alienated your children from you when she sided with your former spouse during your divorce. Or your mother-in-law who wouldn't accept you as being worthy of her son or daughter. Or the father-in-law who showers your wife with everything that you can't afford to provide? Or the black son-in-law who married your white daughter against your wishes? Or the partner of your lesbian daughter who treats you with disdain because she knows you disapprove of their lifestyle? Or the stepsister . . . Enough! You get the picture.

Now, let's try one of those tough ones. Let's go through the steps toward forgiveness and reconciliation with someone where there is no history of love, but where the person has too much control over someone we love and want to be with again. The daughter who hates her stepmother for taking her father away is a challenge. How does the daughter—let's call her Lauren—begin the process of forgiveness so that she can reconnect with her father? First of all, Lauren must realize that the reconnection she wants is not likely to happen if hatred for her stepmother persists.

Lauren has to take a look at what happened outside of her narrow part in the drama. Maybe the marriage between her parents was intolerable for her father. Maybe her mother drank or went out with other men or she just didn't love Lauren's father anymore. He may have had similar problems, but because of the unhappiness he was hurt and vulnerable. Through his work he met a woman and developed a friendship that turned into love. Did Lauren think she couldn't have any respect for a woman who entered into a relationship with a married man with a family? She has to realize the woman is the same kind of person as the man who entered into the "illicit" relationship—her father. They're both people who have strengths and weaknesses and susceptibilities. They're not all good nor are they all bad. But one thing is certain: If Lauren cuts her father out of her life because of his failure to keep in as close touch with her as she wants, she will be losing the only natural father she'll ever have. According to Dr. Paul Hirschfield, estranged fathers still love their children even if they don't show it. So if

Lauren wants a relationship with him, she'll have to unlock the door by forgiving him for leaving. And she will have to stop hating his wife for falling in love with her father when he was still married to her mother. And if Lauren's memories of her stepmother are so bad, either from her own limited contact with her during the time of upheaval or because she was influenced by her mother to believe that this "other woman" was rotten to the core and stole her father away, then she will have to wipe that slate clean. As an adult woman who wants a relationship with her father, that image of his wife has to be obliterated or the hatred will never cease. Getting acquainted with her on the right terms can go a long way toward dispelling that evil image of her that's been created.

The reconciliation has to begin with contact. Lauren needs to call her father and say something like, "I realize that no matter what's happened, you're still my father, and I can't stop loving you. I'm sorry we've lost so much time and I hope we can make up for it."

Most fathers would be brought to their knees by such a statement. Then the next step—the question of his wife. Lauren must remember that her father loves her and lives with this woman.

She might say, "I'd like to get to know Mona. Can't we all meet sometime?" This should be enough of a gesture toward reconciliation to restart the relationship. They are far more likely to be receptive than Lauren probably expects. But now comes another hurdle—keeping an open mind about her stepmother. Lauren needs to reevaluate the situation in light of her own maturity and desire to reconnect with her father.

More hurdles may have to be negotiated. If Lauren's mother is still living and has a close relationship with her daughter, she may consider Lauren's reconnection with her father and acceptance of his wife as a betrayal. In the divorce chapter, there is a story similar to this one: "The Addicted Mother," in which a daughter never allowed herself to lose contact with her father even though it meant a period of estrangement with her mother. That could happen in this situation, but an estrangement between Lauren and her mother would be far easier to mend even with the mother's perception of her daughter's actions as betrayal. If Lauren wants a relationship with her father badly enough, then her mother will have to understand that she can't extort her daughter's love and devotion for herself to the exclusion of her ex-husband. In time, Lauren's mother will face the unfairness of her ultimatum that her daughter can't have a relationship with her and a separate one with her father and stepmother. Bear in mind that mothers don't easily give up their children. Lauren's reconciliation with her father would not be enough to cause her mother to *permanently* cast her from her life, not if she really loves her daughter. But she has to give her mother time to accept the situation.

All of these hurdles—forgiving a wrong and dispelling hatred—are difficult to overcome unless there is a strong desire to reconnect with a loved one.

Family estrangements among "the rich and famous" occur for the same variety of reasons as they do in our own families. The only difference is the whole world is privy to their private pain.

The public first learned about the bitter estrangements in Ronald and Nancy Reagan's family from their daughter, Patti Davis, who wrote a scathing memoir, *Home Front*, in which she described her mother as a manipulating pill popper and her father as an island of ice. Patti made a practice of scorning her parents by taking her mother's maiden name as her own last name—an act of disrespect for her father—writing three different books that, in neon lights, revealed the family dysfunction, and appearing nude in *Playboy.* Patti broadcast to the whole world that she wanted nothing to do with her famous father and mother, and why.

Furthermore, in *On the Outside Looking In—The Intimate Autobiography of the Eldest Son of President Ronald Reagan and Jane Wyman*, Michael Reagan reveals the kind of relationship he had with his father. At Michael's high school graduation, his father, then governor of California, delivered a commencement address and shook hands with members of the graduating class. "As Michael stood proudly before him in cap and gown, his dad cheerfully announced, 'My name is Ronald Reagan. What's yours?'"

There are only two possible reasons for such bizarre behavior: one, that Reagan's Alzheimer's disease started before he took the presidential oath of office—a frightening thought—or, two, that Michael was of such little importance to him that he couldn't recall his son's face. Michael believed it was the latter. He, too, revealed the embittered feelings he had for his father in a tell-all book of their estrangement.

In 1994, a few weeks after her father's Alzheimer's was made public, Patti decided to apologize to her parents for the pain and humiliation she had wrought on them through her memoir exposés. Michael, too, has found his way home after a long estrangement. Alzheimer's disease is a sad and terrible ordeal for a family to have to cope with, but in the case of the Reagans, it was ironically the catalyst that brought them all together again.

ROAD MAP TO RECONCILIATION

Most estrangements don't mend as abruptly as they did in the case of the Reagans. Ronald Reagan's Alzheimer's put the family on fast forward. Serious illness of an elderly matriarch or patriarch often produces a family unity that might otherwise not be there. But sometimes it does just the opposite: it heightens emotions and turns people against one another. Usually reconciliation comes about in fits and starts, two steps forward and one back. Most of us can't zero in on the right course of action that results in an immediate love-fest with the person who seriously hurt us because we're not free of resentment. There are crosscurrents at play. Though the resentments may not be healed yet, time has surely obscured the details that caused the breach. Who did what to whom is often unclear. Exactly what happened is often muddled in our minds. But don't go to rewind, because you'll be prone to cast the facts in a light most favorable to you, and that will certainly hamper moving forward toward your goal of mending the estrangement. It will only reinforce and intensify your resentment. To expect two people (or factions) caught in mutual hatred to sort out their differences is like asking two tribal armies to draw straws to see who won the war.

In researching hundreds of stories of estrangements for this book, the ones that mended successfully usually skipped the rewind—the rehashing of the hurtful events. Instead they went directly toward a heartfelt gesture of reaching out, one to the other.

In one story, in the divorce chapter, a divorced father spent years asking his estranged son to meet him for lunch, for dinner, for a walk, and even for a drink when the son was older. After 16 years of refusals, and when the son was 35, the father invited the son to join him for a game of golf. To the father's delight, the son accepted the invitation. What was the dynamic for that change of heart? All the prior invitations meant the father and son would be face-to-face with nothing to do but rehash the painful course that led to the breach in their relationship. Playing golf allowed them to be together without confronting the past. It worked. Another few games of golf put father and son together again.

In another story, a young homosexual man cast out by his mother was able to finally effect reconciliation by sending her a video of a TV movie he had taped. *Doing Time on Maple Drive* portrayed a young man's struggle with his homosexuality, his shame, his near suicide, his love for his family and his desire to have their approval. The mother put her religious convictions aside to reconnect with the son she loved. Again, no confrontation occurred.

One sister who had been bitterly estranged from her brother because of an inheritance fight allowed bygones to be bygones. When her brother's wife was diagnosed with cancer, the sister called and offered to drive her sister-in-law to the hospital for chemotherapy and anything else they might need in the way of help. She and her brother never discussed the conflict over the inheritance, but their relationship mended.

A grandmother who had been alienated from her grandchildren because of her son-in-law's influence on her daughter was able to mend a long-term estrangement by a gesture of good will. After a court granted her visitation with her grandchildren, the son-in-law was inflamed and tried to do everything in his power to turn the children against their grandmother. Eventually, he drove his 12-year-old son from home and into the arms of the grandmother. Instead of gloating over her victory, the grandmother persuaded the child to forgive his father and return home. She knew vengeance would mire them all in the pain of past events. Finally, the son-in-law was able to see her as a loving person, a peacemaker, and not as the enemy.

An interracial couple who had been cast out by the wife's family sent a kind note and pictures of their new baby. Time, and the joy of a new grandchild, persuaded the family to mend the relationship with their daughter and her family.

Another divorced father who had been alienated from his three children for several years persisted in calling the children, sending gifts for special occasions and birthday cards. His persistence paid off. As the children reached their teens, realizing that his love for them was steady and consistent, one by one they reconnected with their father.

Many others who were guided by professional therapists also used the same methods. Nevertheless, while it is more likely that mending will occur when the past is buried, that isn't always the case. In certain situations the past must be explored and resolved, particularly where matters of inheritance or family business problems are a part of the mix. Often the presence of an objective third party is helpful under such circumstances. A person both sides respect can sometimes work magic. For example, a family lawyer or even a professional mediator can often hit the right chords of conciliation over an issue that would otherwise have dismal prospects for resolving.

Mending estrangements is really hard work, and there's no easy way back to togetherness. Every situation has its own set of ingredients—its own dynamic. Every knotted relationship is seen in a different light depending on who's looking at it and from which vantage point they view it. No matter how much you want to set the record straight about what happened in the past, that route is filled with perils and could get you lost on a road to nowhere. Replaying the pain of being wronged, the hurt of being betrayed, cheated, demeaned or stung, ignites the fires of hatred all over again. Beware of becoming a prisoner of those past hurts, or of becoming hooked on them like addicts. That is truly self-destructive. For everyone connected to the conflict, it's best to get rid of the tape that plays unending reruns of grievances.

In taking that first step toward reunion when you're the one who's doing the forgiving, use general terms rather than the details of the wrong. You might even say, "I can't remember all the details of what happened, and I don't want to remember them. I just want us to be together again. I miss you and love you. I don't want to waste any more time being estranged."

I APOLOGIZE

If you've played a role in the wrongdoing, then it's important to take the apology route toward reconciliation. This is the time to throw away obstinate pride. A genuine apology is key. How often have you received an apology that really sounded genuine? Not often. Apologies usually sound something like this: "Listen, I'm sorry, OK? Look, you don't have to make a federal case out of it." Or: "I'm sorry you feel that way." Or: "I'm sorry I hurt you, but you've got to develop a thicker skin." In other words, the tone of real contrition was absent or negated by rationalization or an insinuation that the one doing the apologizing really thought you were hypersensitive or even the one really at fault. Let's face it, most of us can spot an insincere apology a mile away. So if you're thinking about making amends, be certain that you really mean it, because if you're doing it to be manipulative or because you're under duress, the insincerity will show and the situation could worsen. For instance, if you want to reconnect with your father and you have to make amends with your stepmother through an apology, the words, the gestures, the tone will all matter. Lines such as these, genuinely conveyed should be of enormous help: "I know I can't take back what I did, but I would if I could. My actions were wrong and insensitive. Obviously, I have hurt you deeply, for which I am so profoundly sorry. [If you want to spell out the wrong you committed, do so, but be as brief as possible.] I want to do anything that will make this up to you. Please let me back into your life. I miss you and I really want a loving relationship with you."

In chapter 5, under the heading, "To the Letter," there's a letter written by a daughter to her parents begging to be reconnected with them. It strikes all the right notes with a tone of genuine sincerity and love.

One caveat: When estrangement occurs, usually the wrong is serious, so in making an apology, *don't try to be cute or funny*. It could come across as trivializing the situation.

Lastly, in the matter of mending an estrangement, how do you go about it when you haven't a clue as to *why* someone walked out of your life? For example, in several interviews, newly married sons (rarely daughters) exiled themselves from their own family with virtually no explanation of why. You may be aware that the new in-law was a factor for reasons of control or jealousy, but why did your son (occasionally daughter) play the enabler? Even if he offered reasons, they were so trite and transparent that it was evident he was unwilling to admit the real cause for the estrangement, perhaps because it might involve disclosing serious problems with the spouse. If you've made repeated attempts to find out what you may have done to cause the rift, and still the person is not forthcoming, the best you can do is comb your memory and figure out what it might be. Were you thoughtless or inconsiderate? Did you fail to do something you said you would do? If you didn't, did you explain why? You have to put yourself through a third degree. If you're still unable to get to the root of the problem, then try to enlist the intervention of a therapist, one who specializes in family counseling. If the other person is a close relative and wants to work through the problem, he or she might go to a therapist with you.

If that's not possible, then make a general but profuse apology: "I'm sincerely and deeply sorry for whatever it is I may have done to hurt you. I wish you felt comfortable enough to be candid with me, but in the meantime, I love you and miss you and want to do whatever I can to bring us together again. . . ."

You can't expect that once you've made this heartfelt gesture, the other person will automatically respond. You may have to work at it by repeating your desire to reconnect. If that doesn't work, then do what both Drs. Fitzgerald and Hirschfield recommend: keep the door open. Send birthday cards, notes, e-mails and make occasional phone calls just so that your loved one knows that you're always receptive to him, and whenever he's ready to reenter your life, you'll be there.

If, however, an in-law or a stepparent has a stranglehold on your loved one, then the resolution might entail a long wait, possibly until a divorce occurs. Unfortunately, while that situation prevails, no one involved can be happy about it, particularly your estranged family member, who is allowing his or her spouse to exercise such control and ruin an otherwise loving relationship.

Where reconciliation is your objective, there are some basic thoughts to keep in mind while you're engaged in the process.

- One person has to have enough courage and love to initiate contact.

- The aim cannot be to restore the relationship to that place where it was before, because the breach has changed it permanently.

- Everyone involved has to be willing to listen.

- Everyone involved has to be willing to forgive.

- Everyone involved has to be willing to give up the need to be right.

- Everyone involved has to be flexible in reviewing the past if that review is demanded by any of the parties to the estrangement.

- Everyone has to make the effort to see the problem from the other person's point of view.

- Bury your feelings of revenge and redirect them into a search for solutions.

- Think of a better future of togetherness, pleasure and wholesomeness, rather than a past of anger, bitterness and hatred.

- Recognize that reconciliation with a relative removes negative feelings that add stress to your life. Lastly, in those step and in-law relationships where there is no prior common history or period of love on which to build, recognize that reconciliation doesn't have to mean a full and loving embrace. You can start with just learning to be comfortable in the presence of the other person. The goal is to reconcile with your own feelings and to see the other person not as evil but as a person with imperfections just like the rest of us.

✻ And don't punish yourself if you experience some leftover anger after you've forgiven the other person. The best you can do is to not focus on the anger. In time, it will dissipate.

COPING WHEN WE FAIL TO MEND

We've run out of options. We've tried repeatedly to reconnect with that person who has walked out of our lives, but we haven't succeeded. We've made every effort to reestablish the relationship, but for whatever reason, the other person continues to resist our overtures. In some cases, we know the reason for the estrangement; in others we haven't the vaguest notion of why the breach occurred. Whether we know why it happened or we don't, the estrangement remains unresolved. We're still miserably unhappy with the void in our lives, and *we need to get beyond it.* If we continue to dwell on the breach, we may continue to be disappointed, even angry and embittered. Because those feelings lead to emotional and physical suffering, *we need to learn to cope* with a situation we can't change. We need to learn to live with it or beside it, and without despair, knowing that we have no control over the outcome.

The best way to achieve that end is to *keep busy, happy and involved.* We need to feel connected, to know that we matter to someone, hopefully to more than one person. Strengthen ties with other family members. If you feel a need to talk to someone about these problems, a close family member might be exactly the right person. If there are siblings you haven't been seeing as often as you'd like to, make arrangements to see them. Call them up and say you've missed seeing them. Invite them to come for a visit or go visit them. If they live far away, take a trip. That can be one of your first diversions. If that sibling doesn't know what has been going on in your life and is someone you're emotionally close to and has good judgment you can trust, you might air it with that sister or brother. In fact, that sister or brother who knows you probably also knows the estranged relative and might be able to shed some light on the problem. They might see your part in the conflict because they know you so well. Be receptive to their insights. They could be the most perceptive ones.

If there is no close family member who can give you advice and counsel, enlist the help of close and trustworthy friends. So many of the people who shared their stories in this book proved that one of the best coping mechanisms was talking to friends, and this was particularly true with women. But men should heed this lesson and do what women do: confide in friends. This is especially true for very depressed fathers who have lost contact with their children because a vindictive ex-wife has poisoned their impressionable minds against him. Most friends will lend a willing ear and offer comfort and support, and sometimes they have wonderful insights and observations to share with you.

If there's no one else you can think of who falls into the category of a close friend, then you really need to get yourself out there and make a friend or two. Remove the shackles of house arrest. Get out there and do things. Stay involved and active. If you can take a trip, do so. It will get you away from the hurtful memories of the estrangement because they are so often tied to your own familiar surroundings. If you love your work, put more of yourself into it. It's a good escape from painful thoughts. And think of your community as an untapped resource filled with opportunities to stay busy. Whatever your age or gender, find activities to interest you. Keep yourself stimulated with sports activities, exercise groups, support groups, volunteer organizations and classes if they're available—in short, stay occupied enough to avoid dwelling on the hurt or anger you might be feeling. Most importantly, let friends and acquaintances know you'd like to spend time with them.

Coping means coming to terms with what you can do and what you can't do. You need to remind yourself that you have the ability to make healthy decisions about what you can no longer tolerate. You're responsible for what you let into your life.

⟫⟪

On a personal note . . .

My own estrangement is not yet fully resolved. But after several years of struggling with the situation and feeling angry and frustrated with my inability to mend the breach, I am now coping successfully while continuing with the process of reconciliation. With help from those professionals who contributed to this book, the interviews herein, family and friends, I found my way to that place we all seek—a place where we can feel inner peace.

In the past, the focus of most of my energy was on trying to place blame on others, or on things outside my control, rather than addressing what I could have done and what I can now do to resolve the conflicts. For a period of years, I had to work hard not to let it get to me, not to let it drain me of energy and weaken my own self-image. These lessons are not easy to learn, especially the one that teaches you not to allow yourself to suffer. For a time, it became too easy to curl up on the sofa in a dark room and replay all the anguish of the lost relationship. That doesn't mean I've parked those issues somewhere far away. I still go there, not to suffer, but to reexamine if there's anything more I can do to move things toward to a complete reconciliation.

I acknowledged to myself that there had been other times in my life in which I had been locked in conflict with someone who resembled the antagonist who manipulated the relationship with my loved one into a hurtful estrangement. I learned that I'm a person who takes things to the wall. I have a tendency to see the worst and then overreact to it. This knowledge was liberating. I realized that I no longer had to feel like a victim of unfair treatment, and that I could only change my behavior and reactions to the situation. Every story in this book helped me to get to the bottom of what was most damaging to me—deep-seated resentment and, yes, hatred of the person who orchestrated the estrangement. It took a long time for me to understand this person's motivation—that my very existence, my personality, may have posed an enormous threat to this person's need to have center stage and also maintain control of the relative I love and didn't want to lose. To get over my hatred and move on to forgiveness for the hurt inflicted on my husband, my daughter and me was one of the toughest challenges I've ever had to face.

As we all know, there is certainly no shortage of people in the world who revel in trying to satisfy their need for power and control. And sometimes we have to learn to deal with them when that relative we love is tethered to such a person. But if we hate that person, we'll never get to where we want to be—in contact with our loved ones. I also learned that this domineering type of personality ignites the worst in me and that my reactions were as much a part of the problem as the actions of others. Accepting that there was nothing I could do to make this person want to be with our family or to change this type of person was a big accomplishment. Another major accomplishment was learning that I was inflicting harm to myself by wallowing in self-pity and feeding on rage.

I proceeded on a course that worked. I did what I suggest you do—stay active, busy and happy. But I couldn't have reached that point had I not heard all the stories I've related to you in this book. I am so grateful to these kind and sharing people who offered the intimate details of their estrangements, because without those details, we wouldn't know how widespread and profound the problems are and how many mending and coping strategies are available.

It's been a long, hard journey for me, and yet, a vital experience especially because I learned how to cope with a hurt that I never believed I could remove from my everyday conscious thoughts.

Most of us have been, to some degree, a hostage to past hurts, but if I can escape, then so can you. The stories, research and professional advice offered in this book have enabled me to do what you will also be able to do. I have given you the road map to take the same route I've taken. I believe the information contained in all of the chapters of this book will lead you to reconciliation or to healthy coping with a fractured relationship until it is mended. Now, I have faith that I will travel from this position of healthy coping to the ultimate goal—a full reconnection with the person I love.

The emotionally draining ordeal of family estrangements will always be with us—it is so often woven into the fabric of human flaws and frailties. But hope and help are within our grasp. You're holding both in your hands right now.

BIBLIOGRAPHY

Adler, Jerry and Wingert, Pat. "A Matter of Faith." *Newsweek*, Vol. 130, Dec. 15, 1997.

Africano, Lillian. "The Importance of Grandparents." *Woman's Day*, Nov. 25, 1980.

Akaskie, Jay. "House Fight." *Forbes*, June 14, 1999.

Allen, James P. and Turner, Eugene J. *We the People: An Atlas of America's Ethnic Diversity*. New York: Macmillan, 1988.

Ascher, Barbara Lazear. "When Families Fight." *Redbook*, Vol. 180, Nov. 1992.

Baliga, Wayne. "Baby Boomers Slated for Inheritance Windfall." *Journal of Accountancy*, Vol. 178, July 1994.

Barboza, David. "Father Divides a Business to Keep the Children

United." *New York Times,* Aug. 1999.

Bettelheim, Bruno. *The Uses of Enchantment.* New York: Random House, 1977.

Bigelsen, Sylvia. *The Ties That Bind: A Survival Guide to In-Law Relationships.* Boston: Element Books, 1999.

Bilofsky, Penny and Sacharow, Fredda. *In-laws/Outlaws.* New York: Villard Books, 1991.

Boyd-Franklin, Nancy. *Black Families in Therapy: A Multisystems Approach.* New York: Guilford Press, 1989.

Bramson, Robert M. *Coping with Difficult People.* New York: Doubleday, 1981.

Browne, Joy. *Nobody's Perfect: How to Stop Blaming and Start Living.* New York: Simon and Schuster, 1988.

Cain, Barbara S. "Older Children and Divorce." *New York Times Magazine*, Feb. 18, 1990.

Carter, Les. *Imperative People: Those Who Must Be in Control.* Nashville: Thomas Nelson, 1991.

Chatzky, Jean Sherman. "Test of Wills." *Money*, Vol. 29, March 2000.

Clift, Eleanor and Sonenshine, Tara. "The Long Goodbye." *Newsweek*, Vol. 126, Oct. 1995.

Conroy, Pat. *The Prince of Tides.* New York: Houghton Mifflin, 1988.

Davidson, James D. "Interfaith Marriage." *Commonweal*, Vol. 125, Sept. 11, 1998.

Davis, Patti. *Home Front.* New York: Crown, 1986.

Eaton, Sandra C. "Marriage Between Jews and Non-Jews: Counseling Implications." *Journal of Multicultural Counseling & Development*, Vol. 22, Oct. 1994.

Furstenberg, Frank F. Jr. *Divided Families: What Happens to Children When Parents Part.* Cambridge: Harvard University Press, 1991.

Gates, Philomene. *Suddenly Alone: A Woman's Guide to Widowhood, Divorce and Loneliness.* Atlanta: Gridiron Publishers, 1997.

Gay, Kathlyn. *The Rainbow Effect: Interracial Families.* New York: Franklin Watts, 1987.

Greenberg, Vivian E. *Children of a Certain Age: Adults and their Aging Parents.* New York: Lexington Books, 1994.

Halpern, Howard M. *You and Your Grown-Up Child: Nurturing a Better Relationship.* New York: Fireside, 1992.

Halvorson, Marilyn. *Cowboys Don't Cry.* New York: Delacorte Press, 1984.

Hammer, Joshua. *Chosen by God: A Brother's Journey.* New York: Hyperion, 2000.

Hull, Jon D. "Waiting for the Windfall." *Time*, Vol. 141, Jan. 1993.

Jenny, C. J., et al. "Are Children at Risk for Sexual Abuse by Homosexuals?" *Pediatrics,* Vol. 94, No. 1, July 1994.

Klagsbrun, Francine. "The Ties That Bind." *People*, Oct. 28, 1992.

Kottler, Jeffrey. *Beyond Blame.* San Francisco: Jossey-Bass, 1994.

Lea, James. "Real Cause of Family Feuds May Lurk Beneath Surface." *Business Journal Serving San Jose & Silicon Valley*, Vol. 15, June 1997.

Lerner, Harriet. *The Dance of Anger.* New York: Harper & Row, 1988.

————— *The Dance of Deception.* New York: Harper & Row, 1990.

————— *The Dance of Intimacy.* New York: Harper & Row, 1993.

Lind, Michael. "The Beige and the Black." *New York Times Magazine*, Aug. 16, 1998.

Marer, Eva. "Family Feuds." *Financial Planning*, Vol. 29, Nov. 1999.

McGoldrick, Monica. *You Can Go Home Again: Reconnecting with Your Family.* New York: W. W. Norton & Co., 1995.

Miller, Mark. "To Be Gay—And Mormon." *Newsweek*, May 8, 2000.

Naughton, Keith; Halpert, Julie Edelson and Green, Jeff. "Squabbling Like Children." *Newsweek*, Vol. 135, April 2000.

Newcomb, Peter and Summers, Mary. "The Forbes 400: Divided We Stand." *Forbes*, Vol. 164, Oct. 11, 1999.

Noonan, Peggy. *Life, Liberty and the Pursuit of Happiness.* New York: Random House, 1994.

O'Neill, Eugene. *Long Day's Journey into Night.* New Haven: Yale University Press, 1955.

Perkins, Mitali. "Guess Who's Coming to Church? Confronting Christians' Fear of Interracial Marriage." *Christianity Today*, Mar. 7, 1994.

Pipher, Mary. *The Shelter of Each Other: Rebuilding Our Families.* New York: G. P. Putnam & Sons, 1996.

Reagan, Michael. *On the Outside Looking In—The Intimate Autobiography of the Eldest Son of President Ronald Reagan and Jane Wyman.* New York: Kensington Publishers Corp., 1988.

Samuelson, Robert J. "Darling, It'll All Be Yours—Soon." *Newsweek*, Vol. 135, May 19, 2000.

Savin-Williams, Ritch C. and Dubé, Eric. "Parental Reactions to Their Child's Disclosure of a Gay/Lesbian Identity." *Family Relations*, Vol. 47, 1998.

Secunda, Victoria. *When You and Your Mother Can't Be Friends.* New York: Dell Publishing, 1991.

Sheehy, Gail. *New Passages: Mapping Your Life across Time.* New York: Random House, 1995.

Smolowe, Jill and Aunapu, Greg. "Intermarried . . . With Children." *Time*, Vol. 142, 1993.

Suro, Roberto. "Mixed Doubles." *American Demographics*, Vol. 21, Nov. 1999.

Tyner, Mitchell. "Religious Freedom Issues in Domestic Relations Law." *BYU Journal of Public Law*, Vol. 8, 1984.

Van Dyne, Larry. "And to My Ungrateful Son . . ." *Washingtonian*, Vol. 34, Nov. 1998.

Viorst, Judith. *Necessary Losses.* New York: Simon and Schuster, 1986.

Watts, Richard E. and Henriksen, Richard C. Jr. "Perceptions of a White Female in a Interracial Marriage." *Family Journal*, Vol. 7, Jan. 1999.

Weiss, Michael J. "A Family in Black & White." *Ladies Home Journal,* Vol. 113, Apr. 1996.

White, Joseph L. *The Psychology of Blacks: An Afro-American Perspective.* New Jersey: Prentice-Hall, 1984.

SUGGESTED READING

(From my own reading on the subject, I offer this selected list of both fiction and nonfiction books that deal with family estrangements.)

Anna Karenina, by Leo Tolstoy (available in paperback).
Anna, miserable in her loveless marriage, enters into an affair with Count Vronsky. Anna's husband alienates her from their young son. This is one of literature's most tragic estrangements.

Another View, by Rosamunde Pilcher (available in paperback).
Struggling to understand her remote artist father, who abandoned her to a boarding house, Emma searches for answers as to why he left and what she means to him.

The Desperate Season, by Michael Blaine (RobWeisbach Books, 1999).
This powerful portrait of a family paralyzed by a son's mental illness focuses on the theme of family relationships, and a son's grievance against his parents.

Dinner at the Homesick Restaurant, by Anne Tyler (available in paperback).
Ever since 1944, when her husband left her, Pearl has tried desperately to raise three very different and wayward children on her own. When grown, they reconcile with anger, with hope and with a harsh

but ultimately dazzling story to tell.

Father Melancholy's Daughter, by Gail Godwin (available in paperback). When Ruth, the wife of a minister, abandons her husband and their six-year-old daughter, the estrangement has a profound impact on the family. Once the daughter is a young adult, she searches for answers to the many painful and unresolved questions.

Home Front, by Patti Davis (New York: Crown, 1986).
This story is a fictionalized account of the author's estrangement from her father and mother, President Ronald Reagan and Nancy Reagan. Now that her father has Alzheimers', Patti Davis has reconciled with her family.

Liar, by Jan Burke (available in paperback).
This murder mystery centers on a search into family history that is made more difficult by reason of a family estrangement and a huge chasm separating two sides of an extended family.

On the Outside Looking In, by Michael Reagan (New York: Zebra Books, 1988).
Michael Reagan, adopted son of Ronald Reagan and Jane Wyman, talks about why he became estranged from his father and how he felt about it. He, too, like his sister, Patti Davis, has since reconciled with his famous father.

The Prince of Tides, by Pat Conroy (available in paperback).
Spanning 40 years, this is the story of turbulent Tom Wingo, his gifted and troubled twin sister, Savannah, and the dark and violent past of the extraordinary family into which they were born. The family members' estrangements from each other are overcome by their love and their persistent desire to reconcile.

Sons and Lovers, by D. H. Lawrence (available in paperback).
Never was a son more indentured to his mother's love and full of
hatred for his father than Paul Morel. Paul and his two brothers
come to manhood with an inability to love because of their mother's emotional dominance of their lives.

You Can't Go Home Again, by Thomas Wolfe (available in paperback).
George Webber has written a successful novel about his family and
hometown. When he returns to that town, he is shaken by the force
of outrage and hatred that greets him. Family and friends feel
stripped and exposed by the truths they have seen in his book.
Their fury drives him from his home. George begins his search for
his own identity and a means of reconciling with his family and his
former life.

I ♡ My Mom